Changing Practices of Doctoral Education

Postgraduate research has undergone unprecedented change in the past ten years, in response to major shifts in the role of the university and the disciplines in knowledge production, and the management of intellectual work.

New kinds of doctorates have been established that have expanded the scope and direction of doctoral education. A new audience of supervisors, academic managers and graduate school personnel is engaging in debates about the nature, purpose and future of doctoral education and how institutions and departments can best respond to the increasing demands that are being made.

Discussion of the emerging issues and agendas is set within the context of the international policy shifts that are occurring and considers the implications of these shifts on the changing external environment. This engaging book

- acquaints readers with new international trends in doctoral education;
- identifies new practices in supervision, research, teaching and learning;
- enables practitioners of doctoral education to contribute to the debates and help shape new understandings;
- questions the purposes of doctoral study and how they are changing; and
- considers the balance between equipping students as researchers and the conduct of original research.

Including contributions from both those who have conducted formal research on research education and those whose own practice is breaking new ground within their universities, *Changing Practices of Doctoral Education* draws on the expertise of those currently making a stimulating contribution to the literature on doctoral education.

David Boud is Dean of the University Graduate School and Professor of Adult Education at the University of Technology, Sydney, Australia. He has written widely on teaching, learning and assessment in higher and professional education and workplace learning.

Alison Lee is Professor of Education in the Faculty of Arts and Social Sciences, University of Technology, Sydney, Australia. She has written extensively in doctoral education, including professional doctorate research, supervision and doctoral writing.

Changing Practices of Doctoral Education

Edited by David Boud and Alison Lee

Routledge
Taylor & Francis Group

LONDON AND NEW YORK

First published 2009
by Routledge
2 Park Square, Milton Park, Abingdon, Oxon, OX14 4RN

Simultaneously published in the USA and Canada
by Taylor & Francis Inc
270 Madison Avenue, New York, NY 10016

Routledge is an imprint of the Taylor & Francis Group, an informa business

Typeset in GaramondMT
by Jayvee, Trivandrum, India
Printed and bound in Great Britain by CPI Antony Rowe,
Chippenham, Wiltshire

Every effort has been made to ensure that the advice and information
in this book is true and accurate at the time of going to press. However,
neither the publisher nor the authors can accept any legal responsibility or
liability for any errors or omissions that may be made. In the case of drug
administration, any medical procedure or the use of technical equipment
mentioned within this book, you are strongly advised to consult the
manufacturer's guidelines.

British Library Cataloguing in Publication Data
A catalogue record for this book is available from the British Library

Library of Congress Cataloging in Publication Data
Changing practices of doctoral education/
edited by David Boud & Alison Lee.
p. cm.
Includes bibliographical references and index.
1. Doctor of philosophy degree. 2. Universities and colleges—
Graduate work. I. Boud, David. II. Lee, Alison, 1952–
LB 2386.C54 2008
378.24—dc22
2008005149

ISBN 10: 0–415–44269–9 (hbk)
ISBN 10: 0–415–44270–2 (pbk)

ISBN 13: 978–0–415–44269–5 (hbk)
ISBN 13: 978–0–415–44270–1 (pbk)

Contents

Figures and Tables

Figures

Tables

Contributors

Claire Aitchison is a Senior Lecturer in the Student Learning Unit at the University of Western Sydney.

Brent Allpress is Architecture Research Director at the RMIT University, Melbourne.

Robyn Barnacle is a Senior Research Fellow of the Graduate Research Office at the RMIT University, Melbourne.

Rosa Becker works at the Observatory on Borderless Higher Education in London.

Alexandra Bitusikova is a senior researcher in social anthropology at the Matej Bel University, Banska Bystrica, Slovakia, and advisor to the European University Association, Brussels, Belgium.

David Boud is Dean of the University Graduate School and Professor of Adult Education at the University of Technology, Sydney.

Angela Brew is an Associate Professor at the Institute for Teaching and Learning, University of Sydney.

Andrew Brown is Dean of the Research School and Professor of Education at the Institute of Education, University of London.

Carol Costley is Reader in Work-Based Learning at the Institute for Work-Based Learning, Middlesex University.

Anna Cowan is Associate Dean (HDR) at the College of Medicine and Health Sciences, Australian National University.

Jim Cumming works at the Centre for Educational Development and Academic Methods, Australian National University.

Rob Gilbert is Professor of Education at the School of Education, University of Queensland.

Bill Green is Professor of Education at the Faculty of Education, Charles Sturt University.

Laura Jones is Director of Heritage Services and University Archaeologist, Stanford University and a Consulting Scholar with the Carnegie Foundation for the Advancement of Teaching.

Alison Lee is Professor of Education in the Faculty of Arts and Social Sciences, University of Technology, Sydney.

Diana Leonard is Professor of Sociology of Education and Gender at the Institute of Education, University of London.

Adrian Liston is a senior fellow, Department of Immunology, University of Washington and John Curtin School of Medical Research, Australian National University.

Ingrid Lunt is Professor of Education, Department of Educational Studies, University of Oxford.

Lynn McAlpine is Professor of Education, McGill University, on secondment to the University of Oxford.

Erica McWilliam is Professor of Education and Assistant Dean Research, Faculty of Education, Queensland University of Technology.

Ruth Neumann is an Associate Professor in Higher Education and Management, Office of the Dean, Higher Degree Research, Macquarie University.

Anthony Paré is Professor in Education and Director of the Centre for the Study and Teaching of Writing, McGill University.

Margot Pearson is a Visiting Fellow at the Centre for Educational Development and Academic Methods, The Australian National University.

Tai Peseta is a Lecturer at the Institute for Teaching and Learning, University of Sydney.

David Scott is Professor of Curriculum, Pedagogy and Assessment at the Institute of Education, University of London.

Doreen Starke-Meyerring is Assistant Professor of Rhetoric and Writing Studies and Co-Director of the Centre for the Study and Teaching of Writing, McGill University.

John Stephenson is Emeritus Professor of Middlesex University, formerly Head of the International Centre for Learner Managed Learning and Academic Director of the DProf programme at Middlesex University.

Mark Tennant is Dean, Faculty of Education and Professor of Education and was formerly Dean of the University Graduate School, University of Technology, Sydney.

Lucy Thorne is a Senior Faculty Administrator in the Faculty of Science and Technology, University of Lancaster.

Chapter 1

Introduction

David Boud and Alison Lee

Research in universities is under scrutiny as never before. Can and should all universities and all parts of universities be funded to do research? How can research be best supported? What does it produce and can this be produced better under different conditions? What should be encouraged? Within this debate sits the vital role of preparing the next generation of researchers. How should this be done, by whom and under what circumstances? The domain of academic practice that was traditionally thought of as most characteristically the purview of universities, the research doctorate, is now the focus of public policy and the gaze of governments. In different countries, in different ways, the doctorate has become a site of contestation: What is it for? How should it be done? No longer is it simply a matter of disciplines reproducing their own; instead, as research has become a vital part of a global, competitive knowledge economy, the doctorate is increasingly becoming subject to the influence of policy-makers and others wanting to shape directions for development.

One important consequence of the increasing scrutiny and intervention into the doctorate over the past decade or so has been the emergence of a set of practices concerned with *doctoral education*, focusing attention explicitly on the educative work involved in preparing doctoral graduates. In fact, this term signals a shift from the organising idea of *postgraduate research*, which attended primarily to the production of research outputs, to the activities and relationships involved in doing doctoral work and producing doctoral graduates. Prior to this period, knowledge about postgraduate research was sporadic and informal, and there was relatively little literature. At the same time there was always a certain ambiguity with respect to the intended outcomes of doctoral work, whether these be primarily focused on the research product or the licensed researcher – the doctoral graduate. New interest in the educative work of doctoral programs has surfaced at a time of major social and policy-led change in the field of doctoral research and practice. In the light of growth and expansion, changes in modes of knowledge production, modes of institutional and state governance, in forms of doctoral programs and in pedagogies, there is, we argue, a growing need to systematically account for the extent and range of practices in the field.

Under these changing conditions, a set of questions has emerged concerning the kinds of person being produced through the doctoral education process and the kinds of attributes required for new conditions of research and work. In this environment, it appears that the commonplace, day-to-day activities involved in doing research and being supervised in this process are increasingly being seen as wanting. The adequacy of older, informal practices to the production of the high level contributor to the knowledge economy and the investigator of new problems as imagined in policy documents is increasingly being questioned. Should there be a different kind of education – new kinds of coursework, or other kinds of training programme and new kinds of output – and how should this relate to the conduct of the project and the supervisory relationship?

A related question concerns whether the reproduction of disciplinary academics is, or should be, the sole goal of doctoral study. The PhD has traditionally been the training ground for 'stewards of the discipline' (Golde and Walker, 2006), and so its practices have been largely shaped by this purpose. Yet many, if not most, who complete the PhD today do not take this direction (Wulff, Austin and Associates, 2004). Who then does it prepare? And, for what? How is this changing?

To situate these changes within a broader context, it is useful to reflect briefly on where the modern doctorate comes from and where and when it emerged as the highest formal educational qualification awarded by universities. The research doctorate, typically known as the PhD, is universally acknowledged as representing the 'pinnacle of scholarship' (Gilbert, 2004). It is commonly characterised as a research degree, a fact that distinguishes it from older forms of doctoral award dating back to medieval times. The early history of the PhD, and the education of doctoral students, was intimately caught up in the shifts in the early nineteenth century in Europe towards a disciplinary base for knowledge production, characterised by a 'research-orientated, individually responsible, specialised search for universal knowledge' (Cowan, 1997). The US adopted this new European form of advanced learning early, in the mid-nineteenth century, while in Britain and its outposts, including Australia, this happened much later: in Britain in 1917, in Australia not until 1948 and elsewhere in the world later still. Countries that have had disrupted educational histories in recent times, for example in Eastern Europe, and those undertaking rapid development of research degree programs, such as many Asian countries, are also contributing to an increasing globalisation of the doctorate and an expanding frame of reference for its study. Many of these diverse histories as yet remaining undocumented in the world literature, it is fair to say that the recency of the modern research doctorate often comes as a surprise to those who have not studied its history.

From its early beginnings, the PhD developed considerable variation, in different national systems and in different disciplines and fields of study (Noble, 1994). Typical variation concerns the degree of structure, through coursework and associated methods of education (i.e. into a canon) or of 'training' (i.e. in research methods and procedures), and hence the relative weighting of the research dissertation. Connecting these disparate and diverse practices, however, has been an emphasis on the central role of the doctorate in the reproduction, maintenance and transformation of disciplines. The role of the PhD was to license scholars to profess a discipline, to replenish communities of scholars within universities and to advance disciplinary knowledge production (Golde and Walker, 2006; Parry, 2007).

Table 1.1 International growth in doctoral education, 1991–2005

	1991	1995/96	2002	2005
Australia		2,905	4,291	5,244
China	2,556	4,363	14,706	27,700
France	7,198	9,801	10,000	
Germany	19,100	22,300	23,000	
UK		7,559		16,515
USA		42,437	39,953	43,354

Sources: DEST (2007): Australia; HESA (2007): UK; NSF (2000): China, France and Germany 1991, 1995/6; Ma (2007): China 2002, 2005; NSF (2006): USA; Nerad (2006): France and Germany 2002.

A major expansion in the numbers of doctoral graduates over the past two decades has proceeded together with a significant increase in the numbers of new disciplines and interdisciplinary specialisations in which doctoral research is being conducted (see Table 1.1). This, together with rapidly changing global candidate demographics, paints a picture of significant change. Once the domain of an elite few, today the research doctorate has become a professional qualification across a wide range of high-order intellectual, professional and work domains.

More recently, in response to the broad changes outlined here, there have emerged a new 'family of doctorates' (Park, 2007), including professional doctorates and other practice-based doctorates, and 'new route PhDs', the 'integrated package of activities that inform the research student experience' (p. 28), including taught courses and assessments. These new doctorates are commonly profession-specific and are more directly aimed at mid-career professionals, or as advanced training grounds for particular professional groups. They have produced a dispersed and diverse landscape of doctoral research and doctoral education, placing the hitherto unquestioned primacy of disciplinary-academic concerns in question and offering a range of alternative avenues for knowledge-making and credentialing (McAlpine and Norton, 2006).

Should these new doctorates follow the same form and path as the PhD? Does the traditional thesis meet the needs of these different kinds of student? If not, what forms and paths are needed? The unprecedented pressures on the doctorate discussed above are driving an agenda for change that is being variously felt across the world. Chris Park has succinctly summarised the key 'drivers' for change:

- *sustaining the supply chain of researchers:* important issues include recruitment, funding, efficiency and cost-effectiveness, the status of researchers, and the growth of interdisciplinary and applied research;
- *preparation for employment:* important issues include the doctorate as a labour market qualification, expectations of doctoral candidates, expectations and requirements of employers, transition and mobility;
- *internationalisation:* important issues include global competition for doctoral students and the need to have internationally competitive doctoral programmes;
- *harmonisation with Europe:* particularly through the Bologna Process (Park, 2007: 2–3).

These drivers of change are accompanied by major changes in modes of knowledge production and flow, captured a decade ago by a changing relation between what was termed 'Mode 1', or disciplinary knowledge production, and 'Mode 2', or trans-disciplinary knowledge, produced in the context of application (Gibbons et al., 1994). As indicated above, the doctorate is becoming requisitioned more and more firmly in the service of national (and regional) economies, as well as being shaped through processes of global 'harmonisation' of qualifications. Through competing policy imperatives, the doctorate is increasingly caught between the need for competitiveness and distinctiveness and the move to standardisation (Labi, 2007). These imperatives push and squeeze doctoral programs in different directions and the result is a level of confusion in the current state of play in the field and an increasingly urgent need for international debates about the future and shape of the doctorate.

In the early years of the twenty-first century, what was once the private and pro-tected sanctuary of university study has found itself opened up to question after ques-tion. What should it do, how should it do it and what form should it take are all queries that are not only exercising academics, but governments too. Interventions are made to improve time to completion, completion rates, the numbers of doctoral graduates, enrolments in economically significant areas and, last but not least, the satisfaction of graduates themselves. Doctoral education can no longer be taken for granted when it is becoming a signifier for a country's competitive success, and academics, it seems, cannot be left alone to look after it.

This book is set in the context of these changes. It takes as its starting point an acceptance that doctoral education is now in play in a global arena, is often seen as in a state of transition, and is likely to continue to change into the next decade and beyond. It has already moved from an internal practice of particular academic disciplines to a field of practices that is regulated, made accountable, reviewed and focused beyond the academy. While there will remain a critical function of the doctorate for the formation of disciplinary scholars and members of the academy, even that will need to change to accommodate the need for a more widely equipped academic profession that directs attention beyond research in the disciplines to teaching and learning, to interdiscipli-nary and trans-disciplinary research and to knowledge formation in different settings and circumstances.

The focus of the contributors of the book is on the many ways in which doctoral education is changing. These changes are occurring at all levels, from the public policy work of governments, to institutional responses to new conditions and to the micro-level of encounters within departments and research groups. The book seeks to redress the dominance of policy narratives that limit and constrain what doctoral education is for – the training of a research workforce to sustain a high-tech economy – on the one hand, and is skeptical about the rhetoric of disciplinary reproduction and the primacy of the unitary supervisory relationship – business as usual – on the other. The contrib-utors are interested in the practices of doctoral education – the particularities of what it does and can do, as well as how they might be made more effective in a variety of ways. They chart the innovations that are occurring, the issues that arise and the contexts in which they take place.

As the doctorate is a rapidly expanding and changing global phenomenon, the book opens up an international conversation about these developments. It is focused on North America, Europe and Australia, since it is in these places that most has been written and the debates are lively. Many of these discussions, however, have been relatively inaccessible from outside the countries in which they are occurring or the publication outlets in which they appear. An important aim of this book, therefore, is to make visible to a general audience interested in doctoral education the nature of these conversations and what they are giving rise to. It is not a handbook, like so many others published recently, but a research-based contribution to this conversation, bringing in some of the key ideas, focusing discussion and presenting some alternatives. It also tells generative stories about where doctoral education is going currently. It captures examples of practice and represents them in ways that make them available to those in other disciplines and those who are not familiar with the settings and circumstances in which they occur.

In order to accomplish this, the book focuses on the practices of doctoral education. The contributions to this collection are all written by researchers who have been engaged in systematic inquiry into the changes in doctoral education over the past decade. They are organised around a set of key themes that position doctoral education within an environment of major changes in higher education and the changing role and purpose of the university worldwide. A range of disciplines – engineering, biological sciences, English, architecture, education – is represented, as well as doctoral work in trans-disciplinary and emerging professional fields. Together with this, the book presents a broad-based view on what will count as practice in doctoral work, ranging from macro-social analyses of the contexts and conditions of change in the doctorate to micro-level studies of the student experience. Hence, in addition to disciplinary perspectives, there are those from policy analysts, doctoral program managers, academic developers, supervisors and educational researchers. The book also includes a chapter from a then current doctoral student (Cumming), whose doctoral research is about the practices of doctoral education. This work represents a growing body of doctoral work producing new insights into the doctorate as an institution and set of cultural practices.

The title of the book, *Changing Practices of Doctoral Education,* construes doctoral work in terms of practice, and defines doctoral work in a broad sense as a social practice or set of practices. Practice is an over-arching conceptual frame for the sets of key themes that organise the book. As Schatzki (2001: 2) writes, practice can be understood as 'embodied, materially mediated arrays of human activity centrally organised around shared practical understanding'. Practice is purposeful, people are invested in it and it generates meanings and outcomes. We take up this framing of practice and argue in Chapter 2 both for an expansion of the range and scope of practice to include the work of a broad range of actors within the field, as discussed above, as well as for robust theory that can build a sophisticated research base for the field of doctoral education.

The following three chapters make up Part II, titled 'Disciplinarity and Change', which focuses on the changing nature of knowledge production within so-called 'traditional' disciplines and the move to make these explicit. In Chapter 3, Laura Jones writes about recent challenges to traditional understandings of differences between science- and humanities-based doctorates, drawing on the Carnegie Foundation's major inquiry into doctoral education in the US (the Carnegie Initiative on the Doctorate). This chapter discusses some insights from this initiative into a new, hybrid approach to producing 'creative scholars' across the disciplines, drawing on strengths from both sides of a traditional disciplinary divide. Chapter 4 follows this with an account of the 'shifting landscape' for English doctoral education drawn from a Canadian case study. Lynn McAlpine, Anthony Paré and Doreen Starke-Meyerring describe the struggles of a discipline in a process of re-definition in a time of dramatic changes in popular culture, publishing and the graduate job market.

In Chapter 5, Rob Gilbert takes up the changes in the way knowledge is framed in doctoral programs through the increasing emphasis of universities on 'research training' – the attempts by universities to articulate the once implicit understandings and skills of the practice of research within disciplines. This chapter reviews recent attempts to specify the goals, knowledge and skills that comprise contemporary doctoral research training and then considers ways in which knowledge is being differently framed into doctoral 'curriculum'.

The following five chapters form the second part of the book, titled 'Pedagogy and Learning'. These chapters move beyond the more traditional focus on supervision as primarily involving an essentially private relationship between a supervisor and a student within a discipline. Instead, they consider the 'distributed' practices of pedagogy and learning within current and emergent doctoral programs in the UK and Australia. Chapter 6 takes up a set of strategies to redress the general neglect of the students' perspectives of doing doctoral work. Diana Leonard and Rosa Becker describe ways in which departments, faculties, schools, research groups and interdisciplinary centres each provide complex opportunities and challenges for doctoral students, beyond the frame of individual study or the relationships with individual supervisors. Claire Aitchison and Alison Lee develop this theme in Chapter 7, with a focus on doctoral writing, arguing that, while it is often neglected and poorly understood, writing is a primary site of both doctoral learning and doctoral output. This chapter describes promising strategies for enhancing doctoral writing, both for the dissertation and beyond into the sphere of publication.

The following two chapters focus explicitly on doctoral education in laboratory science disciplines, making a significant contribution to redressing a lack of systematic documentation of laboratory-based doctoral work. In Chapter 8, Margot Pearson, Anna Cowan and Adrian Liston explore some of the complexities of supervising in the bio-medical sciences in terms of cultivating the professional skills and knowledges essential for developing an independent researcher, as distinct from merely a 'super-technician'. They provide instructive vignettes of a variety of coaching and mentoring strategies for science doctoral candidates, including lab meetings and journal clubs that are geared to establishing strategies to advance optimally the professional and career development of doctoral candidates. This is followed, in Chapter 9, by a detailed case study of doctoral research in molecular biology, in which the progression through the degree of one doctoral candidate is explored from the perspectives of key participants. In this chapter, Jim Cumming, himself a doctoral candidate whose research involved close case narrative work on doctoral research across a range of science-related disciplines, offers important insights into details of the complex and distributed practices and relationships involved in doctoral candidature in this discipline.

This part concludes with an account of a relatively recent development in the expanding field of practices of doctoral education – that of the professional development of doctoral supervisors. In Chapter 10, Angela Brew and Tai Peseta describe a program of supervisor 'training' in a large, research-intensive university that seeks to shift supervisors from simply reproducing their own experiences of having been supervised to a more theorised/more considered position, systematically and critically reflecting on their practice of supervision drawing on scholarly literature in the field.

Part III examines new and emerging forms of doctoral program that have engaged explicitly with changing influences on the doctorate as a form of research training. These include the rapidly expanding doctorates by publication that are a visible response to policy-led pressures for research productivity within the 'performative' university, as well as innovative practice-based, project-based and professional doctorates. The three chapters in this part describe programs whose purpose is not to prepare candidates for a discipline-based research career within the university but to contribute directly to knowledge work within professional spheres.

Chapter 11 focuses on professional doctorate programs, addressing the tensions between three sites of knowledge production (research, pedagogic and workplace) in relation to professional doctorates in two occupational fields in the UK: education and engineering. In this study, David Scott, Andrew Brown, Ingrid Lunt and Lucy Thorne show how knowledge is reconfigured in response to internal and external pressures at each site, and how the resolution of these conflicts has implications for the development of a specialised body of knowledge for the occupation in each case. Brent Allpress and Robyn Barnacle, in contrast, take the challenge of 'design research' and 'creative practice research' as their focus in Chapter 12, describing a 'PhD by Project' model of doctoral work in architecture. The chapter focuses on the role of disciplinary ways of knowing in the research process and sketches the outlines of a way of understanding project-based research within such disciplines.

Chapter 13 offers a further contrast to the professional and the disciplinary focus of the previous cases, by documenting a doctorate program focusing on the advanced professional development of individuals. Carol Costley and John Stephenson detail the doctorate in professional studies (the DProf) at Middlesex University. This chapter shows how the particular practices of this doctorate emerged from work-based learning and how, through case example, the program is constructed, implemented and assessed.

Part IV, titled 'Policy and Governance', takes up the changing influences on, and tensions within, doctoral education in an international context. The four chapters position doctoral education within the contemporary 'performative' and global university. In Chapter 14, Erica McWilliam explores risk-consciousness as an organisational imperative for the (post)modern university, with powerful implications for the production and legitimation of knowledge within the doctorate worldwide and for the practices of doctoral programs and participation at all levels.

In Chapter 15, Alexandra Bitusikova introduces what is arguably the most influential large-scale intervention into the doctorate in recent years, the unfolding of the Bologna Agreement in Europe, which seeks to 'harmonise' qualifications across national boundaries and to facilitate mobility of doctoral candidates and enhance regional competitiveness. The Bologna process and subsequent policy developments have a wide-ranging effect in bringing doctoral education into a global conversation beyond the boundaries of Europe. The chapter discusses the implications of the changes and details a range of strategies for development in doctoral programs that have emerged from them.

The two chapters that follow are examples of the pace and reach of the changes in the governance of doctoral programs. In Chapter 16, Ruth Neumann details the adaptations made by universities from a time of funding enrolled doctoral places to an era of competitive performance-based allocations. She notes the risk to diversity in the context of these developments, as university managements are tempted to adopt risk-minimisation strategies under the pressures of more competitive funding and narrow outcomes-based performance measures. In Chapter 17, Mark Tennant details the establishment in universities of Graduate Schools or their equivalent, which have the remit to manage candidatures of research students, develop policy and strategic directions, provide management information, and to foster innovations in doctoral education.

The final chapter brings the book to a close through reflecting on the preceding contributions and identifying directions in which doctoral education is moving. Bill Green considers this within the context of increasing globalisation of doctoral education, including the movement of staff and students internationally within programs, greater interchanges between practices in different countries and different disciplines, and the need for doctoral education to meet a wider range of purposes than preparing researchers for the next generation of academics. The chapter considers the implications of the expansion of the role and purpose of the doctorate within knowledge-based economies, and the distribution of knowledge production across university, professional and industry-based settings, as well as within and across more traditional disciplinary boundaries. It summarises the contribution of the book as one involving the imagining and documenting of diverse futures for doctoral education.

References

Cowan, R. (1997) Comparative perspectives on the British PhD, in N. Graves and V. Varma (eds), *Working for a Doctorate: A Guide for the Humanities and Social Sciences*, London: Routledge.

Department of Education, Science and Training (DEST) (2007) Australian Government, Canberra, at: http://www.dest.gov.au/sectors/higher_education/publications_resources/ profiles/students_2005_award_course_completions.htm.

Gibbons, M., Limoges, C., Nowotny, H., Schwartzman, S., Scott, P. and Trow, M. (1994) *The New Production of Knowledge: The Dynamics of Science and Research in Contemporary Societies*, London: Sage.

Gilbert, R. (2004) A framework for evaluating the doctoral curriculum, *Assessment and Evaluation in Higher Education*, 29(3): 299–309.

Golde, C.M. and Walker, G.E. (2006) *Envisioning the Future of Doctoral Education: Preparing Stewards of the Discipline*, San Francisco, CA: Jossey-Bass.

Higher Education Statistics Agency (HEST) (2007) at: http://www.hesa.ac.uk/index. php?option=com_datatables&Itemid=121&task=show_category&catdex=3#quals.

Labi, A. (2007) As Europe harmonizes degrees, report calls for more cooperation among Ph.D. programs, *Chronicle of Higher Education*, 5 September, at: http://chronicle.com/daily/ 2007/09/2007090503n.htm.

Ma, W. (2007) *The Trajectory of Chinese Doctoral Education and Scientific Research,* Research and Occasional Paper 12.07, August, Center for Studies in Higher Education, University of California, Berkeley, at: http://cshe.berkeley.edu/news/ index.php?id=34.

McAlpine, L. and Norton, J. (2006) Reframing our approach to doctoral programs: an integrative framework for action and research, *Higher Education Research and Development*, 25(1): 3–17.

National Science Foundation, Division of Science Resources Statistics (NSF) (2006) *Science and Engineering Doctorate Awards: 2005*, NSF 07-305, Susan T. Hill, project officer, Arlington, VA.

National Science Foundation, Division of Science Resources Studies (2000) *Graduate Education Reform in Europe, Asia, and the Americas and International Mobility of Scientists and Engineers: Proceedings of an NSF Workshop*, NSF 00-318, Jean M. Johnson, project officer, Arlington, VA.

Nerad, M. (2006) Globalization and its impact on research education: trends and emerging best practices for the doctorate of the future, in M. Kiley and G. Mullins (eds), *Quality in Postgraduate Research: Knowledge Creation in Testing Times*, CEDAM, Australian National University, Canberra, pp. 5–12.

Noble, K.A. (1994) *Changing Doctoral Degrees, An International Perspective,* Buckingham: Society for Research into Higher Education/Open University Press.

Park, C. (2007) *Redefining the Doctorate*, London: Higher Education Academy, at: http://www.hea.ac.uk.

Parry, S. (2007) *Disciplines and Doctorates*, Dordrecht: Springer.

Schatzki, T.R. (2001) Introduction: practice theory, in T. Schatzki, K. Knorr Cetina and E. von Savigny E (eds), *The Practice Turn in Contemporary Theory*, London: Routledge, pp. 1–14.

Wulff, D.H., Austin, A.E. and Associates (2004) *Paths to the Professoriate: Strategies for Enriching the Preparation of Future Faculty*, San Francisco, CA: Jossey-Bass.

Chapter 2

Framing doctoral education as practice

Alison Lee and David Boud

In order to think clearly about doctoral education and identify priorities for change, it is necessary to frame it in ways that open up productive discussions about what doctoral education does and how it might do it. The perspective we take on this task is to view doctoral work, and doctoral education, as forms of social practice. We do this in order to understand the complex features of current debates and to direct attention to new kinds of question about how doctoral education might be pursued.

In framing this discussion we concentrate on an expansion, distribution and diversification of the practices of doctoral education, focusing in particular on how the broad economic, political and intellectual agendas shape the ways in which knowledge is produced and exchanged, how doctoral graduates are formed as particular kinds of selves – in terms of identities, or skills, capabilities and dispositions – and the activities involved in doctoral work. Of course, none of these areas of concern is distinct from the others and all are overlapping, embedded and mutually constitutive. Our emphasis in this chapter is on the multiple determinants of change and their effects on practice.

Current conceptualisations of doctoral work tend to be limited to particular and different levels – of policy, of program development, of institutional provision, of the learning experiences of students – and there is often a lack of articulation of concerns across levels. There have been substantial developments in doctoral education at governmental, institutional and local levels, but they often work to different agendas: at the policy level, to needs for workforce planning and economic development; at the institutional level, to needs for accountability and risk management; and at local level, to needs for disciplinary maintenance, reproduction and transformation and for appropriate experiences for doctoral students.

Policy has been produced, in general, from a rather thin conceptualisation of what the doctorate is and what it does. What commonly results is a set of prescriptions for research degrees that follow economic imperatives but are simplistic in terms of the complexities of the multiple agendas at work in doing doctorate work. One outcome of this reductive approach to policy development is an over-emphasis on 'inputs' to the system, for example: differential funding to strategic discipline areas, blanket requirements for 'research training' of a certain kind, such as the requirement for a formal year of research study (e.g. the MRes in the UK), or the need for more generic or broader skill development (e.g. research commercialisation training in Australia). The point here is not that programs of this kind might not be of considerable value, but rather that such policy-driven 'solutions' to perceived deficiencies in the sector are a blunt instrument that assumes that more front-end 'training' is a 'good' in itself. What is missing from the policy process is a focus on what doctoral work actually produces and how it is produced. The result of a lack of good policy process is that government prescriptions are often resisted and found wanting by those directly involved in delivery of doctoral programs.

At the level of program development and provision in individual institutions, the picture is often reactive and poorly informed. There is a great deal of re-invention of the wheel in a field that is still generally information-poor (e.g. adding courses on research methods and methodology). Older traditions of doctoral work focus more on 'research' than 'education' and see the practices of supervisors and program coordinators at university and department level implicitly reproducing the ways in which they themselves were inducted into their discipline (see Brew and Peseta, this volume). There are few good studies documenting informed responses and innovative practices in different discipline areas.

At the same time, universities are greatly reactive to policy and funding imperatives. Often change is driven by intensifying accountability requirements as governments increase scrutiny on matters such as time to completion, the distribution of candidature across key fields, the need to skill graduates in terms of employability indicators and so on. One outcome of this is a sense in universities of being both micro-managed and overloaded, for example in relation to new 'capability-driven' course requirements. The pressure is on to produce, not just a successful doctoral thesis as evidence of the achievement of an original contribution to knowledge in a field, but also and at the same time graduates who are work-ready and knowledgeable about research policy, including such matters as intellectual property and commercialisation. There is a scant information base and lack of a forum from which universities, which also have 'stewardship' of disciplines and their imperatives, can dialogue with governments about such matters.

In terms of research into doctoral education, knowledge is fragmented and partial. While there has been a pleasing increase in the number and range of studies, there is at best a patchy empirical picture of the international scene of the doctorate and a lack of coherence in conceptual terms. It is difficult to 'scale' up from the current knowledge base. This is particularly true of work conducted within the US on one hand and British, European and Australian work on the other. For example, in the US there are large-scale surveys of graduate destinations that are not available elsewhere; in the UK and Australia there are important conceptual debates about the nature and purpose of the doctorate and its pedagogy, as well as a body of inquiry into new and different kinds of doctoral program not available for other national systems. And in Europe there are major policy-led debates about the status of doctoral-level work, with important debates about diversity and convergence. There is an almost complete lack of systematic inquiry into developments in doctoral research in Asia, Africa and elsewhere.

One example of how this is a problem is the assumption within much research and policy that differences between programs will fall out along the lines of disciplinary differences (Pearson, 2005a). Yet there is the beginning of a body of work that questions that assumption, drawing attention through detailed empirical work to the considerable degrees of overlap between different disciplines in relation to supervisory practices (e.g. Jones, this volume).

Much of the available literature in doctoral education to this point focuses on one or another aspect, or level, of a large and complex field. A major focus in much of the literature is on policy-driven change; hence many studies report on systemic changes – in numbers of students, types of programs, disciplines and fields of research, etc. – the factors driving these changes, and the effects of the changes, e.g. in attrition rates. At the opposite end of the spectrum are bodies of work describing the micro-interactions between participants in doctoral processes, often supervisors and students or groups of students. Somewhere between these two poles is a growing body of literature focusing on the improvement of the practices of supervision and the management of candidature. However, there has in general been a lack of study of the relationships among all of these elements, together with a still largely unexamined set of assumptions about these relationships.

In other words, there has been insufficient conceptual attention paid to doctoral education as a complex social field consisting of an interconnected array of different kinds of activities at different levels of abstraction, with often conflicting purposes and with varying expectations of outcome. To this end, we echo Pearson's (2005a) concerns about the 'limiting gaps' in available accounts of the practices of doctoral work. Pearson argues that the 'micro-level studies of educational practice and the doctoral experience have too often been decontextualised, with disciplinary differences assumed to be of most significance in explaining variation of practice' (p. 130). To address this problem and address her concern to bring a more global perspective to research into doctoral education, she calls for:

> more complementary macro- and micro-level studies, more critical analysis grounded in empirical data, more fine-grained analysis of local activity and agency and more recognition of the broad range of stakeholder interests. Such studies would provide richer and critical accounts of how changes and developments are enacted and choices made at many levels (p. 130).

In this chapter we explore how a practice perspective on doctoral education can enable us to address such a challenge.

Why focus on practice?

Practice is a commonplace term and is to be found liberally spread within the published literature in the doctoral education field. It refers to many things and is used in many different ways, some deliberate and others less so. In fact, anything can in principle be a practice since, in its most literal sense, the term refers simply to the action of doing something. Increasingly, however, scholarly disciplines concerned with the conduct of social life see human activity – practice – as a primary building block of the social.

Practices are, in a theoretical sense, as we noted in Chapter 1, 'embodied, materially mediated arrays of human activity centrally organised around shared practical understanding' (Schatzki, 2001: 2). Further, practice can be understood as a 'nexus of doings and sayings organised by understandings, rules, and teleoaffective structures' (Schatzki, 1997: 283) By this Schatzki is referring to the 'linking of ends, means, and moods appropriate to a particular practice or set of practices and that governs what it makes sense to do beyond what is specified by particular understandings and rules'. That is, it is purposeful (teleo), people are invested in it (affective) and it generates meanings of its own (understandings and actions).

Practices occur at any point in a given domain. They involve actors, actions, settings, tools and artefacts, rules, roles and relationships. In this sense, doctoral education can be seen to exceed any particular instance or manifestation in local settings and environments. It can be understood as a diverse and complex field of intersecting, overlapping and changing practices. We see at the heart of the doctorate a set of practices that produce both objects (knowledges, artefacts, institutions) and subjects (persons with skills, capabilities and attributes).

There are important benefits in taking a broad practice perspective on the growing field of doctoral education. We suggested in the opening chapter that the term *doctoral education* has arisen in the past decade or so to focus attention explicitly on the role of 'education' in the work of preparing doctoral graduates. In fact, it signals a shift in institutional attention to the practices involved in doing doctoral work and producing doctoral graduates, rather than merely to the production of research outputs. Prior to this period, knowledge about postgraduate research tended to be sporadic and informal. There was relatively little literature and this was limited by uncertainty of what it was that was produced – the doctoral graduate or the research outcome? New interest in the educative work of doctoral programs has surfaced at a time of major social and policy-led change in the field of doctoral research and practice. In the light of growth and expansion, changes in modes of knowledge production, forms of institutional and state governance, in types of doctorate programs and in pedagogies, there is, we argue, a growing need to systematically account for the extent and range of practices in the field.

The first consequence of a focus on practice is a requirement to attend to the materiality of the activities and experiences that go to make up doctoral work across the spectrum. Directing attention to the literal everydayness of doctoral work includes and encompasses widely divergent conceptual and physical spaces and spheres of activity – the laboratory, the 'field' (wherever and whatever that might be), the discipline (whatever and wherever that might also be), the policy text, the conference, the seminar, the examination room, teaching, supervision, management and administration, writing and doctoral 'study' (in all of its undocumented mystery (Green, 2005)). The focus on materiality suggests inquiry into how practices are distributed and achieved, what counts as practical knowledge in relation to these spheres of activity, and so on.

Second, a focus on practice requires us to understand changes in the activities and experiences of doctoral work in their local and particular settings in relation to and within the larger spheres and networks of activity, such as the globalising policy processes of the Bologna Agreement (European University Association, 2005), national policy processes in higher education and research and changing relationships among universities, industries, professions and the state (Etzkowitz and Leidesdorff, 2000; Lee et al., 2000). This focus construes the territory of the doctorate as a complex network of intersecting practices, or as a dynamic and changing open system, thus expanding the scope of what comes into the sphere of practice and hence within the scope of scholars of doctoral education.

Third, then, a focus on practice directs our attention to what is produced: objects, as we have suggested, and subjects. Arguably, at the heart of doctoral work is the production of the knowledgeable subject, the graduate. The skills, dispositions, knowledges and capabilities of the doctoral graduate are increasingly coming under scrutiny through policy work on graduate attributes and doctoral descriptors. Tensions and intersections between the competing agendas for this graduate have become manifest in debates about the purposes of the doctorate. The projected and directed outcomes include 'stewards of the discipline' (e.g. Golde and Walker, 2006), 'knowledge workers' (Usher, 2002), 'self-managing learners' (Stephenson et al., 2006) and so forth.

Elsewhere (Boud and Lee, 2006) we have noted the range of ways in which practice is taken up within the scholarly literature on the doctorate. Most commonly the term is associated with practice/theory oppositions, as for example in Evans and Kamler's (2005: 116) distinction between 'practice-wisdom' and 'systematic scholarship' on the doctorate. That is, 'practice' is either the 'real' against which is posited abstruse theory or empty rhetoric, or else the daily logics and imperatives of practice are invoked as subordinate to, and even a problem for, serious scholarship. Second, practice is invoked in relation to the quality assurance discourses governing higher education, through notions of best practice and the increasing codification of relations of accountability, such as codes of practice for supervisors, candidates and institutions. Third, an emerging theme in the literature is that of communities of practice (invoking Lave and Wenger (1991) and Wenger et al. (2002)). Most often in the doctoral education literature the term 'communities of practice' refers to local groupings of students and researchers within departments or disciplines or research teams (e.g. Pearson, 2005b). However, it can also refer to external targeted practice communities, particularly in relation to the doctoral programs concerned with researching practice, such as professional doctorates (there are many examples of this usage in the sets of proceedings of professional doctorates conferences. A good example is Green et al. (2001)). It might be fair to say that in this latter range of literatures, the focus is more on defining the community than conceptualising the practice.

It is important to clarify a further use of the word practice that has become common in current discussions. There is a distinction to be drawn between the practices *of* doctoral education, such as those sketched briefly above, and the idea of doctoral education *for* practice, which often focuses on knowledge acquired for application in subsequent professional practice. Government policy agendas often focus on the latter, but we suggest that it is the former that needs more attention. It is clear that systematic inquiry is needed to interrogate the meanings of practice and what it is to research practice within that latter sense (Lee et al., forthcoming). We will return later to the importance of practice settings, but our main point here is that the educative, administrative, policy and research practices of the doctorate itself are a distinct sphere of activity within the university. These require systematic documentation, analysis and critique.

A focus on the practices of doctoral education allows us to map, on the one hand, the instrumental and technical concerns of policy, quality and institutional governance, and, on the other, the concerns of practitioners, students, supervisors, program designers, institutional managers, graduate school deans, academic developers and so on. One of the important implications of attending focally to practice rather than, say, knowledge, as the central conceptual organiser for understanding and researching doctoral education, is the notion of embodiment and practical understanding. That is, practice necessarily includes the person and what they bring, as well as what they are involved in doing. Foucault, for example, shows in his historical studies, how practices constitute intelligible forms of embodiment, in the sense of capacities and aptitudes as well as experiences and even physical properties (e.g. Foucault, 1985). Schwandt (2005) and Kemmis (2005) offer analyses of a wide variety of traditions focusing on the study of practice.

We suggest that there is a need to expand the domains of practice beyond those usually considered and to suggest that they need to be more effectively framed and related to each other rather than rely on happenstance. To date, the bulk of the published literature on the practices of the doctorate has concentrated on supervision, often in the form of guidebooks on the protocols and dynamics of the relationship between student and supervisor (e.g. Delamont et al., 1998; Philips and Pugh, 2000; Taylor and Beasley, 2005). An adjacent body of work directs attention to policy-led change (e.g. EUA, 2005; Nerad, 2006; Park, 2007) and to management and development (e.g. Green and Powell, 2005; Pearson and Brew 2002). The latter have typically focused on improvements to existing practices and broadly involve a formalisation of the processes of managing, supervising and completing a doctoral degree. Emphasis has therefore been on 'professionalising the supervisor' by developing requirements for supervisors to undertake and evidence professional training, developing the tools and programs to facilitate these developments and establishing structures within universities to manage candidature, such as graduate schools. More recently, a policy-led process of deliberately embedding doctoral candidates into university research concentrations has led to changes in selection, focus, supervision and provision of resources. This has particularly impacted on fields and research cultures where doctoral research and candidature were understood more in individualistic terms of personal interest rather than as building a shared set of research outputs (Golde, 2007; Pearson, 2005b; also see Jones, this volume).

Recent developments in the literature are international volumes focusing on the role of doctoral education in relation to the disciplinary work of universities (e.g. Golde and Walker, 2006; Parry, 2007). At the same time, a collection of specialist volumes is emerging, discussing particular issues in research education, for example new forms of doctoral education (e.g. Scott et al., 2004), or aspects of the doctoral process such as examination of theses (e.g. Tinkler and Jackson, 2004). These volumes add a necessary richness and complexity to the international conversation about doctoral education and raise the stakes in terms of the need to better understand this complex and increasingly important sphere.

In all of this literature there are elements that can be construed within an overall practice frame. One way to imagine a connection among these elements is through the developing experience and awareness of the student. As we have discussed elsewhere (Boud and Lee, 2005), what is important is not just what is provided, but how it is perceived and taken up. The practices of others need necessarily to be drawn together in the practice of the student in their doctoral work, since it is the student – the one who studies and who is to become the new doctor – who is the object and the subject of the practice. Indeed, the practice of doctoral work could be seen as a taking up and utilisation of the affordances provided by the programs in which candidates operate, the research environment in which they are embedded, the people they encounter and, in turn, the practices they develop from these opportunities.

In summary, a focus on practice allows a set of critical questions to emerge, concerning the still largely undocumented activities of doctoral work, as well as the changing role of the university and the place of doctoral work within it. What are the purposes of doctoral study and how are current practices realising these purposes? How are the purposes of the doctorate changing and how can this be understood by focusing on the practices of provision, management, pedagogy, study and research? What are the shifting emphases between the dual role of the doctoral degree of 'training' and equipping students as researchers and the conduct of original research? How are the demands for doctoral level education being met for those who do not primarily wish to proceed to be researchers or academics? What are the changes in doctoral outcomes, how are they understood and practised, by students, supervisors and examiners? How can practices of supervision be rethought in these new contexts? How can practitioners of doctoral education engage effectively in the policy process? How can institutions and departments effectively build capacity to support doctoral education when they are subject to substantial economic constraints?

In the remainder of this chapter we briefly outline two key dimensions of the changing scene: the change in the nature and status of knowledge, and the consequent changes in the fashioning, through research and pedagogy, of graduates capable of producing new knowledge and forms of knowledge. Finally, we return to focus on the practices that are implicated in these changes and how they come together in the changing nature of the doctoral work of students.

Knowledge production and the knowledge economy

Major changes in the nature of knowledge, understandings about the role and value of knowledge, and in its modes of production, have become a hallmark of the last decades of the previous century and the first decades of the current one. These impact in fundamental ways on the doctorate and its practices.

There are several different aspects of these changes. The first is a shift from knowledge understood as governed through the logics and imperatives of disciplines and disciplinarity to one governed by the economic needs of nation states and national systems – the 'knowledge economy' (see, for example, Marginson and Van der Wende, 2007). The second, related shift comes from within disciplines themselves, as they proliferate and transform, in response to major increases in the store of knowledge and knowledge-producing capacity through information and communications technologies, and to the emergence of 'big questions' such as environmental crises that require the resources of more than one discipline (e.g. Moran, 2002; Somerville and Rapport, 2003).

Together, these changes are summarised in the now-classic labels of Mode 1 and Mode 2 knowledge production (Gibbons et al., 1994; Nowotny et al., 2001). Mode 1, or disciplinary knowledge production, is seen as the province of the university but the boundaries of the university increasingly become permeable to Mode 2, transdisciplinary knowledge production, created in the context of application. Knowledge is increasingly seen as contested, as rapidly changing with more temporary and heterogeneous practitioners collaborating on problems situated in and defined by a 'specific and localised context', rather than being autonomous and universal (Gibbons et al., 1994).

The idea of the 'knowledge economy' is one that, according to Usher (2002: 144), 'replaces an epistemological with an economic definition of Knowledge'. Knowledge becomes more and more an issue of *production*, more and more critical as economic performance comes to rely more and more heavily on knowledge inputs. Universities are increasingly seen as significant knowledge producers, taking on 'a hitherto unrecognised role as agents of economic growth'.

The implications for doctoral education are many and far-reaching. The knowledge economy is one where knowledge itself is the most important source of economic value. Further, knowledge is potentially infinitely capable of expanding. In national policy terms, doctoral graduates are understood as investments in national economic infrastructure and harnessed in the service of a global and increasingly competitive knowledge economy (EUA, 2005; Usher, 2002). The stakes are high, as evidenced by major policy-led movements in the US, Europe, the UK and elsewhere. A symptomatic example of the movements in this respect is the US initiative, *Rising Above the Gathering Storm*, in which a crisis in the number, quality, nationality and destination of doctoral graduates in science and engineering is seen as evidence of a US loss of competitive advantage over Europe and Asia (Committee on Prospering in the Global Economy of the 21st Century, 2007). On the other side of the Atlantic, Marginson and Van der Wende's report to the OECD on globalisation and higher education (2007) and the EUA (2005) report on doctoral programs for the European knowledge society reflect continuing concern about the 'uneven-ness of global knowledge flows', the continuing global hegemony of US higher education, and the need to focus on the doctorate to produce greater numbers of researchers. More recently, Marginson and Van der Wende (2007) warn of the Anglo- and Euro-centric nature of the knowledge wars and sketch the rise of the 'new Asia-Pacific science powers' (Korea, Turkey, Singapore, Taiwan, Portugal, China, Brazil and Australia).

As 'knowledge-intensive' organisations, universities are inevitably involved in the production of knowledge, the licensing of knowledge workers and hence in economic development. This means that universities have to ensure that these workers take their place with the appropriate amount and kind of human capital. In this environment, doctoral education is now, as Usher (2002: 145) writes, 'right in the middle of a fierce contestation that pits the traditional values of the academy against the new values of the knowledge economy'. These tensions can clearly be seen in policy work across different national and regional settings. They influence what counts as doctoral work and hence they are played out graphically in relation to the practices of knowledge-making, including changing relationships among disciplinary and post- or trans-disciplinary, or Mode 2, forms of knowledge production. They also influence the selecting, focusing, training and credentialing of doctoral students, sweeping them up in broader processes of redefinition and focus that are taking place at the departmental, university or sectoral level.

A practice perspective on knowledge production directs attention to three levels of issue: at the highest and most abstract, to ways of approaching knowledge production; at the intermediate, to the *effects* of political and economic change on doctoral programs and the ways governments and institutions grapple with these; and most immediately at the local level, with the world of the practitioner-producer, what they do and how they are formed. A practice perspective focuses on the activities and dynamics of program development and disciplinary, inter- and trans-disciplinary work in terms of topic choice, research methodologies and research partnerships with outside agencies and so on. The focus is more on how knowledge and identity are being produced, how capacities are built and how relationships are forged between those who identify problems and the variety of those who can contribute to their solution. In short, a practice perspective draws attention to the what, where and how of knowledge production.

Doctoral graduates as 'advanced knowledge workers'

As knowledge production changes, and with these changes, the goals and purposes of the doctorate, so too do the kinds of graduates produced through doctoral work. In policy terms, doctoral graduates are understood, resourced and governed more and more in terms of human capital. This means that new kinds of graduates are imagined and projected through doctoral work. They are the 'knowledge workers' with different skills, capabilities, dispositions, memberships and relationships from those of the imagined communities of older ideas of the doctorate within a 'disciplinary economy' of knowledge. Who, then, are these new doctors? What are the environments and practices that produce them and what do we know about these practices?

As knowledge production shifts emphasis from disciplinary, closed systems to post-disciplinary, trans-disciplinary and extra-disciplinary 'open' systems, as links among universities, professions and industry change, as new relationships with the state emerge through changed policy and funding regimes, new skills and capacities emerge. Disciplinary trainings mesh with 'soft', transferable and flexible skills and dispositions, such as communication and problem-solving abilities. The capabilities and attributes of doctoral graduates represented in recent policy texts evidence these qualities, summed up in the following sorts of terms:

> flexible and multi-skilled with an openness to learning. They must be at home in a work environment shaped by globalising processes and the information and communication revolution. They must as a minimum be IT literate. These skills required have been described as 'soft skills' and are themselves knowledge intensive – skills to do with problem-solving, collaborative work, leadership and knowledge application.
>
> (Usher, 2002: 145)

One response to this intensifying environment of change is an explicit focus, by national and regional governments, sectors and systems, on the formation of the graduate in terms of descriptors of outcomes and attributes (e.g. SEEC, 2003). In policy terms, sets of 'doctoral descriptors' have emerged that attempt to capture knowledge products as well as the qualities of the graduate produced though the processes and practices of the doctorate. The doctorate is in these ways being repositioned away from simpler, older and more implicit emphases on a 'product' in the form of a thesis text as the sole measured outcome of a period of doctoral study and more and more explicitly towards a graduate as the 'knowing subject' of doctoral work. The graduate needs to be a certain kind of knower and a certain kind of self: research-capable, reflexive and flexible, with 'generic' as well as discipline- or field-specific knowledges and capabilities (Lee, 2005). These in turn become 'scripts for self-fashioning' (Foucault, 1985) for supervisors and students, research program developers and managers.

At the same time, new kinds of doctoral program express the shifting emphases of universities and systems on new kinds of knowledge, new partnerships and relationships and new practices of research. One important strand of this is in disengagement from the traditional assumption that doctoral graduates are trained as future academics. While there remains a strong need for the doctoral graduate as a future academic, a 'steward of the discipline' (Golde and Walker, 2006) and a teacher of the next generations of students, current and emergent practices of doctoral education are increasingly involved in a business of producing people for beyond the academy. Recent research in the US (Wulff et al., 2004), for example, indicates that fewer than half of the US doctoral graduates surveyed take up career positions as academics.

In summary, many of the political and economic shifts in the positioning of the doctorate are in significant tension with older, more implicit forms of apprenticeship and enculturation into disciplinary knowledges, disciplinary modes of production and disciplinary cultures, that characterised the PhD until recently. These traditional practices are being gradually infiltrated and metamorphosed by new practices producing new kinds of researchers and knowers, where attitudes, capabilities and dispositions become as important as expertise and knowledge. These changes can be traced in graduate destination survey research such as Wulff et al. (2004), through the emergence of new 'families of doctorates' (Park, 2007) and new and different relationships among universities and various partners.

Changing practices of doctoral work

As we have discussed, attention has increased in the past decade and a half to considerations of 'doctoral education', a shift that acknowledges the educative work involved in producing increasing numbers of graduates in an accelerated training environment, under increasing scrutiny, for purposes other and beyond those of disciplinary stewardship and the reproduction of the academy.

One outcome of this is that the doctorate has become a space of increasing complexity, where the practices are distributed (Lea and Nicoll, 2002), complexified and sometimes competing and conflicting. For example, the needs of disciplines and universities to produce academics is potentially in tension with some of the more varied dispersed activities of building transdisciplinary partnerships with professional and industry bodies.

As well, there are potentially competing agendas in relation to the growing need to embed doctoral work into areas of existing or emerging research concentration, in response to policy-led pressure for scale and focus in relation to the research effort of universities. These changes shape the selection, administration, focus, pedagogical practices and the governance of doctoral work in wide-ranging ways, the implications of which are as yet barely documented. Furthermore, pressure for timely completion of doctoral study, together with a significant expansion of numbers and diversification of study profiles of students, produces an increased focus on both managerial formalisation and developmental pedagogical work. The changing practices of the day-to-day work of the doctorate in its increasingly wide range of sites of practice remain important questions for further empirical investigation.

First, we might speak, following Bernstein (1996), of the 'pedagogisation' of doctoral work. This ranges from an increasing emphasis on structured programs of a wide variety of kinds, including in places where the doctorate has been until recently a kind of individual apprenticeship, such as in humanities disciplines. The structure and emphasis of new and emerging programs are becoming matters of more public interest as international pressures on the doctorate mount in terms of transparency, parity and transferability of qualifications (e.g. through Bologna; see the EUA, 2005). What these developments signify is a shift from a hitherto almost exclusive focus on 'research' to one on 'training', which plays out at the level of material practices of seminars, workshops, examinations, etc. In the UK, for example, there is an increasing formalisation of provision of research training, particularly through the Research Councils' mandated Master of Research, which focuses explicitly on preparing students for research studies. In Australia, where the shift is not quite so publicly apparent, there is a quiet and inexorable capture of doctoral research by educational work of one kind or another (Neumann, 2003).

While this latter trend has anecdotally been referred to as an Americanisation of the doctorate, this is not necessarily an appropriate characterisation. The 'pedagogisation' is not typically being driven by a need for greater content coursework in the American sense, as UK and Australian undergraduate degrees are typically much more specialised, but by the need to form a person who thinks and acts like a researcher and can draw on the devices – conceptual and practical – researchers need for their work. More importantly, there is a programmatic shift to diverse and differentiated sets of activities normally undertaken on a group basis to equip a new kind of doctoral graduate with the wide range of capacities and competencies needed to be employed in and operate within knowledge generating economies. These typically involve much more than are necessarily required in the production of a standard doctoral thesis.

Second, this pedagogisation of doctoral work extends the sphere of practice to include an increasing emphasis on doctoral learning and on the environments and cultures in which doctoral work is located. We have written elsewhere (Boud and Lee, 2005) of the 'distributed practices' of doctoral learning, drawing on Lea and Nicoll's (2002) account of networks of learning in which learners take up opportunities in a variety of ways without necessary involvement from teachers or supervisors. In a succession of discursive shifts, postgraduate research becomes a space of pedagogy, construed primarily in terms of narrow conceptions of supervision, then becomes dispersed to include the whole environment in which doctoral research is undertaken. In an influential early account, Cullen et al. (1994: 41) construe doctoral students, not as more or less passive recipients of institutional supervision, but rather as 'self-organising agents of varying effectiveness, accessing resources, one of which is the supervisor'. In their study, students presented themselves as being 'at the centre of a constellation of others' in assembling resources to meet particular research/learning needs (ibid.).

We have argued elsewhere (Boud and Lee, 2005) that close scholarly attention to the learning practices of students is necessary for higher education systems to be able to respond productively to policy pressures of one kind or another for change in research education. We sought to conceptualise the doctoral education environment as a site of pedagogy and learning, rather than a kind of passive 'container' or backdrop. Further, we have sought to document and theorise expanded and distributed pedagogical practices that include but go beyond more traditional practices of supervision, narrowly conceived. These include an expanded notion of 'peer learning', where the doctoral student moves from conceptions and practices of learning with and from each other (students as peers) to involve an extending network of peer relations, including conference presentations, publishing in peer-reviewed journals and so forth, in addition to the solo performance of research and thesis production – becoming a peer. Part of this expanding frame for doctoral pedagogy involves an explicit focus on the practices of writing, publishing, editing and reviewing (see Aitchison and Lee, 2006; Boud and Lee, 2005; Lee and Boud, 2003).

Third, a focus on the distributed work of doctoral education involves an expanded attention to the range of actors in the field. These include, in addition to students and their supervisors, other human actors such as a broad range of program coordinators, learning support and academic development staff, managers, policy-makers, and so on. It also includes what might be called a range of non-human actors such as research conferences, internet networks, international research workshops and the like. The capture of doctoral education by higher education research policy sees an array of practices developed to manage the spaces and practices of doctoral work. These include Quality Assurance, risk management, commercialisation and Intellectual Property protocols. They increasingly frame and shape the experiences of doctoral students and populate the space of doctoral study with a rich array of personnel, policies and practices. The iconic student–supervisor relationship is subsumed into a diverse matrix of opportunities, resources, monitoring processes and expectations. Green (2005: 153) suggests the need to conceptualise doctoral pedagogy, and specifically supervision in 'eco-social' terms as a 'total environment within which postgraduate research activity ("study") is realised'. Green notes that the fullest implication of this formulation has not been grasped and is hence 'unfinished business' within the doctoral education literature. This idea would seem to suggest a way forward for research into the practices of doctoral education.

Conclusion

We have suggested that doctoral education is usefully understood as a social practice, or field of practices. This frame allows us to attend to the increasingly complex array of sites of activity governing and framing the doctorate. Far from being the essentially private activity of individuals within the enclosed spheres of disciplines and departments, the doctorate is now the much more complex and public site of practices of governance, regulation and planning, as well as of research itself, the educative work of supervision and teaching and the activities and experiences of candidature.

The current literature on the doctorate commonly takes up one dimension or another of the doctorate. Much of it is policy-based or policy-dominated, as higher education systems in different countries come to terms with the major increase in governance and regulation of the doctorate within an economically-driven change agenda. Alternatively, the focus is on the micro-levels of practice, most commonly attending to the dynamics of supervision and the experiences of candidature. Each of these accounts of change tells different stories of the doctorate that serve different purposes. But in each case they delimit the scope of reference, with the result that the emerging field of scholarship on the doctorate remains rather fragmented. This is perhaps true of any new scholarly field, and doctoral education research is in many respects still in an emergent or immature phase.

In this regard we would endorse Pearson's (2005a: 130) call, cited at the beginning of the chapter for macro- and micro-level empirical studies, including fine-grained analysis of local practices, together with a stronger recognition of stakeholder interests. At the same time as moving towards a more expansive and integrated empirical inquiry, however, we also note an absence of a strong theoretical base to much research and scholarship in doctoral education. In the light of this, we suggest that various forms of practice theory, such as those outlined by Schatzki (2001) and Kemmis (2005), may offer opportunities to build richer understandings. There may be productive resources for further inquiry within the conceptual frames of, for example, activity theory, actor-network theory or communities of practice theory, together with theories of complexity such as Green's (2005) 'eco-social' conception of the doctoral education environment – to explore the still largely undocumented activities of doctoral work, as well as the changing role of the university and the place of doctoral work within it.

References

Aitchison, C., and Lee, A (2006) Research writing: problems and pedagogies, *Teaching in Higher Education*, 11(3): 265–278.

Bernstein, B. (1996) *Pedagogy, Symbolic Control and Identity*, London: Taylor and Francis.

Boud, D. and Lee, A. (2005) Peer learning as pedagogic discourse for research education, *Studies in Higher Education*, 30(3): 501–515.

Boud, D. and Lee, A. (2006) What counts as practice in doctoral education?, in M. Kiley and J. Mullins (eds), *Knowledge Creation in Testing Times: Proceedings of the Quality in Postgraduate Research Conference, Adelaide, April 2006. Part 2*, Canberra: Centre for Educational Development and Academic Methods, Australian National University, 45–54, at: http://www.qpr.edu.au/2006/.

Committee on Prospering in the Global Economy of the 21st Century: An Agenda for American Science and Technology, National Academy of Sciences, National Academy of Engineering, Institute of Medicine (2007) *Rising Above the Gathering Storm: Energizing and Employing America for a Brighter Economic Future*, Washington, DC: National Academies Press.

Cullen, D., Pearson, M., Saha, L.J. and Spear, R.H. (1994) *Establishing Effective PhD Supervision*, Canberra: Australian Government Publishing Service.

Delamont, S., Atkinson, P. and Parry, O. (1998) *Supervising the PhD: A Guide to Success*, London: Society for Research into Higher Education.

Etzkowitz, H. and Leydesdorff, L. (2000) The dynamics of innovation: from national systems and 'Mode 2' to a triple helix of university–industry–government relations, *Research Policy*, 29(2): 109–123.

European University Association (2005) *Doctoral Programs for the European Knowledge Society*, final report, at: www.eua.be.

Evans, T. and Kamler, B. (2005) The need for counter-scrutiny: taking a broad view of doctoral education research, *Higher Education Research and Development*, 24(2): 115–118.

Foucault, M. (1985) *The Use of Pleasure: The History of Sexuality, Vol. 2* (translated by Robert Hurley), London: Penguin.

Gibbons, M., Limoges, C., Nowotny, H., Schwartzman, S., Scott, P. and Trow, M. (1994) *The New Production of Knowledge: The Dynamics of Science and Research in Contemporary Societies*, London: Sage.

Golde, C.M. (2007) Signature pedagogies in doctoral education: are they adaptable for the preparation of education researchers?, *Educational Researcher*, 36(6): 344–351.

Golde, C.M. and Walker, G.E. (2006) *Envisioning the Future of Doctoral Education: Preparing Stewards of the Discipline*. San Francisco, CA: Jossey-Bass.

Green, B. (2005) Unfinished business: subjectivity and supervision, *Higher Education Research and Development*, 24(2): 151–163.

Green, B., Maxwell, T.W. and Shanahan, P. (eds) (2001) *Doctoral Education and Professional Practice: The Next Generation?*, Armidale, NSW: Kardoorair Press.

Green, H. and Powell, S. (2005) *Doctoral Study in Contemporary Higher Education,* Buckingham: Open University Press.

Kemmis, S. (2005) Knowing practice: searching for saliences, *Pedagogy, Culture and Society*, 13(3): 391–426.

Lave, J. and Wenger, E. (1991) *Situated Learning: Legitimate Peripheral Participation*, Cambridge: Cambridge University Press.

Lea, M.R. and Nicoll, K. (eds) (2002) *Distributed Learning: Social and Cultural Approaches to Practice*, London: Routledge.

Lee, A. (2005) 'Thinking Curriculum': framing research/education, in T.W. Maxwell, C. Hickey and T. Evans (eds), *Professional Doctorates: Working Towards Impact, Proceedings of the 5th Biennial International Conference on Professional Doctorates*, Geelong: Deakin University Press, pp. 75–86, at: http://www.deakin.edu.au/education/rads/conferences/publications/prodoc/index.php.

Lee, A. and Boud, D. (2003) Writing groups, change and academic identity: research development as local practice, *Studies in Higher Education*, 28(2): 187–200.

Lee, A., Brennan, M. and Green, B. (forthcoming) Re-imagining doctoral education: professional doctorates and beyond, *Higher Education Research and Development*.

Lee, A., Green, B. and Brennan, M. (2000) Organisational knowledge, professional practice and the professional doctorate at work, in J. Garrick and C. Rhodes (eds), *Research and Knowledge at Work: Perspectives, Case Studies and Innovative Strategies*, New York and London: Routledge, pp. 117–136.

Marginson, S. and Van der Wende, M. (2007) Globalisation and higher education, Education Working Party No. 8, Paris: OECD Directorate for Education.

Moran, J. (2002) *Interdisciplinarity*, London and New York: Routledge.

Nerad, M. (2006) Globalization and its impact on research education: trend and emerging best practices for the doctorate of the future, in M. Kiley and G. Mullins (eds), *Quality in Postgraduate Research: Knowledge Creation in Testing Times*, Canberra: CEDAM, Australian National University, pp. 5–12.

Neumann, R. (2003) *The Doctoral Education Experience: Diversity and Complexity*, Canberra: Department of Education, Science and Training, Evaluations and Investigations Program.

Nowotny, H., Scott, P. and Gibbons, M. (2001) *Re-thinking Science: Knowledge and the Public in an Age of Uncertainty*, Cambridge: Polity Press.

Park, C. (2007) PhD quo vadis? Envisioning futures for the UK doctorate, in R. Hinchcliffe, T. Bromley and S. Hutchinson (eds), *Skills Training in Research Degree Programmes: Politics and Practice,* London: Open University Press.

Parry, S. (2007) *Disciplines and Doctorates*, Dordrecht: Springer.

Pearson, M. (2005a) Framing research on doctoral education in Australia in a global context, *Higher Education Research and Development*, 24(2): 119–134.

Pearson, M. (2005b) Changing contexts for research education: implications for supervisor development, in P. Green (ed.), *Supervising Postgraduate Research: Contexts and Processes, Theories and Practices*, Melbourne: RMIT University Press, pp. 11–29.

Pearson, M. and Brew, A. (2002) Research training and supervision development, *Studies in Higher Education*, 27(2): 135–150.

Phillips, E. and Pugh, D.S. (2000) *How to Get a PhD: A Handbook for Students and their Supervisors*, third edition, Buckingham: Open University Press.

Schatzki, T.R. (1997) Practices and actions: a Wittgensteinian critique of Bourdieu and Giddens, *Philosophy of The Social Sciences*, 27: 283–308.

Schatzki, T.R. (2001) Introduction: practice theory, in T. Schatzki, K. Knorr Cetina and E. von Savigny (eds), *The Practice Turn in Contemporary Theory*, London: Routledge, pp. 1–14.

Schwandt, T. (2005) On modelling our understanding of the practice fields, *Pedagogy, Culture and Society*, 13(3): 313–332.

Scott, D., Brown, A., Lunt, I. and Thorne, L. (2004) *Professional Doctorates: Integrating Professional and Academic Knowledge*, Maidenhead: Society for Research into Higher Education and Open University Press.

SEEC (2003) SEEC Southern England Consortium for Credit Accumulation and Transfer,

Credit Level Descriptors for Further and Higher Education, at: www.seec-office.org.uk/ SEEC%20FE-HECLDs-mar03def-1.doc.

Somerville, M.A. and Rapport, D. (eds) (2003) *Transdisciplinarity: Recreating Integrated Knowledge*, Montreal: McGill-Queens University Press.

Stephenson J., Malloch, M., and Cairns, L. (2006) Managing their own programme: a case study of the first graduates of a new kind of doctorate in professional practice, *Studies in Continuing Education*, 28(1): 17–32.

Taylor, S. and Beasley, N. (2005) *A Handbook for Doctoral Supervisors*, New York: Routledge.

Tinkler, P. and Jackson, C. (2004) *The Doctoral Examination Process: A Handbook for Students, Examiners and Supervisors*, Maidenhead: Open University Press.

Usher, R. (2002) A diversity of doctorates: fitness for the knowledge economy, *Higher Education Research and Development*, 21(2): 143–153.

Wenger, E., McDermott, R. and Snyder, W. (2002) *Cultivating communities of practice: a guide to managing knowledge*, Boston, MA: Harvard Business School Press.

Wulff, D.H., Austin, A.E., and Associates (2004) *Paths to the Professoriate: Strategies for Enriching the Preparation of Future Faculty*, San Francisco, CA: Jossey-Bass.

Part I

Disciplinarity and change

Chapter 3

Converging paradigms for doctoral training in the sciences and humanities

Laura Jones

Doctoral education in the United States is in an era of change. Recent developments in technology, the emergence of new fields of study and a decline in public support for higher education are gradually transforming the arenas in which PhDs are trained and work (Bell et al., 2007; McGuinness, 1999). The US system of doctoral education is unregulated and highly decentralized, with most authority resting in the hands of faculty supervisors. More than 400 US universities grant doctoral degrees; together they produce more than 40,000 doctoral graduates each year (Thorgood et al., 2006). In contrast to the 'tightening up' of standards for student and supervisor performance in some countries (Parry, 2007: 16), the size and organizational complexity of the US higher education system has limited the spread of well-intentioned national reform efforts (Walker et al., forthcoming).

The Carnegie Foundation for the Advancement of Teaching, funded by a grant from Atlantic Philanthropies, undertook a five-year 'action research' project to encourage creative re-examination of core assumptions in doctoral education. From the beginning, the project accepted that reform efforts would be initiated at the local level and that there would be no 'best practices' recommended for every program. In the Carnegie Initiative on the Doctorate (CID), we worked with more than 80 doctoral programs in six disciplines: chemistry, education, English, history, mathematics and neuroscience. Nearly all of these departments were located in the United States (one was Canadian). The CID was designed to encourage local re-examination and reform of doctoral training practices, because our theory of change assumes that change will rise from the bottom up in US doctoral programs.

A key tool used by the CID to promote critical examination of current practice in partner programs was structured comparison between alternative models from within the discipline, and between disciplines. The CID requested that programs prepare narrative descriptions, collect data and artifacts and make these local practices 'public' in meetings hosted at the Carnegie Foundation, and later in a Web-based exhibition space (http://gallery.carnegiefoundation.org/cid). The first two sets of meetings were organized by discipline and focused on the critical review of the programs' self-study reports and the design of curricular experiments. The variability of practices within each discipline was a revelation to many participants and inspired many to experiment with practices 'borrowed' from a sister program. Fundamental assumptions were rarely challenged in the disciplinary meetings; however, this was a good way to begin the process of self-study and experimentation. Participants were highly motivated to compare themselves with their colleagues in competing programs, and they shared a common frame of reference that promoted collegiality.

The CID wanted to reach a deeper level of critical thinking, however, than we witnessed in the first two years of meetings and site visits to the programs. Our strategy was to mix up the disciplines, hoping we would witness a more lively debate and real questioning of fundamental principles. The third set of multidisciplinary meetings was organized around three topics: learning to teach, learning to conduct research, and becoming a member of an intellectual community. Not surprisingly, in these meetings, participants struggled to overcome the differences between them: in style of scholarly discourse, in the definition of research and in their expectations for students in their doctoral programs. These divergences have been described by many scholars (Becher and Trowler, 2001; Huber and Morrealle, 2002; Parry, 2007): 'What do you mean, the student is assigned a research topic?' from humanities faculty and students, and 'Do you really think it's responsible to expect your students to spend ten years in your program?' from the science side. Though they struggled to find common ground, our participants were forced to justify their paradigms and assumptions, an important step in change.

These situations of high contrast were highly productive in promoting creative thinking about doctoral education: assumptions needed to be made explicit and, once offered, were subject to vigorous challenge. While we witnessed defensiveness and retrenchment in some instances ('Some topics take ten years to address', for example), the comparative process opened up the conversation to new possibilities and more ambitious experiments. In this chapter, the focus is on the re-imagining of doctoral education based on comparisons of high contrast: between the laboratory sciences and the humanities. Our experience in the CID was with chemistry and neuroscience on the one hand, and English and history on the other; it is likely that these insights extend to sister disciplines as well. (Mathematics and education were important partners in the CID project; however, they displayed patterns of practice that did not fall as neatly into the two 'basic' divisions we – and other authors – have noted between the sciences and the humanities.)

Doctoral education in the United States experienced a divergence between the laboratory sciences and the humanities during the mid-twentieth century, as external funding of scientific research transformed the academic workplace in many disciplines. If we look to the most extreme cases, we see many doctoral students in lab sciences admitted to perform a specific laboratory analysis funded by a larger project directed by their primary advisor. This paradigm represents a particular version of academic apprenticeship with a very strong hierarchical relationship between a student and a single advisor/supervisor. In our survey of more than 2,000 doctoral students in programs participating in the CID, more than 60 per cent of chemistry students, and nearly 50 per cent of neuroscience students reported having only one advisor or mentor (see Figure 3.1). These students generally receive their Ph.D.s when the lab analysis is complete (and the grant funding expires), regardless of how well-prepared they may

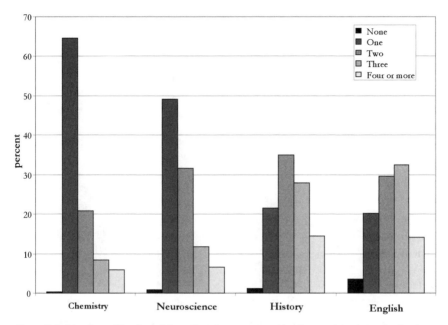

Figure 3.1 Number of faculty advisors/mentors reported by doctoral students, by faculty.

be for their subsequent careers. Indeed, many go on to a series of postdoctoral fellow-ship positions prior to entering the ranks of the faculty.

In the humanities we found a different paradigm: students expected to select and design their own research and spending many years working alone on their projects. In the absence of external grants, these students often teach full time to support themselves through the years of the program. Expectations regarding advising are dif-ferent in the humanities, where students identify more than one faculty advisor (see Figure 3.1), typically the members of the dissertation committee. Interaction with advi-sors is less frequent, with English and history faculty reporting that they meet monthly with students in the final stages of the program while science faculty have frequent contact with students even at this advanced stage (Figure 3.2).

The dissertation is a further area of divergence: in the sciences a series of published papers (which increasingly may be 'published' only in online formats), which may include co-authored reports, forms the basis of a dissertation that may be only 50 pages in length. Dissertations in the humanities continue to reach hundreds of pages in length. Co-authored dissertations and alternative media are beginning to appear but remain rare at this time in the humanities; programs continue to expect a book-length monograph for the dissertation.

Each paradigm has strengths and weaknesses. The strengths of the lab science model at its best are: frequent contact between student and advisor (daily–weekly), the immersion of the student into a lab group that forms the basis for peer mentoring and a sense of intellectual community, the process of collaborative research and

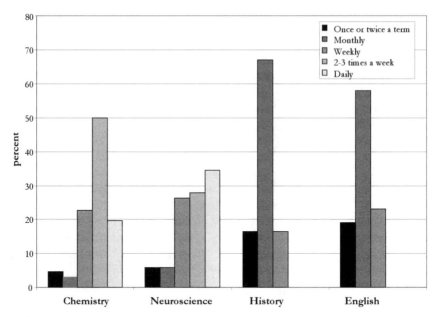

Figure 3.2 Frequency of meetings between advisors and students within one year of completion of the PhD, reported by faculty.

publication, and the relatively short time spent in the program (four–five years). The basic weaknesses are: narrow exposure to the field at large (and to alternative approaches) and few opportunities for students to develop independence and creativity. The strengths of the humanities paradigm are: the expectation of independence (which extends from research into teaching as well), and the flexibility to choose and change topics. Its weaknesses are: infrequent contact between student and advisor(s), isolation of students from peers and advisors due in part to economic realities (many humanities students work full time and many leave campus during the later stages of their study), long time-to-degree, and a tendency to overspecialization that is similar to that found in the sciences.

The CID report offers a comprehensive model of doctoral education, with new forms of apprenticeship – multiple mentors, nonhierarchical mentoring, cascading mentoring – embedded within programs as intellectual communities (Walker et al., forthcoming). In this chapter, I narrow in on two trading zones that build on the 'signature pedagogies' of doctoral education in the sciences and the humanities: offering lessons in collaboration from the sciences, and learning about independence from the humanities (see Golde (2007a, 2007b) for other examples from the CID). The principles of collaboration and independence may seem to be pulling in different directions. A more careful analysis shows that they can in fact both be fostered through deliberate program design and appropriate mentoring relationships. This is not however a simple matter – attention to the needs of individual students and the character of particular research questions will shape the balance between teamwork and individual effort.

Collaboration

Early in our CID project, we commissioned a set of essays from leading scholars in the disciplines (Golde and Walker, 2006). Kenneth Prewitt was one of three scholars asked to comment on the entire collection of essays. Prewitt observed that, 'on the testimony of the Carnegie Essays on the Doctorate, building doctoral training around practices that are interdisciplinary and collaborative is our future' (2006: 31). Chemistry professor Angelica Stacey's remark that, 'cutting edge research requires cooperation' (2006: 189) echoes English scholar Andrea Lunsford's suggestion that students be offered the 'opportunity to engage in the kind of project that calls for more than one researcher' (2006: 366). A recent National Science Foundation report clearly recognizes the trend towards multiple author, and multidisciplinary publications (Bell et al., 2007).

How do students develop the interpersonal skills, work habits and ethical sensibilities that support intellectual collaboration? In successful science labs, they enter a context in which collaboration is expected, and in which they participate in a nested set of intellectual communities where collaborative practices are common. Three of these practices – lab group meetings, journal clubs and poster presentations – showed some portability into humanities departments based on our experiences in the CID.

The lab group is interdependent: the success of each (and all) depends on the contributions of the others, which can create a social setting of cooperation and mutual support, as well as pressure to make timely progress. The weekly lab group meeting is a critical venue for helping each other overcome obstacles but is also the venue for negotiating the messy issues of co-authorship (each paper may be authored by all the members of the lab group – and some outside partners – and the order in which their names appear is a carefully orchestrated statement of intellectual ownership). Leadership by the faculty director and advanced students (and postdoctoral fellows) is critical to setting the standards for collegiality, trust and cooperation in the group. One faculty member in Chemistry reported:

> The most effective tool is the mentor relationship within a research group. My students learn from frequent discussions and examples from me and from working together with fellow graduate students.

A faculty member from neuroscience echoes this approach:

> My most effective teaching tool is direct and frequent interaction with me. Also interaction with my collaborators and other students in the laboratory.

Here is a detailed description of how this works from one lab (this one from an education research group):

> The lab context involves new students working with more advanced students. Analyses and findings for 1–2 research projects are discussed at each lab meeting, usually with myself and 3–4 graduate students who are familiar with the data that is being analyzed. Ideas are brainstormed, analyses are sometimes done right then,

and new directions are discussed. Drafts of written papers are brought to the lab group, as well as to my Co-PI, and feedback cycles are extensive. Although in the first project with the student, I tend to take charge of the analyzing and interpreting, the second project's analyses are typically completed by the student or a small group of students. Each project, I tend to have to scaffold less and less.

The pedagogy of research in lab sciences is social and one of its key objectives is learning to conduct collaborative research. Another faculty member, again from chemistry:

I work hard to provide experience not only in the technical skills and data analysis, but the ability to work effectively with others, to resolve conflicts between collaborators and colleagues.

A chemistry faculty member defines 'overall student success' as:

The ability to do science in an honest and ethical fashion; to ensure that relevant background material is understood and credited; to work effectively and congenially with others, regardless of whether they are peers, superiors or subordinates; to exhibit a strong work ethic and high standards for the quality of the 'results' they produce whether that 'result' be a student's education, a piece of research or the management of a group of people.

Science departments also host organized groups of scholars with overlapping areas of interest: journal clubs. In journal clubs (which may persist for decades in a program), participants take turns presenting an important recent article from a major journal in the field. The goal is to create a common understanding of the direction scholarship in the field is moving, but pedagogical goals are met as well when students practice scholarly debate in a cooperative setting. This is also an opportunity for students to engage with colleagues outside their lab group in a context of cooperative inquiry. Participation in the intellectual community of the journal club is a powerful socializing force in science programs. The journal club format has the potential to address a number of problems reported by humanities doctoral students, for example:

I think we are weaker, however, in training students to develop research and write for publication. I'm speaking about a literature program, so in many subfields there seems to be a pretty intense saturation of work already done. The process is more or less taken for granted; when in reality there are identifiable strategies that would demystify that step from class paper/project to more fully professional work. I also wonder if the standards of our professional work are being brought down by obscuring the distinction between a passable project and what really enters a conversation or makes a contribution.

And by faculty who want their students to succeed, for example from an English professor:

> Success is their ability to formulate their interests into compelling questions, knowing how these questions fit into the larger conversations, and being able to analyze the issues in writing effectively ... The most effective thing is to treat them as colleagues and enact these scenarios over and over.

The journal club is tailored to address these critical issues – by taking a piece of recently published work and placing it in context, subjecting it to critical evaluation and doing this in a social setting. Regular participation and attendance is expected and would help address the sense of isolation reported by advanced students in the humanities (see Golde 2007b). Hear a voice from English:

> One of the big disappointments of graduate school has been how little interaction there is between students of different subfields in my department. I'm not sure how the department itself could foster this interaction more, but sometimes I feel that our drive to specialise prevents us from emphasizing the common ground we have in our field.

And another from history:

> We spend so little time focusing on real research or how to go about it. And once one is done with coursework you really feel out of the loop with your discipline since you are virtually alone in your field.

In contrast, healthy science programs are highly social and students are active members. Science students are expected to regularly report on work progress in the small lab group setting, summarize and critique major contributions to the field in journal club presentations, and to represent the lab's research efforts in poster sessions at regional and national conferences. The poster presentation is a form that is highly developed in most science disciplines, and entirely lacking in most humanities disciplines. The poster may focus on the narrow topic of the student's dissertation project but must link that work to the larger problem addressed by the lab (the grant-funded research project directed by the advisor). The students prepare their posters under the watchful eyes of their lab group colleagues and understand that they are representing the group as they stand by their poster. Early on in their graduate studies they learn to identify their role in the larger project, to give credit to others, and to understand that representation is negotiated with collaborative partners. As they stand by their posters in the conference hall, they are expected both to present the lab's work strongly and to be alert for opportunities for collaboration with people who stop to ask for more information. The student is then expected to report back to lab group about how the poster was received and often continues to correspond with new colleagues encountered in the poster session.

We found some similar practices in the humanities: groups of teachers and teaching assistants for large undergraduate courses who meet regularly, seminars where students and faculty discuss recent work and writing groups, for example. An example is described by a faculty member from English:

> I meet bi-weekly with the doctoral students who are writing their dissertations with me. During these meetings we focus on the research of one of the participants for half the meeting and discuss ways to develop a project and improve the writing they've submitted. During the second half of the meeting we set some goals such as grant application, article publication, and check on work towards previous goals. This group meeting is invaluable in keeping students on track, sharing resources and experience with each other.

Unless they address a common research problem, however, they may not succeed in creating the social/intellectual dynamic of interdependence that drives collaboration. In the co-teaching groups, if the individual teachers are evaluated separately they may not feel responsibility for each other's success or failure. The humanities seminar may not seek to move knowledge forward in any particular direction; it may not identify any common problem for the participants to collaborate on. The writing group generally focuses on giving feedback to individual authors. The norms of reciprocity and collegiality are critical skills in collaboration. A sense of shared intellectual responsibility that characterizes the lab group, journal club and poster presentation in the sciences is less common in the humanities.

Co-authorship remains rare in literary and historical publications. The emphasis on elaborated practices of reading and writing in doctoral programs in English and history produces astonishingly literate scholars. However, students recognize that isolation and overspecialization may hinder their future success. An English graduate student describes his/her department as:

> Very much tradition-bound in many ways. Very text-centric and not very accepting of 'cultural studies'. While this is good to some degree in that the job market looks for people who are bound to literary periods and can show themselves to be experts in the literature of period this tendency has some bad side effects with regard to supporting non-literary historical and cultural work. Also the MA exam with its emphasis on knowledge-over-imagination still hobbles this department and its acceptance of really innovative research.... What good is knowledge if you can't think outside the box? Sure you need to know the box to think outside of it, but you don't need to know every last inch of the box and be able to draw the box in your sleep.

In the CID, several humanities departments experimented with adapting lab groups, journal clubs and poster presentations to their disciplinary contexts. What does a lab group look like in history or English? We found examples where faculty built on the success of learning communities and project-based learning in undergraduate education by assigning group work around a common problem, source of evidence or text in their graduate courses. We also found many examples using teaching as an opportunity to form collaborative groups of faculty and course assistants. The subfield of public history provided examples of groups of students working with a faculty member (and often other mentors as well) on a common project. Interdependence is the key attribute of collaboration: this is possible in the humanities but the long tradition of individualism continues to work against innovations in this area.

Many US humanities programs offer students the opportunity to collaborate in the organization of conferences or as editors of journals. These are important venues for learning organizational skills and conventions of professional communication in a teamwork setting. By and large, the scholarly products remain a loosely connected collection of individual efforts rather than a collaborative project. The shift to acceptance of group projects and co-authorship in the humanities requires a cultural shift away from the emphasis on the author as individual, which is deeply embedded in these disciplines, to viewing scholarship as a collaborative social endeavor.

Journal clubs may seem easy to adapt; after all, there are certainly many journals in the humanities. The challenge in the face of persistent bias towards individualism and specialization (and the dominant paradigm of the seminar) is to find a format that addresses the interests of a self-sustaining group of scholars in the program. In the absence of a common project, humanities scholars struggle to find common ground reviewing research that often adds even more complexity to divergent, hyperspecialized interests. The emphasis on theory in many humanities seminars must be balanced by a discussion of the practices of research and knowledge creation – this is where the journal club in the sciences excels and has the potential to link theory and practice in the humanities by redirecting the focus to the question of 'how does this journal article advance the field?' In the humanities, common interests in geographic areas, time periods or genres may offer the opportunity for interdisciplinary journal clubs and further expand the opportunities for meaningful collaboration. In the sciences, some journal clubs are forming that focus on the major international journals such as *Nature* or *Science* rather than the most focused publications of the subdiscipline. A chemistry faculty member identified the practice of having students present research from other fields to the journal club as critical to 'develop a broad understanding of science so that they can critically evaluate and learn from experiences in other disciplines'.

The use of posters as a device for entering a scholarly conversation is catching on in history, but as a genre it has yet to take hold in English. The opportunity for students to prepare posters and enter the professional conference setting gradually creates opportunities for mentoring around the difficult tasks of defining the research question and approach, recognizing when the student has achieved presentable results and, of course, the representation of the significance of these achievements to the field at large. The poster is thus a prelude to the conference paper, journal article and the dissertation. As history has a longstanding commitment to public outreach, preparation of the poster is also seen as good practice for communicating complex ideas to a more general audience. Is it necessarily collaborative? In the sciences, the poster presents work that is the result of collaboration and the poster product is produced collaboratively. In the CID, our participants produced posters that presented innovative practices in their doctoral programs and thus exemplified the work of a collaborative group. As the poster format emerges into humanities conferences, the collaborative value of this experience for students must be consciously developed (by their programs and/or conference organizers) or it will not meet its full educational potential.

The successful transfer of the practices of collaboration from the sciences into the humanities requires a shift in thinking about the traditional notion that the goal of doctoral education is the formation of scholars capable of independent, original work. This shift asks us to think about how to prepare scholars to participate in collaboration: to make original contributions to group projects, to meet the needs and expectations of the group (or partner), and to identify the unique perspective that they can offer to complement the different strengths of their collaborative partners.

Independence

How does this vision of collaborative interdependence relate to the formation of scholars capable of independently generating original research? Our CID work suggests that independence is a necessary stage in student development: students ideally move from dependence on the ideas and assistance of others to independent production of ideas and products, and the ability to produce high quality results independently forms the basis of interdependent collaboration. We suggested above that humanities doctoral programs overemphasize the development of independence and ignore opportunities to develop the necessary skills for collaboration. In the sciences, on the other hand, many students never move beyond dependence, and while their collaborative skills are well-developed, both students and faculty identified the development of intellectual independence as an important area for development. A student in chemistry voiced a common (but not universal) complaint:

> I think most advisors in my program see grad students as cheap lab labor and don't care about their intellectual development. In my lab group, we are not allowed to design our own research. We do the experiments we are told to do and we have no say in the direction of our research. There is no incentive in my program to become an independent researcher capable of designing and developing our own research projects.

Science faculty see independence as a gradual development. A faculty member in neuroscience describes the process:

> Motivate the student to feel that they are 'in charge' of their research program and responsible for their discoveries, i.e. to take ownership of their intellectual contributions even though at an early stage these may not in reality belong to the student entirely – but over time they will become so.

How do students in the humanities develop scholarly independence? By being given a great deal of autonomy and responsibility from the beginning of their studies, in particular by being given freedom to choose their topic and advisors. Science students have some choice in these matters, but not the wide latitude given to students in the humanities. Humanities students report more confidence in their ability to design and conduct research projects of their own devising than science students. Are there lessons from the humanities that can be adapted to the constraints of laboratory science?

In the chemistry and neuroscience programs we worked with, students take a series of common content-based examinations (after the first year or two of coursework) and defend a narrowly defined research project in order to advance to candidacy for the PhD. In the humanities, our programs reported that students are given primary responsibility for defining the content of the examinations through development of a reading list that represents mastery of their chosen field of study (see Golde 2007a, 2007b) on the pedagogy of the 'List'). In addition, the development and defense of the research proposal is a critical test of the students' ability to independently formulate an interesting question and address the question in an appropriate theoretical and methodological framework. This effort is guided by the students' advisors but the burden of initiative is placed squarely on the student.

Several CID science programs experimented with a new form of qualifying examination, in which one task was for the student to prepare and defend a proposal for a large scale research project – larger in scope than their dissertation project and perhaps in another subfield. The format is a fully-fledged formal grant proposal (which is however not submitted for funding). The educational goals were to introduce students to the important practice of grant-writing, to encourage breadth of knowledge and to foster independent thinking.

One CID neuroscience program, at the University of Minnesota, had a unique approach to offering students opportunities to develop independence. The program built a state-of-the-art science lab from funds not related to any faculty grant or project and during the summer session doctoral students have the opportunity to experiment with independent (or collaborative) projects in this lab. The setting is off-campus at the university's remote Lake Itasca center and functions in part as the orientation for new doctoral students (a number of faculty and advanced students also participate). The principle of free inquiry is a central focus. During the regular academic term, students are working in their advisors' labs on grant-funded projects but the freedom to experiment is given special importance by the program. As an orientation setting for new doctoral students, this forms the basis for entering their first-year research rotations within a culture that expects them to contribute original insights and independent thinking to their lab groups.

Where the scientific enterprise requires an expensive investment in facilities and equipment, it is unlikely that students will be afforded the opportunity to pursue entirely independent lines of research. And, in fact, in their professional lives as researchers after the PhD they will rarely be working alone. Science programs must seek out opportunities to cultivate independent thinking, respect freedom of inquiry, and allow students to develop the level of initiative and responsibility they need to succeed in their careers. The qualifying examination process and summer programs are important opportunities for innovation that can balance the constraints created by their support from grant-funded research. The lessons from the humanities – where students are routinely expected to define their own areas of inquiry – can be adapted within even the limited 'free' space of science programs.

Looking forward

Scholarship in both the humanities and the sciences is moving towards the boundaries between traditional disciplines and to new and surprising areas of intersection. Intellectual versatility and the skills that underlie successful collaboration are essential for success. The cultivation of breadth and collaboration skills in doctoral programs calls into question the traditional one-to-one apprenticeship model of doctoral supervision. The CID advocates retaining the positive aspects of apprenticeship – frequent interaction, conscious modeling and mutual responsibility – in a new framework where students are 'apprenticed' to multiple mentors (one-to-many) and where in principle all members of the department are responsible for every member's success (many-to-many). We elaborate on these models of apprenticeship within community in our project report (Walker et al., forthcoming).

Preparing students for careers as scholars, teachers and public intellectuals in a rapidly changing world suggests a shift in emphasis from independence as the ultimate goal of doctoral training to developing confidence, competence and the skills and practices of collaboration. Both the sciences and the humanities have important insights to offer on how to balance individual effort and teamwork. It is clear from our work in the CID that all programs, regardless of discipline, need to take a step back and examine their practices and assumptions.

The impressive accomplishments of recent efforts to reform standards for doctoral supervision in Europe, Australia and the UK may be more difficult to achieve in the highly decentralized higher education system of the US. Nonetheless, the challenge of maintaining excellence requires critical examination of current practices and long-standing traditions. The aim of doctoral education – the formation of scholars capable of creating new forms of knowledge and understanding – remains constant. Our work suggests however that we have much to learn from each other – across disciplines and across borders – about how to support students as they enter an exciting and unpredictable future. It is my belief that this future will bring new approaches to the dissertation project, and that the interplay of freedom of inquiry and collaborative research is key to the formation of the next generation of scholars.

References

Becher, T. and Trowler, P.R. (2001) *Academic Tribes and Territories,* second edition, Philadelphia: Society for Research into Higher Education and Open University Press.

Bell R.K., Hill, D. and Lehming, R.F. (2007) *The Changing Research and Publication Environment in American Research Universities,* Working Paper SRS 07-204, Arlington, VA: Division of Science Resources Statistics, National Science Foundation, at: http://www.nsf.gov/statistics/srs09204/.

Golde, C.M. (2007a) Signature practices and disciplinary stewardship: observations from the Carnegie Initiative on the Doctorate, *ADE Bulletin,* 16–23, 141–142.

Golde, C.M. (2007b) Signature pedagogies in doctoral education: are they adaptable for the preparation of education researchers?, *Educational Researcher*, August–September: 1–8.

Golde, C.M. and Walker, G.E. (eds) (2006) *Envisioning the Future of Doctoral Education: Preparing Stewards of the Discipline,* San Francisco, CA: Jossey-Bass.

Huber, M. and Morreale, S. (2002) *Disciplinary Styles in the Scholarship of Teaching and Learning: Exploring Common Ground,* Washington, DC: American Association for Higher Education and Carnegie Foundation for the Advancement of Teaching.

Lunsford, A.A. (2006) Rethinking the Ph.D. in English, in C.M. Golde and G. Walker (eds), *Envisioning the Future of Doctoral Education: Preparing Stewards of the Discipline*, San Francisco, CA: Jossey-Bass, pp. 357–369.

McGuinness, A.C. (1999) The States and higher education, in P.G. Altbach, R.O. Berdahl and P.J. Gumport (eds), *American Higher Education in the Twenty-first Century: Social, Political and Economic Challenges*, Baltimore, MD: Johns Hopkins University Press, pp. 183–215.

Parry, S. (2007) *Disciplines and Doctorates: Higher Education Dynamics 16*, Dordrecht: Springer.

Prewitt, K. (2006) Who should do what: implications for institutional and national leaders, in C.M. Golde and G.E. Walker (eds), *Envisioning the Future of Doctoral Education: Preparing Stewards of the Discipline*, San Francisco, CA: Jossey-Bass, pp. 23–33.

Stacey, A.M. (2006) Training future leaders, in C.M. Golde and Walker G.E. (eds), *Envisioning the Future of Doctoral Education: Preparing Stewards of the Discipline*, San Francisco, CA: Jossey-Bass, pp. 187–206.

Thorgood, L., Golladay, M.J. and Hill, S.T. (2006) *U.S. Doctorates in the Twentieth Century*, Washington, DC: National Science Foundation Division of Science Resources Statistics, at: http://www.nsf.gov/statistics/nsf06319/pdf/nsf06319.pdf.

Walker, G.E., Golde, C.M., Jones, L., Bueschel. A.C. and Hutchings, P. (forthcoming) *The Formation of Scholars: Doctoral Education for the 21st Century,* San Francisco, CA: Jossey-Bass.

Chapter 4

Disciplinary voices

A shifting landscape for English doctoral education in the twenty-first century

Lynn McAlpine, Anthony Paré and Doreen Starke-Meyerring

What is appropriately done in a doctorate (Golde and Walker, 2006; Noble, 1994)? To what extent should disciplinary differences, changing economic conditions, the technological revolution, or societal need influence the answer (Woollard, 2002)? What is the doctorate preparation for – work in an academic field or in society (Golde and Dore, 2001)? These questions highlight for us the shifting, contested nature of the doctorate both within and beyond academe, and are questions of scholarly (as well as professional) interest to us. And, the questions assume even greater urgency in the face of a significant problem in Canadian and US universities: increasing times to completion (Elgar, 2003) and doctoral attrition rates as high as 30 per cent to 50 per cent, with the higher rates common in the humanities (Lovitts, 2001; Yeates, 2003).

In this chapter, with the help of academics and students in a Department of English – a discipline representative of the humanities – we examine issues around the changing nature of the doctorate. For us, this was an opportunity to look within another discipline and learn more about doctoral education from that border crossing (McAlpine and Harris, 1999). And this visit to another disciplinary culture – quite distinct from ours – has been an object lesson, since we face different but equally forceful policies and societal trends in our own field – Education.

What emerged was an intriguing picture of a discipline struggling with whether and how to re-define itself in a time of dramatic changes in popular culture, publishing, and the job market for English PhD graduates. In the words of Gerald Graff (2006: 372), 'the English doctorate needs to be rethought from the ground up'. This moment of flux provides a context for considering how disciplines can and might change their doctoral practices and how those in English specifically imagine and propose to move forward. In effect, we make the argument that there are opportunities for the revitalization and growth of the English PhD, but only with a thoughtful re-examination of the shifting landscape of the field; what may be required is the transforming of many traditional cultural practices – a change process not easy for any discipline to achieve.

How this account was developed

We used a grounded approach, beginning in a particular department of English, using focus groups (one with academics and one with PhD students) since we were interested in the negotiated and constructed ideas of the community (Wilkinson, 2003). During these conversations, we also asked for suggestions of published sources in the field of English that addressed doctoral education – in this way accessing the literature these individuals were aware of.

After analyzing the transcripts and notes from the interviews to identify themes pertinent to each group, the drafts of the themes were sent to each to ensure authenticity. Next, we drew on the literature suggested by our English colleagues to see the ways in which the themes in this department were mirrored in others' experiences in the same field. At this point, we also drew on our own knowledge – Anthony's and Doreen's in literacy studies, and Lynn's in higher education pedagogy and academic development. By incorporating our own understandings and interpretations, we were able to consider the implications for the doctorate beyond this outpost of English. In using this grounded approach, we attempted to be sensitive to context, to be transparent yet rigorous (Smith, 2003) in order to represent as best as possible insiders' perspectives.

The department: an outpost of the discipline

This story is embedded in a particular time – 2005 – and place – McGill University, an English language-based institution in a predominantly French-speaking province of Canada. The Canadian political system is extremely decentralized, and the division of fiduciary and fiscal powers, different from more centralized jurisdictions such as the UK and Australia, limits the creation of national standards in higher education. This creates, perhaps, more degrees of freedom for universities and departments to decide how to respond to the mixture of societal expectations and government policies that they are experiencing.

The PhD program in this department was rethought 13 or so years ago and consists of one year of coursework, one year of 'fieldwork' (study with substantial report and exam), and then the dissertation, with an expected five years in total to complete. The program is intended to 'give [students] an understanding of a particular field but also a deep understanding of a number of important theoretical questions that bear on work in the discipline' (P). [Initials refer to the individual: D–Dorothy, M–Maggie, P–Paul.]

The professors' voices: fetishizing completion as a Platonic good

It is late afternoon in mid-November. It's already dark and snow is falling outside the window deadening the sounds on campus as we gather around a table in Paul's office. Paul, the Chair of English, with Shakespeare his academic interest, is a relative newcomer to McGill, having arrived only four years ago. Maggie, at McGill for roughly 20 years, is the previous Chair and has also been Graduate Director; her interest, the Renaissance, overlaps somewhat with Paul's. Dorothy, the present Graduate Director, also acted in this position from 1999–2002; she is a medievalist and has been here about as long as Maggie. *In these areas of expertise, we see fields which have been central to traditional departments of English.* [Italics represent our comments on the descriptions and statements.]

We ask a couple of questions and are launched on a lively, animated conversation for the next hour and a half, discussing a range of things; the two we highlight here – since they represented the central issues of the group – are institutional and societal pressures on time to completion that conflict with disciplinary perceptions of what it takes to become a member of the discipline, and issues around attracting the best students.

Maggie and Paul are particularly vehement concerning the institution's increasing emphasis on PhD completion in four years regardless of subject area. Maggie sees it as 'dangerous thinking'. Paul believes there is a 'deep misunderstanding between some disciplines in the humanities and the university. Time to completion is the wrong proposition; it should be time *for* completion'. All three want students to complete relatively quickly, but not without the chance to 'follow their noses' (P), 'do some intellectual exploration in a relatively risk free environment [and] not at the sacrifice of the quality of research' (M). This is 'truly distressing and highly detrimental to research in arts and humanities. Whatever happened to exploring the frontiers of knowledge and ideas for the sake of intellectual expansion and scholarly enhancement?' (D). *At issue here is the contrast between Mode 1 and Mode 2 forms of knowledge (Gibbons, 2000). What is valued here is a more traditional academic view of knowledge rather than the one that prizes socially useful knowledge (Golde and Walker, 2006).*

And, there are bigger, longer-term issues at stake: 'reverberations down the line for the next generation of scholars and I think that these things were not adequately being considered . . . these are not understood. The administration does not seem concerned with the potential long-term effect on certain fields that might require field work or time-consuming archival research' (M). 'Being told *how long to take* is going to determine some choices. . . . It is therefore vitally important our discipline is adequately represented in discussions that could determine the directions of future scholarship for some time' (M). 'It needs to be talked out' (P). *While there have been ongoing conversations within the Modern Languages Association for two decades about the nature of the discipline and the purpose of the doctorate (Delbanco, 2000), the discussion does not appear to have been taken up with those outside of English (Graff, 2006). Thus, institutional awareness of variation in disciplinary expectations of the PhD is not common.*

When asked whether these issues were discussed in the field, Maggie and Paul note the competition among the English departments for the best students. 'I went to a meeting of chairs of English . . . and the question came up of topping up students [ones who have already received funding council fellowships] – because departments compete to get these students. . . . And this wonderful guy from [X University] said 'maybe we should call a moratorium on this'; and we all looked at him and said 'that's a wonderful idea but we are not going to do it' . . . and we all knew why we weren't going to do it . . . because it would disadvantage us' (P) . . . 'That's what you try and compete with' (M) . . . 'We want to attract the best students not just in Canada, but in North America and from Europe and so we want to do anything we can to bring them here' (P) . . . 'And usually that means money' (M). *The challenge with increasing global competitiveness (e.g. the Bologna Declaration in Europe) is to find a way to preserve 'an edge'. Attractive funding packages offered by departments can be a deciding factor in choosing a program for many students.*

Overall, these issues represent concerns about the future of the discipline and who controls it. *The issues are largely represented as difficulties with institutional and funding council expectations and how competition among programs seems to limit collective action. There was no reference to how changes in the nature of the field might influence the PhD, although Graff (2006) and Lunsford (2006) both point to the extraordinary changes in the field as a source of tension in and a motivation for the revision of the English doctorate.* We turn now to the students' perspectives.

The students' voices: entering the profession – grooming us for what? Where?

A month later, mid-December – again late in the afternoon, dark; it isn't snowing and the lights of the city can be seen from Lynn's window. Sitting at the table are Joel, Jenn, Janet and Lynn. During the next hour and a half, the conversation flows around the challenges and tensions they are experiencing becoming academics.

Joel, who did his MA elsewhere and has just completed his first semester, begins: '[I] was unsure if I would like teaching and found a sessional lecturer position. . . . By about the third year, I had absolutely peaked, hit the ceiling . . . . I didn't really see any future . . . and I wanted to do some more research and writing and thought that the PhD would be a good place to start'. *Joel represents an increasingly common career in English – sessional lecturer hired part-time or on an annual contract with no career prospects (Graff, 2006; Zimmerman, 2006) – though surely not the career envisioned by English faculty, whose focus is on preparing scholars, predominantly in literature.*

Jenn, is a new post doc, having just completed her degree at McGill in four years. She 'could have done a "better" dissertation' if she had taken longer, but 'basically I was speedy because of the money issue'. Janet, who will finish shortly, has taken a bit more time than the five years named by the professors as 'the time it takes'. 'Fairly early on in my undergrad degree I had a feeling I would like to do a PhD and now . . . at the end of it . . . I am often in the position of evaluating what I thought it would be like with what it has *really* been like . . . certainly, my expectations have changed' (Ja). (As before, initials designate individuals: Ja – Janet, Je – Jenn, Jo – Joel.)

This launches us into a discussion of expectations. Why were they doing this? 'Hoping for tenure track' (Je) . . . 'Yeah' (Jo). 'I thought of course I'd get a tenure-track position' (Ja). And, is this consistent with their program? 'We're being groomed for tenure-track positions and they don't discuss other options' (Ja). Joel adds: 'Because there's a real competition among research-intensive universities. And that's the reason our departments are preparing us as researcher-scholars rather than teacher-scholars. So, we have virtually no attention paid in our school to teaching because they are working on the assumption that they're gearing us up as the next generation of research-intensive scholars'. This goal is reinforced by 'a list going around the department of who has ended up where – you don't count if you ended up at a [junior college] . . . the faculty members don't give that the same validity' (Ja). *This lack of change to doctoral programs to incorporate alternate career prospects rather than a focus on tenure-track positions in literature has been described as quite common in English (Golde and Walker, 2006) despite calls to reform programs (Graff, 2006). At the same time, there are programs pursuing alternatives in composition and rhetoric, or English in the sciences. Yet, such program changes can be difficult given the general tendency to re-produce cultural patterns and practices; such change may engender departmental rifts as well as a major re-thinking of departmental priorities for hiring, supervision, etc.*

While their hope is – *was* – for tenure-track positions in research-intensive universities, they are aware that this is not, in fact, what the future holds. In a jumble of voices, this reality emerges. 'There are maybe about half the tenure-track jobs available for those who graduate' (Ja). 'And where you get those jobs may not be where you expect – they may not be at research-intensive institutions' (Je). Janet adds the facts (all three seem to know them) from the Modern Languages Association: in North America, there are something like 900 graduates each year and 400 tenure-track positions – counting the 'many, many liberal arts colleges . . . in small town no-wheresville' (Ja). Jenn asserts 'nor do they tell us that you are not likely to end up at McGill because you can never go above your PhD, you can only go below when it comes to the job market. They didn't say that it's not McGill or [another Canadian research-intensive university] that's going to hire you'. Further, they know the department is hiring from outside the country; in fact, they researched the issue and found 80 per cent of recent hires have been from the US – 'What message does that send?' (Je). *Academic hiring is increasingly international, so that graduates not only compete for positions with colleagues in Canada, but also from other countries, especially the United States. Bidwell (2005) confirms the students' statements that only 50 per cent of the individuals hired in Canadian universities into tenure-track positions that year had Canadian PhDs. This contrasts with contractual limited-term appointments for which all positions were held by those with Canadian PhDs (ibid.). And their situation is not a happy one; Zimmerman (2006:42) notes the 'humiliation of applying for work every year, the lack of security, the desire for 'new blood' in the department so graduates are not hired . . . some call it a feudal system'.*

So, what of the future? In Canada with a small number of research-intensive universities, that leaves few options, especially as Jenn notes that the number of sessionals is increasing and now represents close to half of academic staff in some Canadian institutions. 'You need to lower your expectations a bit' (Je), accept the 'realization that perhaps that ideal job in a research-intensive institution in an urban centre is not going to be as attainable as something . . . with a lower profile' (Ja). *This pattern also exists in the US (De Naples, 2003).*

On this depressing note, we shift to issues within the PhD. 'There's a lot of difficulty because of the funding. . . . Basically most of us realize we are going to sink or swim based on our funding. So if we don't get decent funding, we are slaves to [teaching assistantships] and other work, which is valuable work experience for most of us. But it's really valuable to the university because it's such cheap labour. They're [administration] . . . willing to exploit it to any extent possible without worrying too much whether a grad student should still be in university in seven or eight years' (Jo). *North et al. (2000) believe that universities have taken advantage of the lack of consensus within the discipline about the value of literacy and communication studies to hire part-time lecturers for the bulk of communication and writing courses. Graff (2006) echoes that analysis.*

'Yeah, and it's soft funding' (Jo) . . . 'Funding which is actually work and there's this awful distinction, which is not made, between funding and work' (Je) . . . 'Yeah, they call it funding but it means 'slave labor' . . . what is really at issue here is not the unpleasantness of teaching assistantships – they're actually quite enjoyable! – but rather their capacity to suck all time and energy away from the research and writing a grad student is supposed to be doing. Thus, the administrative pressure to complete the degree in four years is unreasonable, given the hours of labour (many unpaid) that are involved in TA-ships, the only "guaranteed form of funding"' (Ja). *TA-ships are the norm in English doctoral programs, with more than half of reporting institutions offering them to all first-year students (wysiwyg://35/http://www.mla.org/sum_tables). Indeed, time to completion ideals, likely derived from conditions in better-funded disciplines where students may work on their theses as research assistants in labs, assume a very different meaning in English, where funding is frequently less related to the student's research.*

Key issues for the students are lack of career opportunities, which is linked to the ways in which their program does (or doesn't) prepare them for the future, and how teaching is a double-edged sword (necessary for survival and appreciated as a learning opportunity but taking time away from the PhD. *These students are experiencing what Graff (2006) has called a disciplinary 'curriculum', that is, a set of negotiated compromises that creates disorientation and confusion because of its mixed messages. Again, there was no reference to how changes in the nature of the field (as opposed to the job market) might influence their preparation.*

The lived experience: mirroring the larger context

The conversations highlighted for us some of the tensions and pressures of the reality of English and the PhD in this department. How do these issues relate more generally to the field? The positioning of English as a discipline within the university clearly emerged as something that both groups – faculty and PhD students – agree is an issue. Their perspectives vary, though, given their different roles, although they emerge with a consensus that the university doesn't understand or acknowledge the differences between the sciences and humanities and, in fact, may – as predicted by Lyotard (1984) – privilege the sciences over the humanities. As Hyland (2004) notes, the sciences have in many cases been very successful in articulating the relevance and value of their knowledge in post-industrial society. Delbanco (2000) is also concerned with institutional pressures. He decries the marketplace metaphor and managerialism of university; and, he affirms, the lesser privilege of the humanities in this universe of fiscal reality, describing science envy as driving the institution.

While the students are receiving mixed messages from the university, they also feel they are receiving mixed messages from the department. They understand that the professors want this to be 'the best years of your life'. But the constant struggle for funds – doing the teaching, as well as trying to get published substantially before graduation if they are to have any hope competing for a tenure-track position – leads them to ask 'where is the time to reflect, to enjoy'? Delbanco (2000) notes that those in research-intensive universities (e.g. McGill) are terrorized by publication schedules and graduate students are realizing that they are actually exploited employees mollified with false promises about their future. Folsom (2001) also describes the results of the shift to a more competitive research-driven environment, features of the field that concerned the McGill students (and to some extent the academics): toughening of tenure standards, pre-professionalization of the discipline with graduate students needing teaching and publication files equal to what was expected for tenure 15 years ago, and those hired into colleges having strong publishing rather than teaching records. These thoughts are mirrored by Graff's (2000: 1192) reference to the 'ruthless productivity speedup', the need to have publications in order to even get an interview.

As regards tenure-track positions, again there is agreement among students and professors that such positions are the hope, but there is a certain disappointment and a sense of deception for the students since they see a reality that does not match either their hopes or what the department is preparing them for. Delbanco (2000) echoes the concern of the McGill students, noting that scholars who thought they would be professors at distinguished universities are poorly paid writing masters at colleges. Folsom (2001), former chair of the English department at Iowa State University (interestingly at a large research-intensive university), laments the present expectation of colleges competing with research-intensive universities and sees this shift originating in an administration with institutional goals often based on getting top class talent, thereby becoming a second-rate research-intensive university rather than a unique undergraduate one.

The shifting landscape of knowledge production

There was an issue we found in the literature that didn't emerge in our conversations with the academics and students in the department: the shifting nature of knowledge production and its impact on the field of English. The shifting nature of knowledge production includes, for instance, radical changes in notions of literacy; new media and electronic technologies; divisions between literature and rhetoric, and between literature and cultural studies; theoretical rifts between traditionalists and post-'everything'. How might changes in knowledge production form/transform disciplines? How might academics deal with potential disruption to disciplinary knowledge production if they wish to respond to changing external environments as well as remain stewards of their disciplines? Since we view such questions as influencing the nature and purpose of the doctorate, we consider them in some detail.

Interestingly, the English Department is situated in Quebec and thus in the educational context that gave rise to Lyotard's (1984) groundbreaking articulation of this changing environment as the 'postmodern condition'. As Lyotard noted, in post-industrial societies, under the conditions of global capitalism, 'knowledge has become the principal force of production', resulting in a fundamental shift in which knowledge is valued and which isn't. Specifically, Lyotard noted that in post-industrial societies, knowledge will be valued increasingly for its instrumental and commercial value and less for its own sake or for the sake of social progress or for societal emancipation: 'Knowledge is and will be produced in order to be sold, it is and will be consumed in order to be valorized in a new production: in both cases, the goal is exchange. Knowledge ceases to be an end in itself; it loses its "use-value"' (pp. 4–5).

There are perhaps few other disciplines that reflect the tensions emerging from this shift more acutely than English. On the one hand, traditional research concerns of the field, e.g. ancient or modern literary works, critical theory, literary hermeneutics, are not easily subordinated to the increasing emphasis on the exchange value of knowledge in post-industrial society. On the other hand, the shift in knowledge production and values is reflected in the emergence and recent boom of various subdisciplines such as Rhetoric and Composition, Literacy Studies, Cultural Studies, Media Studies, Technical and Professional Communication, and the Rhetoric of Science, all of which have extended the study of English from the English of novels and poems to the English of student writers in and outside classrooms; teenagers on the internet; professionals, e.g. engineers or managers, in workplaces; researchers across disciplines; and citizens in public arenas. Over the last 20 to 30 years, these subfields have grown tremendously, with numerous PhD programs, professional associations, large annual scholarly conferences, and numerous scholarly journals attesting to this growth. While the trend originally emerged in response to numerous social, political and disciplinary exigencies in the United States, it has increasingly also developed in Canada.

When such programs arise, they often create considerable tension as curricular space and norms of scholarships are being negotiated between the emerging and the traditional forms of knowledge in English. It is in these emerging disciplines where much of the growth is occurring, where funding is often easier to obtain, and where the demand for job candidates is greatest, with many openings going unfilled because not enough candidates specializing in these emerging areas are available. However, not all English departments have embraced these emerging directions for numerous reasons, including perhaps the overall mission of their university, a sense of resistance to the shift in knowledge represented by these new areas of research, or a lack of resources. The challenge of being a steward of the discipline, entrusted with its care on behalf of those in and beyond the discipline (Golde and Walker, 2006), is to reconcile the tension between conserving the essential features of the past while keeping the discipline relevant and current.

Co-constructing a discipline, a program and a process: the way forward?

Within this shifting landscape, how might the purposes and practices of doctoral education change? As noted earlier, there has been an ongoing but unresolved dialogue about the purposes of the English PhD (for instance, a 1999 conference on the 'Future of the Doctorate'). And, De Naples (2003), a graduate program director, asked: 'What can graduate schools do to improve knowledge of our profession, and what should chairs and senior faculty members do to make sure their junior colleagues reach tenure and promotion?' (p. 40). His answer: Since students often find positions in a two-year college rather than a research-intensive university, they should be prepared to thrive in two-year colleges, to develop knowledge of teaching and service in order to become better candidates and later more successful faculty members in these types of institutions rather than research-intensive ones. This is not a dramatic change, conceivably do-able without substantial disruption to departmental practices.

What are some bolder images of possibility within the discipline for the issues documented above? North et al. (2000) believe what is required is a radical rethink, creating a new single entity distinct from the original components in the discipline; the rationale for this is that what has been tried so far – splitting off rhetorical and cultural studies or holding everything together through compromise to create an 'integrated' curriculum – has simply not worked.

Similarly, Lunsford (2006) proposes English as encompassing literature, language and writing (noting that separating them is counter-productive given the ways in which communicative acts are merging electronically). Programs should include a range of discourses and images of all kinds – film, video, multimedia, cookbooks and tombstone inscriptions. Equally important for her is modifying admission procedures to reduce exclusionary practices which have led to the under-representation of females and minorities. Lastly, she believes it is essential that students experience collaborative projects and, when possible, multidisciplinary ones. She even recommends collaborative dissertations in order to prepare students for the changes that are occurring in society and in expectations for those who complete a doctorate.

Graff (2006) confronts the deepening ideological and methodological conflicts by proposing that the 'contested issues of the discipline' should form the basis of the doctoral curriculum. For instance, introductory graduate courses could focus on disputed issues, e.g. What is English? What are the differences between the new and old ways of historicizing literature? How did the 'publish or perish' system evolve? What is its rationale? What, if anything, should be done about it? He has other suggestions as well that would better integrate the range of fields within the disciplines. For instance, establish and promote alternatives for non-academic employment; and explore the common ground between the research and pedagogical aims of doctoral programs and English teacher education programs by offering jointly taught courses.

Conclusions

In this chapter, we have examined the nature of doctoral education in English – the 'profession' as it is called by those who belong – from a Canadian and a North American perspective. We see the interconnected and contradictory world that professors and students are dealing with as they attempt to reconcile societal drivers, institutional demands and disciplinary expectations in an ever-more complex world. The culture of English (and modern languages) is a 'shifting and fragile homeostatic system – a particular and unique equilibrium of opposing forces, a method for avoiding or attempting to avoid . . . breakdown while evolving and adapting to changing environments' (Evans, 1990: 275).

At the same time, the issues within English parallel those in other disciplines and may provide some insight for us. In fact, we were struck by the ways in which we could see parallels. For instance, in the social sciences there are concerns about the career pathways of new PhDs. In Education and other applied fields, there are efforts to create new kinds of doctoral degrees – ones that are deemed to better prepare individuals to engage in Mode 2 knowledge construction. Projects in the US, such as Preparing Future Faculty and the Carnegie Initiative on the Doctorate, have provided support for departments and disciplines to rethink their doctoral curricula. And, a recent initiative by the Carnegie Foundation is directed explicitly at exploring the professional doctorate in Education as distinct from the research degree.

At the same time, a critique of the disciplinary work on rethinking doctoral education in the Carnegie Initiative (Golde and Walker, 2006) brings to the fore the difficulties of change when undertaken from within. The proposals for change in the Golde and Walker book were written by respected disciplinary experts, and they are described by the editors of the book as representing incremental shifts rather than more radical re-articulations of what doctoral education might become. While such a stance might be interpreted as a desire to avoid breakdown while adapting to changing environments (Evans, 1990), it may also represent the inherent stability and continuity of socio-cultural practices – in fact, the difficulty of not reproducing embedded ways of thinking and acting. Delamont et al. (1997) note that in doctoral education there tends to be an intergenerational transmission of disciplinary knowledge and skills that results in the reproduction of academic practices. Further, academic knowledge is a cultural product mediated by a wider social context (Hyland, 2004) and departments may be more focused on those outside the discipline, e.g. the institution in which they are situated, who are challenging established but different aspects of disciplinary/departmental practices – for instance, at McGill, the push by the institution for shorter times to completion. Yet, some of the examples of change proposed above by those in English represent more radical perspectives. And, they provide a set of broad questions which could reasonably be addressed in all disciplines:

- How might changes in modes of knowledge production be forming/transforming disciplines? What new fields, ways of thinking, are lurking at the boundaries of the disciplines?
- How can we remain stewards of the discipline – both conserving the best in the discipline while responding effectively to these changing circumstances?
- How do the answers to these questions change the purposes and the practices of doctoral education?

Addressing these questions requires simultaneously co-constructing a discipline (a distinct culture of knowledge and ways of thinking, acting, valuing), a program (the doctorate) and a process (developing academic identities). In doctoral programs, both academics and students through their collective inquiries can form and transform the discipline, while finding ways to respond to, re-direct, limit or take advantage of institutional and societal influences. The challenge entails preserving respect for self, finding continuity in personal and disciplinary goals, and sustaining academic authenticity – both supporting the reproduction but also the transformation of identities and relationships of the disciplines. So, we end with Royster's (2000: 1226) still current and challenging question to his colleagues in English: 'Given both our vital differences and our vital alliances amid changing material conditions, how … do we engage each other in meaningful and useful conversation … to negotiate both mutual and non-mutual actions? (1226)

Acknowledgements

We greatly thank D. Bray, M. Kilgour, P. Yachnin, Janet, Jenn and Joel – all from English – who shared their views, read drafts and helped ensure we came to better understand the profession. The three students wished that only their first names be used.

References

Bidwell, P. (2005) CACE/ACCUTE hiring survey, 2004–2005, *ACCUTE*, June: 6–11.

Delamont, S., Atkinson, P. and Parry, O. (1997). *Supervising the PhD*, Buckingham: Open University Press.

Delbanco, A. (2000) What should PhD mean?, *PMLA [Modern Language Association Newsletter]*, 115(5): 1205–1209.

De Naples, F. (2003) Between the undergraduate college and the graduate school: what do undergraduates need? What are doctoral programs doing?, *ADE Bulletin [Association of Departments of English]*, 29–82, 134–135.

Elgar, F. (2003) *PhD Completion in Canadian Universities,* Halifax, NS: University of Dalhousie.

Evans, C. (1990) A cultural view of the discipline of modern languages, *European Journal of Education*, 25 (3): 273–282.

Folsom, E. (2001) Degrees of success, degrees of failure: the changing dynamics of the English PhD and small-college careers, *Profession*, 121–129.

Gibbons, M. (2000) Changing patterns of university–industry relations, *Minerva*, 38: 352–361.

Golde, C.M. and Dore, T.M. (2001) *At Cross Purposes: What the Experiences of Doctoral Students Reveal about Doctoral Education*, Philadelphia, PA: a report for the Pew Charitable Trusts, ERIC Documents ED (www.phdsurvey.org).

Golde, C.M. and Walker, G.E. (eds). (2006) *Envisioning the Future of Doctoral Education: Preparing Stewards of the Discipline.* Carnegie essays on the doctorate, San Francisco, CA: Jossey-Bass.

Graff, G. (2000) Two cheers for professionalizing graduate students, *PMLA*, 115(5): 1192–1193.

Graff, G. (2006) Toward a new consensus: the PhD in English, in C.M. Golde and G.E. Walker (eds), *Envisioning the Future of Doctoral Education: Preparing Stewards of the Discipline*, San Francisco, CA: Jossey-Bass, pp. 370–389.

Hyland, K. (2004) *Disciplinary Discourses: Social Interactions in Academic Writing,* Ann Arbor: University of Michigan Press.

Lovitts, B.E. (2001) *Leaving the Ivory Tower: The Causes and Consequences of Departure from Doctoral Study*, Lanham, MD: Rowman & Littlefield.

Lunsford, A.A. (2006) Rethinking the PhD in English, in C.M. Golde and G.E. Walker (eds), *Envisioning the Future of Doctoral Education: Preparing Stewards of the Discipline.* San Francisco, CA: Jossey-Bass, pp. 357–369.

Lyotard, J.-F. (1984) *The Postmodern Condition: A Report on Knowledge* (Transl. by G. Bennington and B. Massumi) Minneapolis: University of Minnesota Press (original work published in 1979).

McAlpine, L. and Harris, R. (1999) Lessons learned: faculty developer and engineer working as faculty development colleagues, *International Journal of Academic Development*, 4(1): 11–17.

Noble, K.A. (1994) *Changing Doctoral Degrees: An International Perspective*, Buckingham: Society for Research into Higher Education and Open University Press.

North, S., Chepaitis, B.A., Coogan, D., Davidson, L., Maclean, R., Parrish, C.L., Post, J. and Weatherby, B. (2000) *Refiguring the PhD in English Studies: Writing, Doctoral Education, and the Fusion-based Curriculum*, Urbana, IL: National Council of Teachers of English.

Royster, J. (2000) Shifting the paradigms of English studies: continuity and change, *PMLA*, 115(5): 1222–1228.

Smith, J. (2003) Validity and qualitative psychology, in J. Smith (ed.), *Qualitative Psychology*, London: Sage, pp. 232–235.

Wilkinson, S. (2003) Focus groups, in J. Smith (ed.), *Qualitative Psychology*, London: Sage, pp. 184–204.

Woollard, L. (2002) The PhD for the 21st century, paper presented at the annual meeting of the Canadian Society for Studies in Education, Toronto, Canada.

Yeates, M. (2003) Graduate student conundrum. *University Affairs*, February: 38–39.

Zimmerman, B. (2006) The plight of Canada's contractual professors, *University Affairs*, January: 42.

Chapter 5

The doctorate as curriculum

A perspective on goals and outcomes of doctoral education

Rob Gilbert

What counts as knowledge in research was once implicit in the cultural practices of disciplinary traditions and institutions. In the ideals of the medieval university and the monastic tradition, to learn was to be immersed in a scholarly discursive practice borne as much by a set of community relationships as by a body of ideas. Modern universities, and especially their more bureaucratic forms, now codify knowledge in frameworks of goals, outcomes and skills, making what was once implicit in specific communities of discourse now the subject of explicit and anonymous policy and evaluation.

In operationalising research training[1] in policy and procedures, universities have formalised the research degree by specifying the aims of the doctorate and the criteria for examination through definitions, checklists and pro-forma reports. This chapter will review attempts to specify these goals and assessment criteria in the light of challenges to the doctorate and concepts of knowledge said to be involved in the research process.

The discussion will briefly review recent debates around the doctorate, and argue the need to see aspects of these debates as issues of curriculum. Viewing the doctorate as curriculum directs attention to the forms of knowledge in which it is grounded, and how these are articulated in the documentation of the degree. The discussion uses as illustration evidence from a study of the doctoral curriculum in Australian universities, and comparisons with developments elsewhere.

Concerns about the doctorate

Recent decades have seen unprecedented scrutiny of the purposes and practices of doctoral education as a form of research training. Long regarded as the pinnacle of university scholarship, the doctorate has faced a growing range of challenges to its traditional forms and status, and statements of concern about the quality and breadth of research training.

In Australia, such concerns have been expressed in a number of government reports and inquiries (Gallagher, 2000; Kemp, 1999; Review Committee on Higher Education Financing and Policy, 1998). In the US, there are claims that the PhD in the United States is outmoded (Kendall, 2002), and that institutional needs in doctoral training are given precedence over the needs of students after they graduate (Adams and Mathieu,

1999; Association of American Universities, 1998; Geiger, 1997; Raber, 1995). In the UK, similar issues have been raised (Economic and Social Research Council, 2001; Office of Science and Technology, 1992). In reviewing developments in research training in England, Coate and Leonard (2002: 24) note a view among the Research Councils that 'the PhD provides neither a rigorous enough methodology training for those who go into academia, nor an appropriate initial and continuing professional development for those who go outside', though the authors comment that there is little systematic research on which to base these assertions.

A key aspect of the questioning of the traditional PhD curriculum is that academia is no longer the dominant destination for doctoral graduates (Adams and Mathieu, 1999; Golde and Dore, 2001; Raber, 1995; Review Committee on Higher Education Financing and Policy, 1998; Wellcome Trust, 2000). Concerns have been expressed about the relevance of the PhD to the needs of industry and student careers outside the university or industrial research laboratory (Adams and Mathieu, 1999; Association of American Universities; 1998; Bourner, 1998; Economic and Social Research Council (OST), 2001; Geiger, 1997).

In addition, the very purpose of the PhD has come into question. In its discussion document on *The Nature of the PhD*, the UK Office of Science and Technology (OST, 1992) identified a number of competing emphases for PhD programs, including some disagreement about whether the PhD is:

- part of the cycle of education in a mass education system, which the OST sees as the key characteristic of the US system,
- an apprenticeship in scholarship, the traditional European focus,
- a contribution to knowledge, with an emphasis on original research, or
- a research training program.

A number of studies have shown a lack of consensus among academics themselves on whether the emphasis of the PhD should be on producing new knowledge or cohorts of skilled researchers (Hockey, 1995; Johnston, 1999; Pearson and Brew, 2002). There has been a shift from seeing the PhD as aimed at producing a research product (the thesis) to seeing it as a process of research training and the development of skills and expertise (Park, 2005), or what has been termed a shift from a scholarship to a training model of the PhD (Deem and Brehony, 2000: 150). However, concerns have been expressed about the dangers of a narrow technical approach to research training (Pearson, 1996; Pearson and Brew, 2002; Raber, 1995). A significant development in this regard is the emphasis being given in the university sector to the generic skills that might be expected to result from doctoral study (Gilbert et al., 2004a). These questions about the nature, scope and emphasis of the PhD degree are issues of curriculum.

The doctorate as curriculum

Challenges to the doctorate have led to an increasing number of research and evaluation studies into the processes of doctoral education, with particular emphasis on supervision and the cultures of research training (Deem and Brehony, 2000; Delamont et al., 1997).

Over 20 years ago, Connell (1985) noted that a focus on the process of doctoral supervision raises questions of curriculum. However, studies of supervision and pedagogy have not directly addressed what might be called the doctoral curriculum – what it is that graduates learn in their courses of study, as distinct from how they learn or issues of program delivery. The argument here is that there is value in considering doctoral training as an issue of curriculum as well as one of pedagogy.

Burgess (1997: 15) recommends that research into postgraduate education link with enquiries into curriculum, including the structure and content of postgraduate research. McWilliam and Singh (2002: 4) identify 'a strong press to *think* curriculum as a necessary part of research', especially given that the 'rationalities emanating from government, the 'knowledge society', and organisational logic are rendering the processes and products of higher degree research more *calculable* to stakeholders within and outside university settings'.

Hamilton (1987: 34) traces the origins of the English use of the word 'curriculum' to Glasgow University in the late sixteenth century, where it referred to 'notions of order, coherence and intellectual discipline' of an entire program of studies: 'To create a curriculum is to systematise stored-up human experience' (p. 35). The doctoral curriculum is this systematic selection and articulation of experience in order to produce the intended outcomes of doctoral research training. This concurs with the views of McWilliam and Singh (2002), who reject the conventional concept of curriculum as referring only to courses of study and coursework degrees, and argue that guiding individuals in enacting research can be seen as a form of curriculum.

The curriculum can be conceptualised in various ways (Ross, 2000). The most common referent is the *intended* curriculum, those formal statements of purpose, aims or intended outcomes, or, in some cases, lists of content or concepts to be known, or competencies or skills to be mastered. The translation of these formal statements in practice gives rise to the notion of the *enacted* curriculum, which refers to the experiences designed and provided by an educational institution or program in order to achieve the stated aims, and which select from, augment and change the intended curriculum in the process of interpretation and implementation.

The *hidden* curriculum refers to the knowledge, beliefs, values or practices which are implicit in the practice or culture of an institution or program and learned by its participants, but which are not explicitly derived from or openly designed to achieve the stated aims. Examples in the present context might be aspects of the socialisation process into academic identities, where doctoral students may adopt attitudes or values associated with particular disciplines or research groups, whether or not these are explicit aims of the degree program. It is also possible to consider the *informal* curriculum as those learnings which result from participating in the institution or program, but which are not part of the enacted or hidden curriculum. Examples might include learning from other students or student-organised activities, or from other sources not originating in the practices of the institution or program.

It is possible to see the PhD degree as a program of learning which includes all the above forms of curriculum. This view is compatible with studies that focus on the 'doctoral experience' or research training 'cultures'. However, the focus of the current discussion is on statements of intent in university documentation, and is therefore a study of the intended doctoral curriculum.

Issues of curriculum arise from debates about what doctoral research training should aim for and include. Proponents of the traditional doctorate have argued that the capacities required for successful research, and therefore for successful research training, are ineffable, evasive qualities that are only partially captured in any attempt to articulate them. Phillips (1993: 16) quotes a supervisor who said that since PhDs are unique products, it is hard to generalize about them, and that 'Experience teaches one to feel what is interesting and exciting'. Pearson (1996) identifies in the literature on the qualities of the PhD graduate an image of a professional researcher who has the 'astuteness' to identify opportunities to make a useful contribution, the ability to evaluate one's work, to reframe problems in new ways, and to judge when to act. Not surprisingly, Pearson notes that, while these 'matters of "feel" and judgement' were referred to by students in her study, they were not well articulated (p. 307).

A similarly subtle ability is found in Smart and Hagedorn's call (1994: 255) for an emphasis on the 'imaginative abilities and sensitivity to the feelings of others, and reduced attention to assimilative strategies with their dominant focus on abstract ideas and concepts as opposed to people'. McWilliam et al. (2002) refer to creativity, imagination and flair as economically valued qualities in the new knowledge economy to which research training needs to respond. Raber (1995) reports calls for increasing versatility rather than specialisation in US science and engineering programs, and Pearson and Brew (2002) add resourcefulness and adaptability to the list of desired qualities.

The difficulties of articulating the range of elements which comprise knowledge at this highest level of scholarship should not be underestimated. However, an educational enterprise which lacks clarity about its goals will struggle to ensure that they are achieved, and to convince its clientele and funding sources that it is worthy of support. It is for this reason that questions of the nature and purpose of doctoral research training, the doctoral curriculum, need careful consideration (Gilbert, 2004).

A curriculum is an articulation of and from practice. The PhD has conventionally been an apprenticeship in which the practice of research was learned as novices participated in and observed a community of researchers, and was taught ostensively and by example through the close guidance of a mentor. Only recently has this form of teaching and learning been the subject of attempts to describe, formalise and clarify just what the practice aims to achieve, and the elements which comprise it.

Any description of the doctoral curriculum is both retrospective and proactive. It is retrospective in the sense that it tries to fix in language the valued aspects of past practice in order to ensure their continuation. It is proactive in the sense that it tries to influence and guide the practice in ways that are seen to be desirable. Like all official documents, public statements of the aims, objectives and programs of PhD study are multi-vocal, with numerous functions, audiences and intended effects. For instance, descriptions of the PhD will typically be influenced by the desire to attract and encourage potential candidates, to present an image of the university's status, style and research emphases, and to provide a touchstone from which various institutional strategies, procedures and responsibilities can be derived and justified, and in terms of which the program might be evaluated. Accordingly, such descriptions will be designed to address audiences of prospective and current students, supervisors and other staff, administrators, examiners, government and other interested parties.

As a result of this process of textual construction, statements of the aims and elements of the doctoral curriculum will be partial and selective. They will also be abstract and general, since they are intended to apply to a range of disciplines, and to provide flexibility so that the originality of individual research projects is not unnecessarily constrained. However, this generality inevitably means that applying these statements as guides to policy or practice requires considerable interpretation and inference, which may limit their usefulness as guides to practice or the quality of outcomes.

Types of knowledge

If the curriculum is the orderly and coherent articulation of knowledge to be acquired, then its successful description will depend on our ability to represent these qualities in language which is authentic and reproducible in practice. Identifying elements of knowledge for these purposes has usually taken the form of classifications of the range of important types. These classifications are proposed as a result of conceptual analysis rather than empirical studies of knowledge practice, but they are useful in their attempts at comprehensive and systematic description. A synthesis of these classifications (Blackler, 1995; Clegg, 1999; Collins, 1993; Fleck, 1997, cited in Johnston, 1998; OECD, 2000; Pole, 2000) suggests the following major forms:

1   Abstract propositional or declarative knowledge – knowing about facts, theories, generalisations, concepts – often codified in formulae or textual or diagrammatic form.
2   Abstract procedural knowledge involving conceptual skills and cognitive abilities of analysis, explanation and problem solving.
3   Action knowledge involved in performance, interpersonal communication and psychomotor skills.
4   Tacit or habituated knowledge involved in expert practice and professional judgment.
5   Cultural understandings of the perspectives and experiences of others, including empathising and working with others through shared understandings.
6   Embedded knowledge residing in systematic routines, technologies and procedures, including tool and instrument use.

These categories may not be exhaustive; they overlap and do not act independently; and they could be further sub-divided. However, they offer useful models of widely recognised curricular elements, and distinguishing them may be useful in clarifying the expectations of the doctorate. Their interpretation and the priority given to them in different contexts are important questions in judging the quality of programs.

The following discussion considers these typologies as it explores the intended curriculum of the doctorate. The discussion is illustrated by reference to a study of the doctoral curriculum in Australia (Gilbert et al., 2004b). The study analysed the doctoral degree programs of 25 universities, derived from websites, promotional literature, information handbooks, degree regulations and examination criteria provided by the institutions. The first section identifies the nature of the doctorate as represented in descriptions of aims, objectives and intended outcomes. The second section focuses on issues of assessment, and how the doctoral curriculum is reflected in the criteria and guidelines for the examination of the degree. The chapter provides a critical analysis of the nature of the intended doctoral curriculum identified, and relates the findings to the concerns about the doctorate outlined above.

The language of intent in the doctoral curriculum

General descriptions of the doctoral degree reflect the high regard in which the doctorate is held, with concomitantly high expectations. The statements of intent are aspirational, depicting an ambitious set of outcomes aiming for an exceptional level of achievement appropriate for this highest level of qualification.

A typical statement is that from the Australian Vice-Chancellors' Committee Code of Practice for Maintaining and Monitoring Academic Quality and Standards in Higher Degrees (2002: 15). The AVCC Code defines the PhD in the following terms:

> PhD degrees provide training and education with the objective of producing graduates with the capacity to conduct research independently at a high level of originality and quality. The student ought to be capable by the end of his/her candidature of conceiving, designing and carrying to completion a research program without supervision. The PhD candidate should uncover new knowledge either by the discovery of new facts, the formulation of theories or the innovative re-interpretation of known data and established ideas.

An equivalent but more detailed statement can be found in *The Framework for Higher Education Qualifications* developed by the UK Quality Assurance Agency for Higher Education (2001), which states:

> Doctorates are awarded for the creation and interpretation of knowledge, which extends the forefront of a discipline, usually through original research. Holders of doctorates will be able to conceptualise, design and implement projects for the generation of significant new knowledge and/or understanding.

> Holders of doctorates will have the qualities needed for employment requiring the ability to make informed judgements on complex issues in specialist fields, and innovation in tackling and solving problems.

The Framework elaborates the doctoral degree as a series of Qualification Descriptors in the following terms:

Doctorates are awarded to students who have demonstrated:

i   the creation and interpretation of new knowledge, through original research or other advanced scholarship, of a quality to satisfy peer review, extend the forefront of the discipline, and merit publication;

ii   a systematic acquisition and understanding of a substantial body of knowledge which is at the forefront of an academic discipline or area of professional practice;

iii the general ability to conceptualise, design and implement a project for the generation of new knowledge, applications or understanding at the forefront of the discipline, and to adjust the project design in the light of unforeseen problems;

iv   a detailed understanding of applicable techniques for research and advanced academic enquiry.

Typically, holders of the qualification will be able to:

a   make informed judgements on complex issues in specialist fields, often in the absence of complete data, and be able to communicate their ideas and conclusions clearly and effectively to specialist and non-specialist audiences;

b   continue to undertake pure and/or applied research and development at an advanced level, contributing substantially to the development of new techniques, ideas or approaches;

and will have:

c   the qualities and transferable skills necessary for employment requiring the exercise of personal responsibility and largely autonomous initiative in complex and unpredictable situations, in professional or equivalent environments.

In the university literature analysed here, broad statements such as these are typically elaborated by lists of objectives, or by more detailed descriptions of the intended outcomes in terms of graduate abilities, or, in some cases, of the qualities of the thesis, the latter being seen almost universally to embody the outcomes of the degree. These elaborations are the most informative descriptions of the broad doctoral curriculum in its explicitly intended form. The content analysis of the institutional literature revealed references to the range of elements shown in Table 5.1.

The most conspicuous element of this documentation was the frequency of mention of originality as the defining quality of the doctorate, although its particular manifestations varied across facts, knowledge, theories and reinterpreting data or ideas. Obviously, a key issue for the doctoral curriculum is to clarify just what is implied by the idea of originality. As Park (2005: 198) points out:

Table 5.1 Number of institutions specifying outcomes of doctoral degrees (n = 25)

Element of degree objectives or outcomes	Number of institutions referring to element
Original contribution	24
New facts/knowledge	9
Formulating theories	5
Reinterpreting data or ideas	7
Implementing research project	11
Critical review of literature of field	8
Methodological techniques and skills	7
Independent critical thought	7
Communicating research findings	6
Relevance to scholarship in the field	6
Formulating problems	3
Research ethics	2
Personal development	2
Commercialisation and acquiring grants	1

Originality can be a thorny problem, because it means different things in different disciplines, there is no absolute threshold that can be applied, and constraints of time and funding must also be taken into account.

Further questions arise in the variability of mention of other aspects of the aims. Why do some institutions but not others mention the literature review or independent critical thought? Should communication be a standard expectation important enough to be mentioned as an aim? Should it include oral communication as well as written? How do those universities that identify personal development as an aim take steps to ensure that it is achieved? Such questions present considerable challenges to those responsible for developing doctoral programs. From a system perspective, their generality and variability might cause concern about the reliability of doctoral education to produce a clear outcome. These questions reflect the kinds of issues which would be raised if the PhD were viewed from a curriculum perspective, since matters of clarifying goals, aligning goals with teaching and assessment, defining core learnings and the like are part of the discipline of curriculum inquiry.

The language of assessment in the doctoral curriculum

A minimalist concept of curriculum might assume that the doctoral curriculum comprises only what is examined, and that assessment provides the only reliable evidence of what has been learned. It is also the point at which the aims of the doctorate are most directly stated for all involved in the process.

Despite this, at the level of policy, statements about assessment are rare, and when stated, quite general. A typically brief statement is that from the Australian

Vice-Chancellors' Committee Code of Practice for Maintaining and Monitoring Academic Quality and Standards in Higher Degrees (2002: 15):

> Examiners should expect a thesis to be well written and to reveal an independence of thought and approach, a deep knowledge of the field of study and to have made a significant original contribution to knowledge consistent with 3–4 years of supervised research training.

For the purposes of examination, this broad statement of qualities of the thesis is elaborated in particular institutions to describe the criteria to be applied in judging the adequacy of the work of candidates. Specifying criteria for assessment again challenges universities to clarify the aims of the doctorate and the bases for judgement of quality in research training. The UK Quality Assurance Agency for Higher Education Code of Practice (2004: 23) explains the need for such criteria on a number of grounds:

> Applying assessment criteria for postgraduate research degrees helps institutions to safeguard the academic integrity of such programmes and awards, internally and externally. Making assessment criteria available to research students will give them the insight they need into what the institution expects. Criteria should enable students to show the full extent of their abilities and achievements at the level of the qualification they are aiming for.

The diffuseness of the statements of aims in Table 5.1 is no doubt attributable to the variety of purposes and audiences for which the general descriptions of the PhD are developed. In contrast, the statements of examination criteria analysed in the study described here are more systematic, focused and precise in their descriptions, and there is a greater consistency across institutions. On the other hand, considerable diversity remains, and their brevity necessitates substantial interpretation.

The most authoritative statements of assessment are found in the guidelines provided to examiners, which describe the criteria by which the product of the degree is to be judged. It is these statements of guidelines to PhD examiners from 19 Australian universities, which were analysed as shown in Table 5.2. In most cases, a brief description of the overall purposes and/or outcomes is combined with a list of specific features and even checklists to be marked to indicate the presence or absence of the feature described.

General descriptions of criteria are similar to the statements in the introductory literature described in the previous section, commonly referring to the need for candidates to demonstrate an original contribution to knowledge and the ability to design and implement a research project. The more specific and comprehensive descriptions of criteria are elaborated in lists of features to be assessed by examiners.

The most frequently mentioned criterion was the need for doctoral research to be an original contribution to knowledge. Typically, this was extended by the statement that the work should also be substantial, substantive, significant, distinctive or valuable, or that the findings might overturn or challenge previous beliefs, or open up new ideas for future research. Unlike the general descriptions of intent mentioned above, originality

Table 5.2 Number of institutions specifying examination criteria of doctoral degrees (n = 19)

Examination criteria	Number of institutions referring to criteria
Original contribution to knowledge	19
Quality of writing and/or presentation	18
Demonstrated research skills and/or methodology	13
Use of literature	12
Critical or independent thinking and analysis	9
Adequate for publication	8
Analysis of results	6
Comprehensiveness	6
Related to field	5
Evidence of independent planning and research	5
Develops clear hypotheses or questions	4
Shows knowledge of the field or discipline	3

was seldom subdivided further; only a few institutions explained that originality might be the discovery of new facts, the exercise of critical ability or the testing of ideas.

In frequency of mention, the criterion of written presentation was almost as important as originality. In most cases, the elaboration of the criterion described the desired language of the thesis in such terms as clear, concise, correct, accurate, cogent, succinct. Other descriptions referred more broadly to literary quality, general presentation, suitable setting out or presentation appropriate to the research area or discipline. Underlying textual qualities are also occasionally mentioned, such as 'coherent argument', 'adequate exposition and interpretation', or 'authoritative' communication.

Thirteen institutions listed the ability to use skills or methods of research as a criterion of examination. The general requirement was that methods and techniques *appropriate* to the project or discipline were understood and adequately applied. Beyond this, elaborations of the criterion referred to:

- Skills in the gathering and analysis of information and report presentation.
- Justifying the selection of techniques and understanding their limitations.
- Mastery of techniques of analysis and/or synthesis and/or evaluation.
- Competence in selection and application of methods.
- Validation of quantitative methods.

The key to this criterion was the issue of appropriateness. Consequently, while the general intent of the development of methodological skills is clear, just how this is judged across the wide variety of projects, fields and institutions is difficult to determine from the examination criteria themselves. Surveying and using the literature related to the topic of research was a common criterion, though the specification of the desired qualities varied across being critical, comprehensive and detailed. At times the focus was on the review as an end in itself (showing competence in reviewing), while in other cases the literature review was a context for the study, or a means to identifying a problem.

Between the generality of the originality criterion and the detail of presentation and skills lies a group of criteria that connect to the substantive topic and its relation to the field of the research. These include independent thinking and analysis, comprehensiveness, relatedness to the field and knowledge of the discipline.

Of interest here is that, while there is consensus on the criteria of originality and presentation, there remains considerable variation in the extent to which other criteria are specified. In some cases, detailed criteria may be assumed to follow from more general ones such as the ability to plan and conduct research or suitability for publication. Whether or not this assumption is made, a great deal of interpretation and inference is needed in using the criteria to assess any particular thesis.

This is especially obvious when the notion of standards is considered. Criteria specify the dimensions on which a thesis should be assessed, but to judge whether any criterion is satisfactorily achieved requires a concept of the standard that should be expected of research and scholarship at the doctoral level (Sadler, 1987). Only the reference to suitability for publication could be seen to refer to a standard in these examination guidelines. The assumption presumably is that the standards are known by virtue of examiners' experience in research, in examination, or in having completed doctoral study themselves.

An equally important issue is the notion of weighting of the various criteria. Typically, no mention is made of this question, so the presumption must be that the criteria are to be weighted equally in the assessment. However, it is quite likely that this judgement will be made by the individual examiner, whose particular priorities and emphases are to all intents and purposes unknown.

The intended and assessed curriculum compared

This chapter has analysed the documentation relating to the doctoral curriculum in order to describe its contents. The general introductory descriptions and the criteria for examination were the two key sources for the analysis. In general terms, the two sets of documents offered consistent descriptions of the key focus of the doctoral curriculum. The examination criteria indicated a greater consensus among institutions. Over 40 per cent of the examination criteria were mentioned by more than half the sampled institutions, whereas in the general descriptions only the originality feature was mentioned as frequently.

As could be expected, the examination criteria were more specific. The notion of implementing a research project, the second most frequently mentioned of the general features, was in the examination criteria detailed into more specific components. On the other hand, the examination criteria made no mention of research ethics or personal development as outcomes to be assessed.

Common to both sets of data, however, was a high degree of generality. The need to comprehend a very large range of research contexts, traditions and approaches has led to the doctoral curriculum being stated only in very general terms. Even the criteria for examination rely on a large degree of interpretation and inference to give the criteria effect, and make almost no attempt to describe the standards expected on the various criteria. In other words, the intended curriculum, while relatively consistently described across universities at a certain level of generality, depends heavily in its enactment on the understandings and practice of research and scholarship in particular fields.

We can ask to what extent the intended curriculum described here addresses the forms of knowledge described earlier. The elements of the typology can be identified to varying degrees in the documents analysed. Abstract propositional and procedural knowledge, and tacit and embedded knowledge are all identified as part of the documented intended curriculum. However, action knowledge and cultural understandings are not mentioned. Nor are there any references to creativity, a subject of interest in the desire for innovation in knowledge production. Originality is the relevant term here, but since it can be interpreted in many ways, not all of which could be said to be innovative in the sense implied, the question remains as to whether the doctoral curriculum generates this outcome. Notions of entrepreneurship and public engagement are similarly missing from statements of the intended curriculum.

This analysis of the doctoral curriculum, at least as it is described and examined, raises questions about the extent to which it addresses the issues of current debate outlined in the opening sections of this chapter. Since so much of the doctoral curriculum has been shown to be implicit in its practice at the level of the particular field of research, these questions of broader relevance need to be explored in these contexts. This will not be a simple matter, for many devotees of the disciplines, motivated by notions of stewardship and commitment to longstanding traditions of inquiry, may see such demands as a distraction.

Resolving this tension will require clarification of the nature of disciplinarity, and answers to such questions as whether research strategies can be generalised across diverse fields. One response takes an essentialist view that knowledge forms are discrete and that the differences between them are deeply structural. Such a view is difficult to reconcile with notions of generic skill, interdisciplinarity, and even more radical notions of originality, as Hodge (1995) has pointed out in the case of humanities doctorates. An alternative view is that knowledge is more instrumentally and pragmatically derived from processes of problem generation and problem solving in contexts of practice, such as Gibbons' concept of Mode 2 knowledge (Gibbons, 1998; Gibbons et al., 1994). This more open view may facilitate originality, but it will not make it any easier to identify generic skills or to specify in advance clear standards of quality.

As noted earlier, the question of standards and the need to clarify the outcomes of the doctorate are most sharply focused in the assessment process. In many respects the findings here confirm the observations of Tinkler and Jackson (2000) that the PhD examination is conceptualised in diverse ways, a view more recently put by the UK Rugby Team. In 2005, the UK GRAD program established a working group following the Roberts Policy Forum of that year. One of the aims of the group, known as the Rugby team after the location of the Policy Forum, was to consider how to evaluate the effectiveness of skills development amongst postgraduate researchers and research staff. In their report to the Roberts Policy Forum of 2006, the group stated that:

> ... the implications of the research and generic skills agenda on how the PhD is examined has surfaced repeatedly in our consultations. The sector should consider whether the time is appropriate to instigate a debate on the assessment of the PhD.

The Forum Report continued that 'this is clearly beyond the remit of the Rugby Team, but members wished to publicly recognise that there is a growing need for this debate to happen'. The role of assessment in the doctoral degree is clearly a matter for continuing scrutiny, but to clarify doctoral assessment will require a clearer and more systematic concept of the doctoral curriculum than has so far been apparent.

References

Adams, F. and Mathieu, E. (1999) Towards a closer integration of Ph.D. training to industrial and societal needs, *Analytica Chimica Acta*, 393: 147–155.

Association of American Universities (1998) *Graduate Education Report*, at: http://www.aau.edu/reports/GradEdRpt.html.

Australian Vice-Chancellors' Committee (2002) *Code of Practice for Maintaining and Monitoring Academic Quality and Standards in Higher Degrees*, Australian Vice-Chancellors' Committee, at: http://www.avcc.edu.au/policiesactivities/teachinglearning/guidelinescodes/index.htm.

Blackler, F. (1995) Knowledge, knowledge work and organizations: an overview and interpretation, *Organization Studies*, 16(6): 1021–1046.

Bourner, T. (1998) More knowledge, new knowledge: the impact on education and training, *Education + Training*, 40(1): 11–14.

Burgess, R. (1997) The changing context of postgraduate education in the United Kingdom, in R. Burgess (ed.), *Beyond the First Degree: Graduate Education, Lifelong Learning and Careers*, London: Society for Research into Higher Education and Open University Press.

Clegg, S. (1999) Globalizing the intelligent organization: learning organizations, smart workers, (not so) clever countries and the sociological imagination, *Management Learning*, 30(3): 259–280.

Coate, K. and Leonard, D. (2002) The structure of research training in England, *Australian Educational Researcher*, 29(3): 19–42.

Collins, H. (1993) The structure of knowledge, *Social Research*, 60(1): 95–116.

Connell, R. (1985) How to supervise a PhD, *Vestes*, 2: 38–41.

Deem, R. and Brehony, K. (2000) Doctoral students' access to research cultures – are some more unequal than others?, *Studies in Higher Education*, 25(2): 150–165.

Delamont, S., Parry, O. and Atkinson, P. (1997) Critical mass and pedagogic continuity: Studies in academic habitus, *British Journal of Sociology of Education*, 18(4): 533–549.

Economic and Social Research Council (2001) *Postgraduate Training Guidelines*, Swindon: Economic and Social Research Council.

Fleck, J. (1997) Contingent knowledge and technology development, *Technology Analysis and Strategic Management*, 9(4), cited in R. Johnston (1998) *The Changing Nature and Forms of Knowledge: A review*, Canberra: Commonwealth of Australia.

Gallagher, M. (2000) The challenges facing higher education research training, in M. Kiley and

G. Mullins (eds), *Quality in Postgraduate Research: Making Ends Meet*, Proceedings of the 2000 Quality in Postgraduate Research Conference, University of Adelaide.

Geiger, R. (1997) Doctoral education: the short-term crisis vs. long-term challenge, *Review of Higher Education,* 20(3): 239–251.

Gibbons, M. (1998) *Higher Education Relevance in the 21st Century*, Washington, DC: World Bank Human Development Network.

Gibbons, M. Limoges, C., Nowotny, H., Schwartzman, S., Scott, P. and Trow, M. (1994) *The New Production of Knowledge*, London: Sage.

Gilbert, R. (2004) A framework for evaluating the doctoral curriculum, *Assessment and Evaluation in Higher Education.* 29(3): 299–309.

Gilbert, R., Balatti, J., Turner, P. and Whitehouse, H. (2004a) The generic skills debate in research higher degrees, *Higher Education Research and Development*, 23(3): 375–388.

Gilbert, R., Balatti, J., Turner, P. and Whitehouse, H. (2004b) The Doctoral Curriculum: Needs and Directions in Research Training, unpublished report for the Research Programmes and Policy Unit, Higher Education Group, Department of Education, Science and Training, Canberra, Townsville, James Cook University.

Golde, C.M. and Dore, T.M. (2001). *At Cross Purposes: What the Experiences of Doctoral Students Reveal about Doctoral Education*, Philadelphia, PA: Pew Charitable Trusts (www.phd-survey.org).

Hamilton, D. (1987) *Education: An Unfinished Curriculum*, Glasgow: Department of Education, University of Glasgow.

Hockey, J. (1995) Change and the social science PhD: supervisors' responses, *Oxford Review of Education*, 21(2): 195–206.

Hodge, B. (1995) Monstrous knowledge: doing PhDs in the humanities, *Australian Universities Review*, 2: 35–39.

Johnston, R. (1998) *The Changing Nature and Forms of Knowledge: A Review*, Canberra: Commonwealth of Australia.

Johnston, S. (1999) Postgraduate supervision in education: an overview of the literature, in A. Holbrook and S. Johnston (eds), *Supervision of Postgraduate Research in Education*, Review of Australian Research in Education No. 5, Coldstream, VT: Australian Association for Research in Education.

Kemp, D. (1999) *New Knowledge, New Opportunities: A Discussion Paper on Higher Education Research and Research Training.* Canberra: Commonwealth of Australia.

Kendall, G. (2002) The crisis in doctoral education: a sociological diagnosis, *Higher Education Research and Development*, 21(2): 131–141.

McWilliam, E. and Singh, P. (2002) Towards a research training curriculum: what, why, how, who?, *Australian Educational Researcher*, 29(3): 3–18.

McWilliam, E., Taylor, P., Thomson, P., Green, B., Maxwell, T., Wildy, H. and Simons, D. (2002) *Research Training in Doctoral Programs: What Can be Learned from Professional Doctorates?*, Canberra: Higher Education Division, Department of Education, Science and Training.

Office of Science and Technology (1992) *The Nature of the PhD: A Discussion Document*, London: Office of Science and Technology.

Organisation for Economic Co-operation and Development (2000) *Knowledge Management in the Learning Society*, Paris: Centre for Educational Research and Innovation.

Park, C. (2005) New variant PhD: the changing nature of the doctorate in the UK, *Journal of Higher Education Policy and Management*, 27(2): 189–207.

Pearson, M. (1996) Professionalising Ph.D. education to enhance the quality of the student experience, *Higher Education*, 32: 303–320.

Pearson, M. and Brew, A. (2002) Research training and supervision development, *Studies in Higher Education*, 27(2): 135–150.

Phillips, E. (1993) The concept of quality in the PhD, in D. Cullen (ed.), *Quality in PhD Education*, Canberra: Centre for Educational Development and Academic Methods and the Graduate School, Australian National University.

Pole, C. (2000) Technicians and scholars in pursuit of the PhD: some reflections on doctoral study, *Research Papers in Education*, 15(1): 95–111.

Quality Assurance Agency for Higher Education (2001) *The Framework for Higher Education Qualifications in England, Wales and Northern Ireland*, at: http://www.qaa.ac.uk/academicinfrastructure/FHEQ/EWNI/default.asp.

Quality Assurance Agency for Higher Education (2004) *Code of Practice for the Assurance of Academic Quality and Standards in Higher Education*, Mansfield: Quality Assurance Agency for Higher Education.

Raber, L.R. (1995) Chemists give mixed review of NRC Report on doctoral education, *American Chemical Society*, 29 May, p. 44.

Review Committee on Higher Education Financing and Policy (1998) *Learning for Life: Review of Higher Education Financing and Policy*, final report, Canberra: Department of Education, Employment, Training and Youth Affairs (The West Report).

Ross, A. (2000) *Curriculum: Construction and Critique*, London: Falmer Press.

Sadler, D.R. (1987). Specifying and promulgating achievement standards, *Oxford Review of Education*, 13(2): 191–209.

Smart, J. and Hagedorn, L. (1994) Enhancing professional competencies in graduate education, *Review of Higher Education*, 17(3): 241–257.

Tinkler, P. and Jackson, C. (2000) Examining the doctorate: institutional policy and the PhD examination process in Britain, *Studies in Higher Education*, 25(2): 167–180.

UK GRAD Programme (2006) *Report of Proceedings, UK GRAD Programme Roberts Policy Forum January 2006*, at: http://www.grad.ac.uk/cms/ShowPage/Home_page/Policy/National_policy/Rugby_Team/p!ekljFef.

Wellcome Trust (2000) *Career Paths of a 1988–1990 Prize Student Cohort: Review of Wellcome Trust PhD Research Training*. London: Wellcome Trust.

Part II

Pedagogy and learning

Chapter 6

Enhancing the doctoral experience at the local level

Diana Leonard and Rosa Becker

Most of the limited research on the doctorate in the UK over the last 20 years has consisted of reflective, conceptual or philosophical articles and reports, with occasional empirical studies and re-analysis of national statistics, written from the perspectives of policy makers, higher education managers and supervisors. Relatively little empirical work includes the perspective of students. They are increasingly regarded as cogs in the system and not 'key stakeholders'.

Despite this general lack of evidence on which to base new policies, a series of changes have been introduced centrally, aimed at raising the research and employment-related skill levels of the next generation of researchers and improving the efficiency of higher education institutions. These have mostly not yet been evaluated; nor have parallel changes which have been made by universities themselves to try to increase their income, raise their research profiles, and rationalise their administration and teaching.

One result is that many academics feel that certain important understandings of the meaning of research are being over-ridden. These recognise the importance of the person of the researcher and see the doctoral experience (and later research) as a 'journey', an internal process of increased understanding; and as 'trading', producing a product of original knowledge to contribute to the academic community (Brew 2001).

This chapter will suggest some possible ways to redress the imbalance through an understanding of the rather 'messy' processes by which individuals develop personally and produce original ideas. It will concentrate on the contributions which could be made (and in some cases are being made) by the administrative academic units variously called 'departments', 'faculties' or 'schools', and large permanent research groups and interdisciplinary centres (which will here all be referred to as 'academic units'). Support for doctoral students from this level of the university structure has previously been treated piecemeal or largely overlooked.

A review of the literature on the doctoral experience

We can be confident about what empirical research does and doesn't exist on doctoral students in the UK because we recently undertook a review of the literature on 'the learning experiences of doctoral students' for the Higher Education Academy

(Leonard et al., 2006). This was a Systematic Review, working with colleagues in the EPPI-Centre (Evidence for Policy and Practice Information and Co-ordinating Centre) at the Institute of Education to produce an account of 'what is known', based on good research evidence, about the experiences of doctoral students.

We systematically sought out all the existing published and grey literature, and selected from this work which was:

- research-based (i.e. provided empirical evidence – quantitative or qualitative, including evaluations, autobiographies and secondary analysis of data);
- focused on the motivations, experiences and outcomes of research students (MPhil, PhD and professional doctorates);
- included the perspectives of students themselves (not just, for instance, accounts from supervisors of what (they believe) students think;
- methodologically rigorous;
- published since the start of changes to the doctorate (i.e. since 1985).

Time and financial constraints meant we had to focus on UK material. Altogether we found 415 texts, and 120 of these fitted our criteria (several based on the same studies). Subsequent coding, sorting and cross-tabulation of their content on specialised software allowed us to note both the foci of interest and also the numerous gaps in the field.

We found that most UK empirical research which includes students' perspectives is small scale and has often been undertaken by academic and support staff, in their own time, for their own interest and often focused on their own institutions. To this can be added a number of autobiographical accounts by students themselves. Unfortunately the modest original research by our National Postgraduate Committee does not usually differentiate between masters and doctoral level postgraduates and so was not useable. Only a minority of these accounts draw on any specified theories or a broader literature, hence the material they present is largely descriptive.

This literature is heavily weighted towards studies of supervision, and towards the arts and social sciences and especially Education. There are almost no studies of the supervision of doctorates in the high recruiting fields of medicine and health, or business studies. It also discusses mainly full-time and international students. Few look at the supervision of the large numbers of part-time research students, or the effects of gender. Very few indeed have studied the effects (if any) of the social class background and ethnicity of home doctoral researchers – despite the great concern in the UK about social class and differential access to and progress on undergraduate courses.

Alongside the work on supervision, we noted that there were a number of texts exploring specifically the periods before, during and after the UK *viva voce* examination (see Leonard et al., 2006, Section 4); and what can be classed as the relationship between the academic unit (department, faculty, etc.) and students' experiences and outcomes. From the student perspective (or more accurately, for those concerned with the student experience), these appear to be important arenas, and the latter is therefore the focus of this chapter.

However, the present account departs from the mapping provided by the systematic review to use the research it identified as the basis for a more normative/evaluative study. It also departs from the government view of the doctorate as training for young researchers, to consider the integration of the student into the research community and how the person of the researcher develops (is educated) through the research process.

The university-wide context of the doctoral experience

The environment for research students in the UK is now richer – but also more structured and monitored – than 20 years ago. Most universities have established either a central, or several faculty-based, Doctoral (or Graduate) School(s). The senior academics associated with such schools are supported in ensuring the provision of the now required courses and the various institutional arrangements and 'precepts' required by the Quality Assurance Agency (QAA, 2004), by an internal staff of administrators and student support sections. There are also external organisations available for such Deans and support staff: the autonomous membership-funded UK Council for Graduate Education (UKCGE), and a Funding and Research Councils supported UK GRAD Programme. Both broadly aim:

> to build and facilitate networks of academics, PGR support staff, employers, and all those with an interest in personal and professional development for doctoral researchers ... by hosting regional events including Good Practice workshops ... and co-ordinating views from the regions to feed into a national policy debate (UK GRAD Programme website).

How much of the information from these networks and workshops filters down through the Head/Dean of the graduate school to the academics in charge of the research students within each academic unit (who will here be referred to as research tutors), let alone to supervisors and support staff and students themselves, is debatable (as it is unresearched).

Graduate schools encourage recruitment and contribute towards developing a 'thriving research culture' – and also towards providing evidence of it, since this is a key criterion for high rating in the five-yearly Research Assessment Exercise (RAE) of each subject area in each university. The RAE 'score' is in turn a key element in determining the level of funding each university gets from the government. Similarly, the central administration/graduate school of each HEI must periodically complete a questionnaire for the Quality Assurance Agency, detailing the availability of the range of items listed in its *Code of Practice* (QAA, 2004), viz. induction sessions, published regulations and information handbooks, training for supervisors, mechanisms for collecting student feedback, and complaints and appeals procedures, etc. But since position holders are concerned to present a favourable picture of their formal provision, the QAA's first *Review of Research Degree Programmes* (QAA, 2007) is obviously no more than an indicator of current practice. Nonetheless, it has meant that most universities now have at least nominal formal structures in place – even if they are not well known or effective as far as students are concerned. (For example, Lee (1998) found that students who complained of sexual harassment were not helpfully received by heads of academic units, and no mention was made of the doctoral school management as the last port of call for complaints and appeals.)

Despite such reservations, most UK universities do now have a number of central services which are (potentially) of key importance to research students, and especially those from overseas, viz. marketing, admissions, childcare provision (mainly needed by overseas students), accommodation (which is often in chronically short supply, especially for families), English language teaching, short induction programmes, and advising on study skills. Henderson (1996) shows, for instance, the importance of pre-arrival information to anxious students facing the unknown, both the content and the speed with which it is despatched and general criticisms concerning the non-acknowledgement of letters, lack of receipt of money and confirmation of arrangements.

Once they have arrived, research students find that the central student union in most universities focuses on the interests of, and is mainly used by, undergraduates. Moreover, even where specific central postgraduate rooms are made available, with refreshments, bars, TV and social and recreational programmes aimed at building graduate student rapport, these seem to be used mainly by those doing taught (Masters) courses. The literature notes that doctoral students, particularly those who were formerly undergraduates within the same institution, and mature students who hold posts in universities in their own country, frequently wish to distinguish themselves from undergraduates and feel resentful if they are 'integrated' with and/or have to share academic or other resources with others (Humphrey and McCarthy, 1999). They especially dislike living in accommodation alongside undergraduate students. 'Privileges' are symbolic indicators of the beginnings of a researcher's inclusion in the 'inner sanctum' of academia – even if some initially find it unsettling and do not dare to go into the postgraduate room (Hockey 1994; Hockey and Allen-Collinson, 2005). So postgraduate research students are generally less involved in the social life of the university as a whole, and more embedded in – and hence the greater importance to them of – their academic units' provision and processes.

Central student unions do, however, often support groups for specific nationalities or religious groups, and these may be used by some research students. They can provide social activities with other expatriates, run weekend schools staffed by volunteers, and organise the taking over by newcomers of accommodation from departing students.

If research students run into difficulties later in their studies, the central university administration or the graduate school can usually direct those referred by their supervisor or research tutor to counselling support. However, one study shows that overseas students may have difficulty with the available western mode of student counselling. It can be disorientating and counter-cultural for those used to different modes of support, e.g. seeking answers from their supervisors whom they consider 'experts', or only from close family and friends (Okorocha, 1996).

With new Rights legislation, universities have had to review their provisions for students with disabilities, often appointing specialised disabilities officers. A centrally-funded project highlighted good practice (Premia, 2004a, 2004b) and included a number of case studies of postgraduate researchers. Those with mobility or visual impairments had very practical problems where they needed help, such as being unable to move around the campus easily, to take lecture notes, or to handle a lot of reading within a short time. Several individuals reported how much confidence they gained when their prospective supervisor invited them to start a PhD, or when they received efficient help from librarians, or when for the first time in their academic career they felt included on an equal basis thanks to encouraging and supportive attitudes from their supervisors. On the other hand, the isolating experience of the PhD could be magnified when students experience environmental and attitudinal barriers. Many students had negative experiences during their induction period, with staff members not knowing how to react to their disability. One student noted that if they themselves were told that the staff they met knew about their disability and were willing to help, it would make it much easier for them to admit that they would need more help than their peers. Several students were otherwise afraid of asking for extra help because they were worried about looking incompetent.

The impact of the academic unit context on the doctoral experience

Science v non-science

Most researchers continue to stress the dichotomy between science and non-science students established by major studies (e.g. Becher et al., 1994; Delamont et al., 2000) and broader academic units are rarely mentioned for science students because the focus is on the research group and the laboratory. Here they are with fellow doctoral students and postdocs who are doing or have recently completed PhDs on similar topics. There are also research associates and technical staff who are generally supportive and an important source of technical advice (Delamont et al., 1997; Pole, 1998; Wright and Lodwick, 1989). In addition, supervision may be partly a collective responsibility, and should the working relationship with the main supervisor break down, others can come to the rescue and function as a buffer against failure. Indeed the Wellcome Trust found in a survey of its (health-related) doctoral students, and especially in its four-year scheme which allows a PhD student to work on a number of projects in a selection of laboratories in their first year, that a prospective supervisor's encouragement and their potential bench colleagues were more crucial in influencing the decision to do research in a certain place than the actual topic on offer (Frame and Allen, 2002). This produces the tight 'pedagogical continuity' within the science disciplines stressed by Delamont and colleagues.

Science students are therefore usually more content with their studies than those in the humanities and social sciences. They are less socially and intellectually isolated and complete in a shorter time. Non-science students, on the other hand, are presented as having little contact with academic staff other than their supervisor, and less contact with other students. Many 'study in isolation'. They may therefore look for substantial involvement with their supervisors, and can make major demands upon them.

This dichotomy probably needs some questioning. Many science labs are fiercely competitive rather than supportive, with immense peer pressures (see Bunting, 2003), and not all science is done in large research groups or in laboratories. There are also tales of exploitation in science, with students being used to work on what are essentially repetitions of the same procedures in slightly different contexts for the benefit of their supervisor's career. On the other hand, social scientists and others increasingly work on medium-sized projects, or in multidisciplinary centres. It could be that the choice of subject areas for research on the sciences and arts and social sciences, and the focus on full-time students, has blurred some overlaps and that the academic unit has a potential role to play across the board.

Access to supervisors and departmental facilities

The administrative academic unit is generally responsible for administering applications and managing the workload of staff members, and hence for ensuring supervisors have time for however many research students they accept.

Applications are often not well handled. Departments may not interview individuals before offering them places, nor do they suggest to those who are accepted that they should come onto campus to be shown around by an existing student before they accept a place. They also give prospective research students little if any educational guidance (Houghton, 2001). Moreover, although the research tutor may know something of his or her colleagues' research interests, some academic units, at least in the past, have made the connection between student and potential supervisors very casually:

> I was given the names of three possible supervisors. I wasn't introduced to them, I was just given the names. I just wandered around and knocked on people's doors to introduce myself . . .
>
> (Hockey, 1994: 184)

Once started on their studies, the physical support provided for research students varies greatly – between and also within universities. Access to an office and basic academic facilities (desks, labs, materials, computers in locations which are not closed for classes, appropriate software and a good library) are now a requirement for recognition as an 'outlet' for Research Council-funded studentships, and in some cases students are provided with well-equipped shared offices or work places, located centrally within the department, and they can book other rooms for meetings or if they are teaching. They may also have a designated room for socialising. But in less prosperous universities such provision is much more limited, and in urban situations space and facilities can be at a premium (Hockey and Allen-Collinson, 2005). A proportion of students across the disciplines are markedly disappointed with the available facilities and equipment (Chiang, 2004; Gross 1994; Wright, 2003). International students from less affluent countries voice particular concern about lack of photocopying, postage for questionnaires or laboratory consumables, restricted use of the telephone, etc. because being charged or providing them themselves means extra expenditure (Deem and Brehony, 2000). Moreover, facilities work best when they are not just provided but also *managed* by the academic unit staff, who make sure space, etc. is fairly divided and intervene in the event of incompatibilities.

Access to facilities is also important because doctoral students, especially in the social sciences and arts and humanities, feel more involved with their department when they can work in close proximity to their peers, if they can have post and messages delivered, and if they are occasionally engaged with research teams or teaching or conference organisation (Humphrey and McCarthy, 1999). Those who do not have rooms at the university express more need for peer discussion, yet many are seldom seen, preferring to work in the library or at home. This can make institutions, especially in inner cities, into commuter schools and unravel any sense of community (Gross, 1994).

Overall, full-time students tend to be more critical of all aspects of being a research student than part-timers, probably because for them the PhD may be 'their whole life'. The nearer they are to completion, the more anxious and ambivalent they are about their future and financial career prospects in the academic world (Acker et al., 1994). But it is the numerous part-timers, who have jobs and domestic responsibilities elsewhere, who receive the least material benefit from the university. They are rarely given desks or access to other facilities and often know few other students or faculty members (Acker, 1999). They also often find library and archive opening hours very unfriendly (Dickinson et al., 1997).

The symbolic significance of 'special' treatment for postgraduate students, noted above, applies particularly to overseas students across the disciplines. Many come from the elite in their own countries and are used to high status, good living conditions and having professional responsibilities (and secretarial and other support). For them, the passage to postgraduate research study can involve an interruption in a career path and a temporary (but lengthy) lowering of status and power. They may feel aggrieved about their (work and domestic) accommodation and believe that UK universities have a moral or paternalistic responsibility for students and should not take on more than they can house. These are the ones who, from the management perspective, are said to have the most 'unrealistic expectations' of what life in a UK university will be like (Humphrey and McCarthy, 1999).

Courses

Since the mid-1990s, students funded by the UK Research Councils have been required to attend compulsory generic and discipline-specific methodology courses for the equivalent of 60 per cent of the first year full time (Coate and Leonard, 2002). This pattern has also been followed by less elite universities, as far as resources will allow, to enhance their prestige and to increase their numbers of postgraduate students. The research available suggests that full-time home-based social science students were initially cynical and resistant to such research training courses – or at least they were in the late 1990s, when many students and supervisors remembered the time before widespread training was established and before the Research Councils extended their grants to cover a one-year MRes and three years for the thesis. Various myths grew up about the rationale for the changes (Deem and Brehony, 2000; Parry et al., 1994). Self-funding part-time home students still often resent having to learn the range of methods if they are planning to do just one piece of research out of interest, and supervisors may advise students against 'bothering' with unassessed courses. However, international research students, although they were not the ones at whom such courses were originally aimed, seem to welcome this provision and to derive significant academic benefit. They also value having a student cohort, at least for their first years (Deem and Brehony, 2000).

By the mid-1990s, some departments had started to offer their research students certified courses on post-compulsory teaching, and to provide a mentor to support the teaching opportunities they made available (Fischer and Taithe, 1998). But these were overtaken by the required higher education teaching training established in 2002, which is now certified through the Higher Education Academy. Such courses have not been nationally evaluated, nor have the two weeks' worth of courses on personal and work skills which the Research Councils have required their students in all disciplines to attend since 2000. The latter provide 'transferrable skills' training and careers advice, and since 2006 support a Personal Development Planning portfolio. Additional central funding ('Roberts money') has been provided to cover the costs – which some universities have spread to provide these courses for all their students. Wellcome Trust-funded students suggested adding to the areas covered 'grantsmanship' (writing grant applications), writing skills, business accounting and science communication (Wellcome Trust, 2000).

Academic research cultures

Just as the role of the supervisor may be as much to do with moral support and encouragement as with academic help and practical advice, so an academic unit culture which is academically and socially inclusive, and which enables students to make contacts and develop networks, can have a positive impact on student motivation, experience and outcomes. It can provide an important foundation for those seeking to become researchers in or outside academe.

Some academic units have specifically endeavoured to develop collegiality (see e.g. Elton and Pope, 1989; Wright, 2003). Their research tutors take on overall responsibility for systems to support research students, and initiatives to increase a sense of community. The latter include co-opting new students into on-going study groups, regular support groups, special interest groups, task oriented groups, some group supervision, newsletters, networking, and creative use of the Internet. Friendly and helpful administrative staff and communal activity days, together with organised social events, all seem helpful. Moreover, academic staff are encouraged to acknowledge the value of all the unit's research students' views, and their practical experience and networks outside higher education. This helps to sustain students' intellectual self-worth, makes it easier to sort out problems of supervision at an early stage, and gives a sense of value for money to the many who are self-funding. Students feel the institution has a stake in their progress and in return they feel more positively about and contribute to the community (Gross, 1994).

In many departments, however, the amount of student contact with staff is minimal. It is confined to formal supervisions, occasional attendance at seminars and events such as a departmental Christmas party. Older overseas students are especially disappointed at being treated as 'just students', rather than as junior researchers, when UK academics do not recognise their status as lecturers in their home institutions.

Most departments run research seminars, sometimes with a social event attached. But although a high proportion of students know about these seminars, many do not attend them on a regular basis, and some never attend them at all. They say the seminars are inappropriate for their needs: the subject matter is not relevant and/or the setting is too formal. Moreover, even where departments do hold regular events, students may find the contact superficial because academic staff tend to talk among themselves rather than with postgraduate students (Wright and Lodwick, 1989).

Students who do not attend seminars or classes regularly nevertheless often indicate that they want greater opportunity for discussion and more help – but in specific areas. A proportion suggest inter-departmental meetings would be helpful because of the specialised nature of their research, or that contact with others outside the university would be valuable because expertise in a specialised subject is either lacking in the department or not made available. That is to say, feeling under time pressure, they look for narrowly 'relevant topics' and dismiss the rest. They also resist attempts to make attendance compulsory. But those who chose to attend regularly can make serendipitous discoveries of ideas for their theses:

> a lot of it linked quite by chance. I'd find something that would lead me directly to where I wanted to go, although specifically that book [or lecture] wasn't about it . . . I could have been struggling around in certain areas for quite a long time, except for those chance encounters . . .
>
> (Haggis, 2002 p. 216).

Even where there is an ethos of collegiality, some students find it more difficult than others to access departmental social life. Part-time students find research cultures harder to enter and sustain than full-timers and may not always even be aware that they are eligible to attend events or to join professional academic societies due to poor communication by academic units. International students mention encouragement to attend seminars and conferences and informal academic networks much less frequently than home students (Deem and Brehony, 2000). Poverty too can exclude some students from attending conferences and other events.

Even full-time home students feel they are not included in the decisions their departments (or the central graduate school) make about postgraduate researchers. They 'know nothing about the decision-making processes' in their institution; and this is amplified when they feel their particular research area is not a priority – for instance, because staff are moving into other fields.

Peer interaction

From the staff perspective it is frequently noted that doctoral students not only face the challenges of a new phase of learning, but may also have moved location in order to study and left established social networks. In the case of overseas students, it is emphasised that this social isolation is exacerbated by cultural differences and having to spend a long time away from their wider family or even their children.

Students themselves, however, are as likely to describe the pressures they experience as competing demands on their time and having doubts about their capacity to succeed. They worry whether they can finish within four years, and about their intellectual abilities, even when they have previously obtained a first-class degree and been given a competitive award for their doctoral study. This may make them reluctant to take risks in front of their supervisors and to speak in the public domain of seminars when supervisors or other staff are present, especially in departments which have different intellectual traditions from those they have previously encountered (Hockey and Allen-Collinson, 2005). They talk about being confused and frustrated, and 'not knowing what a PhD (or the assessment) is supposed to be about' – and such concerns can recur at different points throughout the process (Haggis, 2002):

> There is a lot of insecurity in postgrad culture. There is a feeling of having to perform all the time, especially in the first year, but as you get further into PhD life, you realise that everyone else doesn't know a lot either. You learn from other postgrads that you don't need to know everything, that is why support networks are so important.
>
> (Male, full-time, home student, cited in Deem and Brehony, 2000: 156)

This is a particular issue for full-time students. Part-time students with full-time jobs outside the university usually have other sources of self-esteem and support, but full-time students often have financial worries and complain more about not getting sufficient supervision. They are particularly in need of not just emotional but also academic support from other students. But even full-time students sometimes know few other students – because the total group in their department/university may be small, or the student him/herself may work away from the university most of the time, or feel they share little in common. Several studies mention students identifying the importance of group support, or the lack of peers with whom they can communicate, as a serious issue. They see learning through relationships as crucial to their progress, and want people in a similar situation to share perspectives and give feedback (Haggis, 2002; Wareing, 1999; Wisker et al., 2002).

This applies especially when normal academic unit venues (such as seminars and supervisions) are perceived as dangerous: as places where academic weaknesses are liable to be exposed. Informal discussions with peer students are a much safer place to explore ideas, especially for first-year students, and some women-only groups get established to make it easier for participants to join in and get noticed (Brina et al., 1999; and on advice for women in mixed groups, Conrad and Phillips, 1995). The peer subculture, like the science research group, can also act as a source of technical advice, e.g. on computer packages, and students frequently mention the usefulness of groups reflecting on theoretical and methodological perspectives and workshops on thesis writing. The presence of a strong peer cohort is one of the main reasons given by those who choose to study for a professional doctorate rather than a PhD.

Discussion groups or weekly informal seminars may be organised by students themselves independently of their supervisors, but several studies suggest departments should facilitate their formation with encouragement and/or some resources – but not institutionalise group structures. Where supervisors set out to lead groups, they may not be aware of the effect of their behaviour on students, and particularly on women students. Reading groups held in the evenings in the homes of staff, which might seem pleasant social occasions to staff, can be especially intimidating for international students from non-English speaking backgrounds. Where such groups exist, few NESB students mention attending them (Deem and Brehony, 2000). In general, it helps if institutions ask all students to pay attention to interaction processes, as well as to the tasks of groups. In addition, they need to provide micro-strategies for improving postgraduate supervision because communication between peers seems to be related to the supervisory culture as a whole (Conrad and Phillips, 1995).

Collective support and friendships among research students typically happen only when there are a sufficient number of full-time students in a given unit. There are also important differences between those where the majority of doctoral students are 25 or younger and those with many over 30 and/or who come from abroad (Humphrey and McCarthy, 1999). But even with a 'critical mass', there appears again to be very unequal access to peer culture. Part-time (usually 'home') students and international students (usually full-time) find it more difficult to join in than home full-timers.

The situation is no better for those part-time students who are employed in the university itself, either as full-time research assistants or as part-time lecturers. This might seem an ideal way of gaining experience, making money and completing a research degree, but such individuals are often marginalised in both the student and the faculty worlds, and many are strikingly discontented with their ambiguous situations (Acker, 1999; Fisher and Taithe,1998). Departments rarely treat them as fully-fledged members of staff, nor are they always part of the postgraduate networks where these exist, though they do feel slightly more involved in the work of the department than other doctoral students (Humphrey and McCarthy, 1999). What they see of academic life tends to make them disillusioned (Acker et al., 1994).

In general, students' strategies to progress and complete their PhD are perforce largely a matter of constructing individual strategies (Acker et al., 1994) and the doctorate gives them little if any experience of the team working which employers are said to value:

> Most home [social sciences] students interviewed held and positively embraced individualistic views of research; [and] international students tended to have such views imposed on them by their working conditions [even if] some would have preferred more collective ways of working.
>
> (Deem and Brehony, 2000: 158)

External sources of support

There is hardly any detailed UK evidence on the kinds of support doctoral candidates receive from employers, though there is some mention of how difficult it is to study without it (Wright, 2003). But several texts mention the importance of family support and the practical help (e.g. with IT problems, or fees) and intellectual support (reading drafts) given by partners – although there is also, of course, sometimes a lack of understanding about, or direct opposition to, doctoral studies from friends and spouses (Haggis, 2002; Leonard et al., 2005; Wisker et al., 2002; Wright, 2003).

Concluding comments

The central formulation of policy on research training in the UK has directed the doctorate towards being a short-term training for future researchers, rather than a high-level education undertaken for personal development, love of learning, to contribute original knowledge and to solve practical problems. There is increased attention to giving potential future employers 'what they want' (though little research to establish what this may be) and a general presumption that research students will keep on enrolling however the doctorate may change. Meanwhile, the universities' shortage of funding has meant they have uncritically complied with instructions from their major paymasters, while being set increasingly in competition with each other, and happy to capitalise on additional fee-paying students.

Since 1990 the Higher Education Funding Councils and the Research Councils seem to have presumed it was unnecessary to justify the need for change by initial research, or to monitor and evaluate the effects of their new policies, other than by occasional surveys – which, as surveys will, have picked up on what they thought to include in the first place. Similarly, the recently introduced (2006) national Postgraduate Research Experience Survey, based on the Australian model and run by the Higher Education Academy, and the annual and leaving evaluations which the QAA *Code of Practice* requires in individual universities, are confirmatory and enumerating rather than exploratory. The interpretations of all this data have also nearly always been limited by their disengagement from general work on (higher) educational curriculum, pedagogy and assessment.

As a consequence of the flurry of directives, and the tying of funding to audit results, the jobs of those appointed to head graduate schools, or to take charge of research students in academic units, have become largely managerial. Most of their time has had to focus on ensuring the required courses are put in place, producing regulations and other documents, ensuring the monitoring of students' progress through written records of supervisions, annual reports and advisory committees, and the writing of returns to external agencies. Some of the more creative things some departments were previously doing to enrich the doctoral experience were initially blown away, and subsequently there has been little time for academic units to innovate or adapt the requirements to their circumstances, or to undertake investigative research for their own use.

The quality of research students' experience has continued to be seen as largely due to their relationship with their supervisor (in the social sciences and humanities), or the supervisor and his/her research group (in the sciences); and the way to improve it is seen as mainly by initial and in-service training of supervisors. As a result, there has been little discussion of the potentially important additional role of the department/faculty/school, or of the graduate school and wider institution, in supporting – as opposed to administering and occasionally trouble shooting – the doctoral experience.

This seems an important omission because all academics/supervisors have increasing workloads, including increasing numbers of doctoral students and additional research projects to direct, which means they cannot easily provide the substantial involvement students want:

> If higher mental functioning in the individual has its origins in relationships between people . . . [i]n the case of the research student . . . the one learning dyad available (the supervisory relationship) may assume a greater importance in the learning process than the relationship can, or is designed to, contain.
>
> (Wright, 2003: 223, citing Vygotsky)

It is an important omission also because becoming part of a departmental research community is a step towards membership of the wider (academic or applied) research community. It is also a significant absence, at a time when there is much concern with doctoral drop-out and time to completion, if it is indeed the case that feeling part of a community is motivating and helps speed up progress.

This suggests many academic units could and should do more to help their research students, though we need up-to-date empirical research to give a fuller picture of the current provisions, activities and the use students make of them. But even the limited existing literature suggests that departments could improve the doctoral experience by:

- Trying to get extra facilities and managing these well.
- Helping students to organise peer support groups of various kinds.
- Establishing mentoring by existing students (Henderson, 1996).
- Monitoring the informal exclusion of some groups from academic networks and supporting whichever groups are currently least involved.
- Encouraging the development of academic networks and helping to establish social relations with staff other than the supervisor.
- Giving research students the opportunity to do some teaching or to be attached, temporarily or long term, to a research project.
- Stressing the complexity, diversity and unpredictability of individual (adult) learning experiences and developing an explicit pedagogic discourse to maximise effective learning in each setting (courses, reading groups, attending seminars, participation in professional societies, etc.).
- Recognising that families and employers may be very involved in the doctoral process; and possibly including them in certain events (ibid.).

These suggestions are based on a more social and developmental view of research students than recent central policies. They would hope to maintain, and to improve, the educational elements of the doctoral experience. They complement the arguments of those who have looked at the broader pedagogy of the doctorate in the light of the general literature on the social situatedness of learning (e.g. Boud and Lee, 2005; Green, 2005; Pearson and Brew, 2002). These authors have stressed the importance of taking the whole research learning environment for doctoral students into account, and not just the supervisory/research group element; and for consideration of how the learning environment operates and can be fostered. But these writers have so far looked at only certain elements of what is discussed above as the overall potential role of the academic unit.

This pedagogic literature also suggests the importance in future of going further than the current UK literature allows, and looking at how individual students take up and assemble the opportunities available in their 'experienced environment' (physical, virtual and metaphorical). Different students have their own diverse situations and understandings of what being a doctoral student/doing a doctoral degree should entail and they will use what is provided in ways which are appropriate for themselves (Boud and Lee, 2005). But this should be a set of positive choices made on the basis of information and understanding and not forced by unavailability of resources or lack of support and guidance.

Acknowledgements

We wish to acknowledge our colleagues Jennifer Evans and Janet Metcalfe, who participated in the systematic review on which this chapter is based. The present interpretation is our own.

References

Acker, S. (1999) Students and supervisors: the ambiguous relationship. Perspectives on the supervisory process in Britain and Canada, *Review of Australian Research in Education*, 5: 75–94.

Acker, S., Transken, S. Hill, T. and Black, E. (1994) Research students in education and psychology: diversity and empowerment, *International Studies in Sociology of Education*, 4(2): 229–251.

Becher, T., Henkel, M. and Kogan, M. (1994) *Graduate Education in Britain*, London: Jessica Kingsley.

Boud, D. and Lee, A. (2005) 'Peer learning' as pedagogic discourse for research education, *Studies in Higher Education*, 30(5): 501–516.

Brew, A. (2001) Conceptions of research: a phenomenographic study, *Studies in Higher Education*, 26(3): 271–285.

Brina, C, Parsons, S. and Early, R. (1999) Doing a higher degree, in S. Hatt, J. Kent and C. Britton (eds), *Women, Research and Careers*, Basingstoke: Macmillan.

Bunting, C. (2003) Loneliness of the long distance runner, *Times Higher Education Supplement*, 17 January.

Chiang, K.H. (2004) Relationship between research and teaching in doctoral education in UK universities, *Higher Education Policy*, 17(1): 71–88.

Coate, K. and Leonard, D. (2002) The structure of research training in England, *Australian Educational Researcher*, 29(3): 19–41.

Conrad, L. and Phillips, E. M. (1995) From isolation to collaboration: a positive change for post-graduate women?, *Higher Education*, 30(2): 313–322.

Deem, R. and Brehony, K. J. (2000) Doctoral students' access to research cultures – are some more unequal than others?, *Studies in Higher Education*, 25(2): 149–165.

Delamont, S., Atkinson, P. and Parry, O. (2000) *The Doctoral Experience: Success and Failure in Graduate School*, London: Falmer Press.

Delamont, S., Parry, O. and Atkinson, P. (1997) Critical mass and pedagogic continuity: studies in academic habitus, *British Journal of Sociology of Education*, 18(4): 533–549.

Dickinson, H.W., Connell, H. and Savage, J. (1997) Student experiences, in N. Graves and V. Varma (eds), *Working for a doctorate: A Guide for the Humanities and Social Sciences*, London: Routledge, pp. 113–130.

Elton, L. and Pope, M. (1989) Research supervision: the value of collegiality, *Cambridge Journal of Education*, 19: 267–275.

Fischer, R and Taithe, B. (1998) Developing university teachers: an account of a scheme designed for postgraduate researchers on a lecturing career path, *Teaching in Higher Education*, 3(1): 37–50.

Frame, I.A. and Allen, L. (2002) A flexible approach to PhD research training, *Quality Assurance in Education*, 10(2): 98–103.

Green, B. (2005) Unfinished business: subjectivity and supervision, *Higher Education Research and Development*, 24(2): 151–163.

Gross, R. (1994) Accommodation of research students, *Journal of Graduate Education*, 1: 21–24.

Haggis, T. (2002) Exploring the 'black box' of process: a comparison of theoretical notions of the 'adult learner' with accounts of postgraduate learning experience, *Studies in Higher Education*, 27(2): 207–220.

Henderson, M.W. (1996) Support provision in higher educational institutions for non-UK post-graduate students, *Journal for Further and Higher Education in Scotland*, 20(1): 18–22.

Hockey, J. (1994) New territory: problems of adjusting to the first year of a social science PhD, *Studies in Higher Education*, 19(2): 177–190.

Hockey, J. and Allen-Collinson, J. (2005) Identity change: doctoral students in art and design, *Arts and Humanities in Higher Education*, 4(1): 77–93.

Houghton, A.-M. (2001) Do experienced educational travellers planning the PhD journey of a lifetime need educational guidance?, in L. West, N. Miller, D. O'Reilly and R. Allen (eds), *Travellers' Tales: From Adult Education to Lifelong Learning . . . and Beyond. Proceedings of the 31st annual conference of SCUTREA*, 4-6 July, pp. 190–194, Standing Conference on University Teaching and Research in the Education of Adults, University of East London.

Humphrey, R. and McCarthy, P. (1999) 'Recognising difference: providing for postgraduate students', *Studies in Higher Education*, 24(3): 371–386.

Lee, D. (1998) 'Sexual harrassment in PhD supervision', *Gender and Education*, 10(3): 299–312.

Leonard, D., Becker, R. and Coate, K. (2005) 'To prove myself at the highest level': the benefits of doctoral study, *Higher Education Research and Development*, 24(2): 135–150.

Leonard, D., Metcalfe, J., Becker, R. and Evans, J. (2006) *Review of the literature on the doctoral experience for the Higher Education Academy* (London and Cambridge: Institute of Education and UK GRAD Programme).

Okorocha, E. (1996) Cultural Clues to Student Experience, *The Times Higher Education Supplement*, 7 June, p.13.

Parry, O., P. Atkinson and S. Delamont (1994) Disciplinary identities and doctoral work, in

R.Burgess (ed.) *Postgraduate Education and Training in the Social Sciences*, London: Jessica Kingsley, pp. 34–52.

Pearson, M. and A. Brew (2002) Research training and supervision development, *Studies in Higher Education* 27(2): 135–150.

Pole, C. (1998) Joint supervision and the PhD: safety net or panacea? *Assessment and Evaluation in Higher Education* 23(3): 259–271.

Premia (2004a) *Case histories of employed graduates with a research degree*. Report produced through the HEFCE funded project Premia – making research education accessible (2003–2005), University of Newcastle upon Tyne <www.premia.ac.uk>

Premia (2004b) *Research Student Case Histories by Disability*. Report produced through the HEFCE funded project Premia – making research education accessible (2003–2005).

QAA (2004) *Code of practice for the assurance of academic quality and standards in higher education*, Section 1 Postgraduate research programmes, Quality Assurance Agency

QAA (2007) *Review of postgraduate research degree programmes in England and Northern Ireland* <www.qaa.ac.uk/reviews/postgraduate/default.asp>

Wareing, S. (1999) 'Doing a research degree', in: G. Wisker and N. Sutcliffe, *Good practice in postgraduate supervision*, Birmingham, SEDA: 7–11.

Wellcome Trust (2000) *Review of Wellcome Trust PhD Training: the student perspective,* London: Wellcome Trust.

Wisker, G., Robinson, V.G., Trafford, M.V. and Warnes, M. (2002) Getting there in the end: contributions to the achievement of the PhD, in M. Kiley and G. Mullins (eds), *Quality in Postgraduate Research: Integrating Perspectives*, Canberra, CELTS, University of Canberra.

Wright, J. and Lodwick, R. (1989) The process of the PhD: a study of the first year of doctoral study, *Research Papers in Education*, 4(1): 22–56.

Wright, T. (2003) Postgraduate research students: people in context?, *British Journal of Guidance and Counselling,* 31(2): 209–227.

Chapter 7

Writing for the doctorate and beyond

Alison Lee and Claire Aitchison

Who is responsible for writing in doctoral education? What difference might it make to current framings of doctoral education if serious attention were to be given to writing as fundamental rather than ancillary to research? What kinds of practices and pedagogies might be imagined? Conversely, what effects are the changes in the purpose and the outcomes of doctoral education having on practices of doctoral writing? What new challenges and possibilities for writing and for pedagogy are emerging in the changing scene of doctoral education?

These are the kinds of questions that are beginning to emerge in the diversifying international landscape of the doctorate. Beginning from a situation in which having written a thesis is most often the primary pedagogical qualification for supervising someone else's, writing has been neglected as a central component of doctoral education. Yet there now appears across the academy to be an increased interest in the writing associated with doctoral work.

This chapter discusses this new attention to writing in the new policy climate of doctoral diversity. It argues that this attention is in some senses reactive and often intellectually poorly resourced, whereby, for example, those engaged to develop research training programs are chosen because of an impressive publication record rather than because of exemplary pedagogical or curriculum expertise. Being a published author or editor is often the main qualification for developing new programs dedicated to writing for dissertation or publication. As a consequence therefore, pedagogies for writing are *ad hoc* and sporadic; critical questions of textuality and of rhetoric appear to be submerged and marginal. Traditionally, while writing pedagogy in universities has remained the 'housework' of university education, it has accordingly been mostly done by women and afforded limited status and prestige (Miller, 1991). Yet in the new climate it appears that there is an emerging recognition of the need for institutional capacity building for writing- and publication-focused pedagogical practices in doctoral work.

In order to sketch an approach to the kinds of questions above, we briefly lay out some key theoretical influences on academic writing research and specifically some current and emergent research on doctoral writing. We then document a selection of institutional and individual responses to the changing demands for writing in the contemporary experience of doctoral candidature. Our purpose is to surface, for examination and discussion, possibilities for advancing the pedagogies of doctoral writing in ways that are cognisant of the increasing and altering demands emanating from outside the academy as well as the very real situated needs of doctoral students struggling to write for their doctorate, their disciplines, their supervisors and themselves.

A literacy crisis in doctoral programs or a new agenda for writing?

We suggest that there is a discernible shift in attention in relation to writing arising from changes in doctoral education policy and research. There are a variety of reasons for this, the first and perhaps the most palpable being the increasing policy-driven attention to managing doctoral degrees as part of an economic efficiency agenda. Government and institutional concerns over poor completion rates for doctoral degrees have generated a number of strategies for the achievement of 'timely completion' in the UK, Europe, Australia and comparable settings. The concerns associated with completion rates connect further to strategies to avert fall-out from public scrutiny over literacy levels and accusations of plagiarism that find their way from undergraduate to graduate levels of enrolment.

Second, the growth and massification of the doctorate as an advanced qualification has led to a diversification in the body of doctoral candidates and an increasing globalisation of doctoral work. Expanded numbers of doctoral students and supervisors do not have English as their first language and nevertheless work together in English, the language of most scholarly publication. While there are complex issues related to the dominance of academic English and the loss of intellectual resources in other languages, writing necessarily becomes a site of struggle for students drawing on diverse linguistic, cultural and socio-economic resources.

A third major cause of increased interest in writing is connected to imperatives within the various national research assessment exercises to increase the rate and focus of publication both during and following doctoral candidature. In addition to pressures for timely completion, increased attention to publication rates is driven by imperatives of governments to maximise 'return on investment' in a global knowledge economy. In response, cash-strapped faculties and departments increasingly turn attention to supporting writing in a bid to improve publication rates as either a direct or longer-term strategic funding strategy. Writing becomes a part of a general policy-led turn to 'training' with regard to the conduct of doctoral work (see, e.g., European University Association (EUA), 2005).

Low publication rates from doctoral degrees have consistently been noted as a problem in the quality and effectiveness of doctoral education for preparing students to participate in research cultures (e.g. McGrail et al., 2005). Two international surveys by Dinham and Scott (2001) confirm the importance of publishing support to increasing actual publication rates among doctoral candidates and graduates. The surveys demonstrate clearly that students who received assistance from supervisors and/or attended an institution with a coherent policy on postgraduate publication were more likely to publish than those who did not.

Finally, the postmodern intellectual environment of the academic work context elicits ever new demands from writing. Contemporary views about writing and language continue to disrupt the traditional boundaries between 'scientific' and other forms of writing; to problematise not only research and disciplinary conventions, but also to challenge basic notions of 'what can be known and what can be told' by whom and to whom (Richardson, 2000).

Problems and struggles with writing can be seen as an impediment to efficient completion and to contribute to a failure to publish. Yet historically there has been a lack of resources directed to building capacity in this area and consequently there is a paucity of pedagogical expertise available to supervisors and program developers to address the challenges of changing the practices and outcomes required of doctoral writing.

Traditionally, there has been very little systematic instruction in high level academic writing offered to graduate students, in the English-speaking world at least (Rose and McClafferty, 2001). Supervisors generally stress the importance of writing when they talk about their supervision pedagogy (Paré et al., forthcoming) yet, despite the increasing array of 'self-help' guides for supervisors and the expanding research into doctoral writing, for most supervisors there remain extraordinarily few resources for developing capacity in writing in the pedagogical relationship.

Major recent initiatives that explicitly target writing for publication include forms such as the doctorate through publication (e.g. EUA, 2005; Powell, 2004). New kinds of doctorate, such as practice-based doctorates, also raise explicit questions of writing in relation to issues of genre, audience and supervisor capacity. These initiatives suggest the need to address issues of writing and publication within a broad reconceptualisation of doctoral pedagogy as more explicitly and tightly linked to research productivity of universities in increasingly competitive environments. At the same time, the increasing focus on doctoral 'training' provides opportunities for the incorporation of writing into a training discourse. For example in the following excerpt from the EUA report on 'doctoral programs for the European knowledge society', the focus on writing is explicit in the following list of forms of research training required for participation in the 'global labour market':

i   Scientific training in core research skills (research methodology and techniques; research management; analysis and diffusion; problem solving; scientific writing and publishing; academic writing in English; awareness of scientific ethics and intellectual property rights etc.)

ii   Training in transferable (generic) personal and professional skills and competences (writing and communication skills; networking and team-working; material/human resources and financial management; leadership skills; time management; career management, including job-seeking techniques etc.

(EUA, 2005: 19)

Changes to doctoral work – including policy-driven structural changes, the impact of changing epistemological orientations across disciplines and the effects of massification of education – are being witnessed at all levels of higher education institutions and most acutely in the changing experiences of doctoral education on the ground. This realisation from the policy level downwards provides new imperatives for reassessing what we know about doctoral writing and to review and renew pedagogical practices around doctoral writing.

What do we know about doctoral writing?

What counts as scholarly knowledge and expertise about doctoral writing? Most attention in the scholarly literature to this point has been conducted within specialist fields of English language teaching, academic English and applied linguistics, with scholars of rhetoric and composition only recently beginning to engage in the field. Initially mostly designed to assist students whose first language is not English, the contributions from these fields of knowledge provide important resources for practice within learning assistance settings where writing is explicitly taught.

Tracing the theoretical underpinnings of doctoral writing research

There is great variation within and between countries regarding where, how (and which) research students can access assistance with writing development. In terms of undergraduate education, North American higher education has had a longer standing institutionalised concern for writing development commencing with common first-year programs on composition and rhetoric, the provision of 'basic writing courses' and other writing programs such as the 'writing across the curriculum' initiatives (Coe et al., 2002; Ivanic and Lea, 2006; Lillis, 2001). This tradition was based on an institutional/structural recognition of the centrality of writing and argument in a democratic milieu, at least for undergraduate learners. By contrast there has been an implicit assumption in the British and similar models that university students can already write by virtue of their admission to the academy.

When it comes to doctoral-level candidature, however, there has been an almost deafening silence. Instead, as Paré et al. (forthcoming) note, apart from one-to-one work with their supervisors, doctoral students in many disciplines are left to learn the normalising ways of writing and speaking in their research communities by observation and trial and error. And, as they demonstrate, supervisors are often poorly equipped to address the need.

A great deal of work on doctoral writing has been developed within the context of language learning. Contemporary practices have grown out of, and alongside, sometimes diametrically opposing views on literacy and language development. The following thumbnail sketch of these developments traces key shifts in the conceptualisation and pedagogies for advanced academic writing.

The teaching of writing and of English for Academic Purposes (EAP) from the mid-1940s to the 1960s was rooted in behaviourist notions of language learning, which were articulated in the classroom, for example, through guided, controlled composition. In the 1960s attention to form broadened beyond sentence-level grammar to include 'rhetorical functions' such as description, narrative, classification, comparison and contrast, exemplification and so on (Paltridge, 2001). Many of the self-help books on doctoral writing still adopt this 'study skills' approach to writing that sees 'good writing' as a unitary, transparent and individuated skill that can be learned by following established linguistic patterns and rules (Kamler and Thomson, 2006).

In the 1970s there was a distinct change of focus in writing teaching from the text as *product* to the *process* of writing. While 'process writing' approaches signalled an advance in writing pedagogy because of their recognition of the centrality of the writer and of writing as creative, by the mid-1980s the restricted ability of 'process' to inform students of the different linguistic requirements of academic contexts was well critiqued (Hyland 2004). Within this orientation, the practical processes of writing were usefully and relatively easily taught; however, process writing on its own failed to 'pay attention to differences in text-type, context and purpose' (Ivanic, 2004: 234).

A major corrective to this lack was the widespread uptake of the concept of 'genre' – a notoriously slippery term. Genre-based approaches to writing vary considerably in their theoretical underpinnings. These include functional linguistic work associated with Halliday (1994) and especially in its school-based application in Australia by Martin (1989); the influential sociolinguistic work of Swales in the US which elaborated a view of genre associated strongly with the notion of discourse community (Swales, 2001; Tribble, 2005) and the rhetorical work emanating largely out of Canada and the US (e.g. Coe et al., 2002, Lundell and Beach, 2003). Linguistic genre approaches to writing are text-focused, and see writing as sets of text-types shaped according to the purposes and needs of the context, while rhetorical approaches see genres as forms of social action and hence focus more on purposes, contexts and relationships.

The most recent directions in the teaching of academic writing are orientations that see writing as a social practice and as social action. These approaches incorporate aspects of the former approaches recognising the importance of genre knowledge, the processes of writing and a familiarity with the textual product itself. In these views of writing, the act of construction and the text as product is conceived of as a socially-situated and socially-constructed communicative or rhetorical event shaped by power relations and with personal and social consequences. In the UK and Australia, these perspectives draw on critical discourse analysis and critical literacy work (e.g. Barton, 1994; Benesch, 2001; Clark and Ivanic, 1997; Cope and Kalantzis, 2000; Ivanic, 1998; Street, 1984), including more recent work on multimodality (e.g. Kress and van Leeuwen, 2002). In Canada and the US, rhetorical work on genre has drawn on activity theory (Lundell and Beach, 2003; Prior, 1998) and ideas associated with situated learning (Lave and Wenger 1991).

Framing writing as a discursive and as socio-rhetorical practice facilitates a finer-grained appreciation of the complexities of writing as an activity that articulates broader social interests alongside the specificities of a discipline or local instance of a writing activity, while at the same time foregrounding the interaction of the individual writer and their text in the act of making meaning. When writing is conceived of as a social act, then writing assistance for higher level academic writers must be socially purposeful and also ideally located within a social context.

Strategies for providing writing assistance for doctoral students are more likely to be successful when they address the desires of the student-writer to become a skilful discipline-specific researcher able to produce the range of genres required in their candidacy and by their disciplinary community. As a consequence, according to the view of writing as a socially constructed enterprise, the best kind of writing assistance is that which is embedded in real-life writing practices offering a range of strategies that focus on the socially situated (institutional and disciplinary) process and practices of text-construction while acknowledging the emerging and multifaceted identity of the writer.

Pedagogical responses to research into doctoral writing

Within specialist fields such as English for Academic Purposes, doctoral writing is part of a broader category known as 'advanced academic literacy'. This is an area where significant advances in research, theory and pedagogy have occurred over the last decade or so (Hyland, 2006). Strategically, an increased professional and disciplinary cohesiveness of these practitioners working in academic literacy has been achieved and a range of national and international peak bodies have been established for the dissemination of information via conferences and publications (these include the European Association for the Teaching of Academic Writing, the Association for Academic Language and Learning in Australia, the British Association of Lecturers in English for Academic Purposes and the Canadian Association for the Study of Language and Learning). Major journals specific to academic literacy, and representing the work of these organisations have consolidated over this time, (for example, the *English for Specific Purposes Journal*, *Written Communication*, and the *Journal of English for Academic Purposes*). In addition articles on writing and academic literacies regularly occur in other international journals such as *Higher Education Research and Development* and *Teaching in Higher Education* as well as discipline-specific journals. These 'mainstream' higher education journals reflect a broadening interest in doctoral writing.

The major focus of doctoral writing research in recent decades has been a concern with key academic genres, most particularly researching the structure and 'moves' within research articles (e.g. Swales and Feak, 2000), disciplinary discourses (Hyland, 2004; Parry, 1998) and more recently other advanced academic genres such as conference abstracts and presentations (Berkenkotter and Huckin, 1995, Kamler and Thomson 2004), literature reviews (Boote and Beile 2005) and specific components of the doctoral thesis such as conclusion chapters (Bunton, 2005).

A review of the recent focus of key journals reveals a growing appreciation of the complexities of advanced academic and doctoral writing. Articles have addressed teaching programs for thesis writing, ethnographic studies of text, comparative studies of components and types of theses and research articles, plagiarism and the social context of writing with special issues on contrastive rhetoric, evaluation in academic discourse and on advanced academic literacy. A feature of the ongoing interest in genre analysis has been the corpus-based studies that employ sophisticated computerised techniques of analysis.

On the one hand then, exciting advances are being made in the theorisation and research into advanced academic writing. At the same time, there is also a great deal of activity around the publication of self-help books on PhD candidature. However, there is a limited transfer of this knowledge to the everyday practices of doctoral education. Both students and supervisors and governmental and institutional stakeholders remain concerned about doctoral writing as a key location for the collapse of high-level scholarly achievement.

Changing demands require new approaches

We began the chapter by arguing that the broad field of doctoral education is intellectually poorly resourced to take up the existing and emerging challenges for doctoral writing in the intensified environment. Unfortunately, the specialist work on doctoral writing sketched above is not readily taken up by supervisors or candidates. Yet as doctoral students are increasingly expected to show mastery of a range of discourse practices over the course of their candidature they and their supervisors are seeking out guidance for strategies for writing development.

Identifying a knowledge and skill gap

Recent institutional research on doctoral pedagogy has been helpful in highlighting some of the challenges faced by supervisors in supporting their supervisees as they navigate the complex demands of doctoral writing. We have found few studies that work closely with the dilemmas associated with teaching writing within the student – supervisor dyad. Recent work by Paré and his colleagues (forthcoming) suggest that supervisors, traditionally the people most closely involved with the student in the production of the dissertation text, are often at a loss as to how to assist students with their written work. They characterise the work of supervision as 'expert and neophyte' engaging in tutorial conditions in 'their discipline's highly specialised knowledge-making practices as preparation for the student's passage to membership in the field'. For them, the pedagogical method is ideally dialectical:

> the supervisor poses critical questions, offers counterarguments, models the discipline's specialised logic, and otherwise helps the student find a voice, identity, and location in the community's conversation. Thus, the ideal process is profoundly rhetorical: the student gains membership by observing and participating in the discipline's discursive practices.

The data in this study suggest that doctoral students generally learn to participate rhetorically in their disciplinary communities without a corresponding ability to articulate the rules of their communities' specialised rhetorical practices. In other words, declarable knowledge of rhetorical convention, like explicit knowledge of grammatical rule, is not necessary for participation in discourse – even highly specialised, polemical discourse. But that inability hampers those who seek to teach others how to participate in that community, for example through writing. Paré et al. (forthcoming) argue that much of the writing advice given by supervisors to doctoral students was vague, a-rhetorical, text-focused, and – for some students – almost useless. Many of the supervisors' suggestions and directives were given without explanatory justification; supervisors groped for words (metaphors, images, structural or architectural analogies) to explain the problems in student texts. The study found that a great deal of the most useful assistance was co-authorship, in the form of sample sentences, suggested passages, re-writes, and so on.

The turn to self-help guide books

In the absence of a skilful pedagogy for supporting writing, doctoral students and supervisors alike are turning in increasing numbers to do-it-yourself guide books for dissertation writing. The burgeoning body of published work on supervision and doctoral education invariably stresses *in principle* the importance of effective writing to the successful undertaking and completion of a doctorate. This work ranges from general guides for supervisors (e.g. Delamont et al., 1997; Taylor and Beasley, 2005), general self-help guides for students on doctoral research and PhD candidature (e.g. Creswell and Plano Clark, 2007; Evans and Gruba, 2002) and more recently a proliferation of guide books on doctoral writing – on the thesis but also writing proposals and literature reviews (Craswell, 2005; Hart, 2001; Punch, 2000; Zerubavel, 1999). Despite the variation in emphasis and approach in this generalist material, most acknowledge the importance of writing. Advice such as 'write early and write often' abounds in these volumes. Often these guidebooks fall short, however. They are frequently prescriptive, failing to take account of the changing identities of doctoral writers and of their writing needs. In general they offer few explicit resources for construing the place and the meaning of writing within the processes of research and doctoral education more generally (Kamler and Thomson 2006).

Both the purpose and the context for doctoral study are undergoing change. The writing demands on doctoral candidates are altering as students are increasingly called upon to produce a greater range of texts: to publish in academic journals, to provide institutional and industry reports, to deliver conference papers, to participate in funding applications, and now also to write 'outside the academy' while simultaneously writing their thesis. The production of these texts, and the opening up of doctoral outcomes to portfolios of different kinds of text and artefacts, frequently involve competing personal and institutional agendas. Each of these genres is defined in explicit ways by the institutional and the disciplinary practices as well as the particularities of the student and their research.

For most doctoral students, the primary location for learning remains prescribed within the student–supervisor dyad. However, as supervisors and students find themselves increasingly pressured to improve completion rates and to publish (McGrail et al., 2006), and to publish for increasingly diverse audiences, this pedagogical space will be increasingly strained. In our respective workplaces and amongst our colleagues internationally, we have become aware of an exciting array of institutional and individual responses to the changing needs of doctoral students to meet the demands on their writing output and requirements for writing dexterity. In the next section we give an account of some initiatives we are familiar with, while being in no doubt that there are many other worthwhile projects underway in multiple sites experiencing similar pressures for change.

Recent pedagogical developments

Increasingly universities have begun to offer their doctoral students some kind of programmed support. Unfortunately, however, reactive institutional responses have all-too-often framed writing support as 'patchup' work, sidelining those who do this teaching, and constructing the recipients of the support as in 'deficit'. In this way, the problem of writing is constructed as the 'dirty linen' of the institution, a source of discomfort for managers and academics alike and is preferably kept hidden, in learning centres which are most often at some distance from the sites of research and knowledge production, or the 'real work' of the doctorate.

Yet there is considerable innovation within the sector of specialist learning and literacy teaching where strategies and programs are being developed to advance doctoral writing. Innovations include, for example, discipline-specific interventions, credit- and non-credit bearing courses on thesis writing, and workshops on collaborative writing for doctoral students (Aitchison and Lee 2006; San Miguel and Nelson, 2007; Skillen and Purser, 2003). Other practices that are being picked up more widely include writing retreats (see Grant and Knowles, 2000; Murray and Moore, 2006), joint writing with supervisors (Kamler and Thomson, 2006), the use of writing buddies and writing mentors as well as writing for publication programs (see Murray and Moore, 2006). In these and other examples of emerging pedagogies we note that successful practices occur in situated, authentic contexts which characteristically incorporate peer review. Such innovations include the deliberate scaffolding of scholarly engagement through local practices such as student-focused conferences or student-facilitated publication projects. In such instances research candidates participate in a rich variety of scholarly writing experiences, including drafting and redrafting, critiquing, reviewing, editing and presenting research within a community of academic peers.

In our own universities we have developed pedagogies for working with doctoral students in writing groups and have borne witness to the value of such groups for their ability to address the particular and changing requirements of doctoral writing. Our experiences with a variety of different kinds of writing groups illustrate the versatility of this pedagogy to adapt to the needs of doctoral students as they progress through their candidature and engage in the development of new and different academic identities. The pedagogy of sharing writing amongst a group of peers with a language facilitator enables the development of a broad range of writing competencies that grow from a close-up, hands-on approach to text that develops an appreciation of language and of writing. The rigorous critique and reworking of texts on a regular basis amongst a small group of writers facilitates not only writing skills but also a deep understanding of how knowledge is created through authoring. In a review of our work we identified that writing groups have 'a strong reliance on the pedagogical principles of identification and peer review, community, and writing as "normal business" in the doing of research' (Aitchison and Lee, 2006: 265). 'Legitimate peripheral participation' (Lave and Wenger, 1991) in communities of writing practice includes many opportunities to make explicit the norms and conventions of the socio-rhetorical practices of writing doctoral dissertations and scholarly publications.

A different kind of response to the intensified environment of doctoral work includes the beginnings of nation-wide strategies to support doctoral students to write beyond the academy (Lee and Kamler, forthcoming). A recent Australian example of a growing practice has been a nationally-funded collaboration by the Australian Academy of the Humanities, in partnership with a number of research-intensive universities, as part of a project entitled 'Promoting Scholarly Writing in the Public Sphere'. In this initiative, doctoral students were invited to a series of workshops and master classes offered around the country to consider ways to write for new and diverse audiences by publishing for the 'common reader' and in interdisciplinary contexts. Workshops included guests from the publishing world and a range of non-academic writers and editors, as well as academics. These initial developments have been followed by increasingly visible initiatives in health and other professional disciplines. In addition some Australian universities have recruited eminent writers and publishers into centres established to encourage doctoral students and academics to write for the public. An example is the recently established Writing Centre for Scholars and Researchers at the University of Melbourne (http://www.gradstudies. unimelb.edu.au/writingcentre/psp/).

Conclusion

In concluding, we return to the question at the beginning of this chapter. Who is responsible for doctoral writing? Writing is of course part of the business of being an academic. In that sense, writing is both everywhere and nowhere. Thus it is not surprising that writing 'know-how' and the ability to 'teach' it are widely attributed to supervisors based primarily, sometimes solely, on the fact that they have themselves written a thesis. At the same time, there is an absence of dissemination and of up take of this specialist knowledge and pedagogical practice of writing into the 'mainstream' work of academic disciplines and research degree programs; into general academic development units; and into the self-help guide books on doctoral candidature (Aitchison and Lee, 2006).

We suggest that at the heart of this issue lies the paradoxical place of writing in dominant understandings about research, a general underplaying of language, textuality and writing in English language academic culture throughout its history and, as a result, a generally low level of engagement with the conceptual dynamics of writing and knowledge production. In this sense the problem of writing is an epistemological and cultural as well as a pedagogical one. We would argue for rigorous conceptual and empirical inquiry into the theoretical and cultural underpinnings of doctoral pedagogies in their relation to disciplinary modes of knowledge production as an essential resource for advancing effective and knowing engagements with questions of writing.

In the intensifying climate of pressure for doctoral completions, diversification of outcomes and textual productions, the inclusion of writing capabilities as doctoral graduate outcomes, and the pressure to publish through and from doctoral research, writing becomes a site of more explicit pedagogical intervention. Current research on doctoral writing has largely constructed images of the dissertation as product or text type almost universally described and measured against a notion of the 'traditional science-based thesis'. Yet this form may be disappearing as fast as it is being documented. Here we argue for rigorous conceptual and empirical inquiry into changing writing practices, in order to afford a more sophisticated response from the sector to the new challenges of writing.

References

Aitchison, C. and Lee, A. (2006) Research writing: problems and pedagogies, *Teaching in Higher Education,* 11(3): 265–278.

Barton, D. (1994) *Literacy: An Introduction to the Ecology of Written Language,* Oxford: Blackwell.

Benesch, S. (2001) *Critical English for Academic Purposes: Theory, Politics, and Practice,* Mahwah, NJ: Lawrence Erlbaum.

Berkenkotter, C. and Huckin, T. (1995). *Genre Knowledge in Disciplinary Communication: Cognition/Culture/Power,* Hillsdale, NJ: Lawrence Erlbaum.

Boote, D. and Beile, P. (2005) Scholars before researchers: on the centrality of the dissertation literature review in dissertation preparation, *Educational Researcher,* 34(6): 3–15.

Bunton, D. (2005) The structure of PhD conclusion chapters, *Journal of English for Academic Purposes,* 4(3): 207–224.

Clark, R. and Ivanic, R. (1997) *The Politics of Writing,* London: Routledge.

Coe, R., Lingard, L. and Teslenko, T. (eds) (2002) *The Rhetoric and Ideology of Genre,* Cresskill, NJ: Hampton Press.

Cope B. and Kalantzis, M. (eds) (2000) *Multiliteracies: Literacy Learning and the Design of Social Futures,* London: Routledge.

Craswell, G. (2005) *Writing for Academic Success: A Postgraduate Guide,* London: Sage.

Creswell, J.W. and Plano Clark, V.L. (2007) *Designing and Conducting Mixed Methods Research,* Thousand Oaks, CA: Sage.

Delamont, S., Atkinson, P. and Parry, O. (1997) *Supervising the PhD – A Guide to Success,* Buckingham: Society for Research into Higher Education and Open University Press.

Dinham, S. and Scott, C. (2001) The experience of disseminating the results of doctoral research, *Journal of Further and Higher Education,* 25(1): 45–55.

European University Association (2005) *Doctoral Programs for the European Knowledge Society,* final report, European University Association (www.eua.be).

Evans, D. and Gruba, P. (2002) *How to Write a Better Thesis,* second edition, Melbourne: Melbourne University Press.

Grant B. and Knowles, S. (2000) Flights of imagination: academic writers be(com)ing writers, *International Journal for Academic Development,* 5(1): 6–19.

Halliday, M.A.K. (1994) *An Introduction to Functional Grammar,* second edition, London: Edward Arnold.

Hart, C. (2001) *Doing a Literature Review,* London: Sage.

Hyland, K. (2004) *Disciplinary Discourses: Social Interactions in Academic Writing*, Ann Arbor: University of Michigan Press.

Hyland, K. (2006) *English for Academic Purposes: An Advanced Resource Book*, Abingdon: Routledge.

Ivanic, R. (1998) *Writing and Identity: The Discoursal Construction of Identity in Academic Writing*, Amsterdam: John Benjamins.

Ivanic, R. (2004) Discourses on writing and learning to write, *Language and Learning*, 18(3): 220–245.

Ivanic, R. and Lea, M.R. (2006) New contexts, new challenges: the teaching of writing in UK higher education, in L. Ganobcsik-Williams (ed.), *Teaching Academic Writing in UK Higher Education: Theories, Practices and Models*, Basingstoke: Palgrave Macmillan, pp. 6–15.

Kamler, B. and Thomson, P. (2004) Driven to abstraction: doctoral supervision and writing pedagogies, *Teaching in Higher Education*, 9(2): 195–209.

Kamler, B. and Thomson, P. (2006) *Helping Doctoral Students Write: Pedagogies for Supervision*, London: Routledge.

Kress, G. and van Leeuwen, T. (2002) *Multimodal Discourse: The Modes and Media of Contemporary Communication*, London: Edward Arnold.

Lave, J. and Wenger, E. (1991) *Situated Learning: Legitimate Peripheral Participation*, Cambridge: Cambridge University Press.

Lee, A. and Kamler, B. (2008) Bringing pedagogy to doctoral publishing, *Teaching in Higher Education*, 13(5) (in press).

Lillis, T.M. (2001) *Student Writing: Access, Regulation, Desire*, London: Routledge.

Lundell, D.B. and Beach, R. (2003) Dissertation writers' negotiations with competing activity systems, at: http://wac.colostate.edu/books/selves_societies/.

McGrail, M., Rickard, C. and Jones, R. (2006) Publish or perish: a systematic review of interventions to increase academic publication rates, *Higher Education Research and Development*, 25(1): 19–35.

Martin, J.R. (1989) *Factual Writing: Exploring and Challenging Social Reality*, Oxford: Oxford University Press.

Miller, S. (1991) The sad woman in the basement, in *Textual Carnivals: The Politics of Composition*, Carbondale: Southern Illinois University Press.

Murray, R. and Moore, S. (2006) *The Handbook of Academic Writing: A Fresh Approach*, Maidenhead: Open University Press.

Paltridge, B. (2001) Linguistic research and EAP pedagogy, in J. Flowerdew and M. Peacock (eds), *Research Perspectives on English for Academic Purposes*, Cambridge: Cambridge University Press, pp. 55–70.

Paré, A., Starke-Meyerring, D. and McAlpine, L. (forthcoming) The a-rhetorical pedagogy of doctoral supervision, in C. Bazerman, D. Figueiredo and A. Bonini (eds), *Genre in a Changing World*, West Lafayette, IN: Parlor Press and WAC Clearinghouse, at: http://wac.colostate.edu/.

Parry, S. (1998) Disciplinary discourse in doctoral theses, *Higher Education*, 36(3): 273–299.

Powell, S. (2004) *The Award of PhD by Published Work*, UK Council for Graduate Education, at: http://www.ukcge.ac.uk/.

Prior, P. (1998) *Writing/Disciplinarity: A Sociohistoric Account of Literate Activity in the Academy*, Mahwah, NJ: Lawrence Erlbaum.

Punch, K.F. (2000) *Developing Effective Research Proposals*, London: Sage.

Richardson, L. (2000) New writing practices in qualitative research, *Sociology of Sport Journal*, 17: 5–20.

Rose, M. and McClafferty, K. (2001) A call for the teaching of writing in graduate education, *Educational Researcher*, 30(2): 27–33.

San Miguel, C. and Nelson, C.D. (2007) Key writing challenges of practice-based doctorates, *Journal of English for Academic Purposes*, 6(1): 71–86.

Skillen, J. and Purser, E. (2003) Teaching thesis writing: policy and practice at an Australian university, *Thesis and Dissertation Writing at Postgraduate Level: Theory and Classroom Practice, Special Issue of Hong Kong Journal of Applied Linguistics*, 8(2): 17–33.

Street, B. (1984) *Literacy in Theory and Practice,* Cambridge: Cambridge University Press.

Swales, J.M. (2001) EAP-related linguistic research: an intellectual history, in J. Flowerdew and M. Peacock (eds), *Research Perspectives on English for Academic Purposes*, Cambridge: Cambridge University Press, pp. 42–54.

Swales, J.M. and Feak, C.B. (2000) *English in Today's Research World: A Writing Guide*, Ann Arbor: University of Michigan Press.

Taylor, S. and Beasley, N. (2005) *A Handbook for Doctoral Supervisors*, London: Routledge.

Tribble, C. (2005) Reviews, *ELT Journal*, 59(4): 342–346.

Zerubavel, E. (1999) *The Clockwork Muse: A Practical Guide to Writing Theses, Dissertations, and Books*, Harvard, MA: Harvard University Press.

Chapter 8

PhD education in science

Producing the scientific mindset in biomedical sciences

Margot Pearson, Anna Cowan and Adrian Liston

The increasing number of PhD students, and the interest in research and knowledge production as a significant factor in innovation in post-industrial economies, have led to greater interest in ensuring that doctoral education is of high quality and relevant to contemporary needs (Denholm and Evans, 2007; Enders, 2004). Tensions are evident, however, as those responsible for doctoral education face competing pressures: to broaden the curriculum; to prepare students for variable career outcomes; and to do so more efficiently, that is within reduced timeframes. In this chapter we argue that these tensions can best be addressed in science doctoral education by focusing on both a doctoral curriculum and pedagogical practices that recognise the need for producing doctoral graduates who have the higher order skills of analysis and ability to make a scientific assessment of data and do this creatively, an approach which constitutes a scientific mindset. Graduates with a scientific mindset have the capacity for independence and innovation in research. They can identify and formulate responses to novel and complex questions and problems. This is in contrast to a 'super-technician' who is technically proficient but has limited capacity to initiate significant research activity. It is the former who are better equipped to adapt to varying work contexts inside and outside academia.

In this chapter we include data from a survey and interviews with doctoral students and supervisors. The survey focused on the issue of the appropriate scope of the doctoral curriculum, questioning supervisors and students in biomedical sciences about their expectations and priorities for their PhD program. Interviews with a group of postdoctoral fellows who had supervisory responsibilities focused on pedagogical issues, in particular how to develop a scientific mindset. Together the data provide the basis for demonstrating how an enhancement of pedagogical practices in science doctoral education can produce an enriched learning curriculum, one that aims to nurture independent researchers who are creative, adaptive and open to variable career outcomes.

Issues in PhD science education

Issues of concern for PhD science education include many that are of more general concern in doctoral education, e.g. the adequacy of preparation of PhD students for independent learning; the lack of training for supervisors who model practice from their own experience; the impact of rapidly changing technology on what has to be learnt; and the need to broaden skills for diverse career outcomes (Pearson 2005). Employment outcomes have been a concern for many years and in some fields, e.g. chemistry, graduate employment prospects have been the subject of research within that community (Adams and Mathieu, 1999). What is of particular concern more recently in science fields is that while doctoral enrolments have increased, the employment prospects of trained researchers are variable and do not necessarily lead to work in academia in the longer term, or science research elsewhere (Thompson et al., 2001).

In response to pressures for ensuring the quality and relevance of doctoral education, much of the focus of policy at government and institutional levels has been on efficiency and timely completions. Even the recent attention to supervisor training has produced more institutional structuring and regulation of the process to reduce attrition, rather than challenges to individual practice, or strategies for enriching the PhD experience educationally. However, concerns about graduate employability in a fluid job market, and over-specialisation limiting career flexibility, have led numerous stakeholders including academics, industry employers and students themselves, to call for a broadening of the doctoral curriculum to include a broader skill set (Pearson and Brew, 2002; Gilbert et al., 2004). Graduates, it is argued, may need to be able to cross research fields, and be prepared to research in a variety of settings, both academic and industrial. Additionally they will need a range of skills that include interpersonal competence for working with others, and the ability to communicate effectively to non-experts as well as peers (Osborn, 1997). Most institutions now offer a range of short courses on skills such as project management and computing that both equip students for their PhD research and develop them professionally for the future. Less attention has been paid to the issue of broadening the curriculum to ensure that students have sufficient knowledge of the field in which their specialist research sits. Where this issue is discussed, it is the experience of the authors that it is often posed as a debate about the (dis)advantages of coursework. There has been less attention too, to approaches to doctoral research education that produce graduates who will be adaptive and creative researchers in diverse work settings.

Remaining in any response to these curriculum issues is the underlying tension between the pressures for efficiency, for which the proxy is usually timely completions, and the calls for broadening and enriching the PhD. For primary investigators running research laboratories, this tension is heightened by the need to increase publication output, in order to resource increasingly expensive science projects, through progressively more competitive funding sources. Furthermore, the funding context has rendered more acute the pre-existing tensions as to the purpose of a science PhD and the tendency to prioritise research productivity over capacity building. The relative scarcity of funds for science in Australia leads to more reliance on PhD students and their output, as opposed to the contribution of post-doctoral fellows in research. In addition, primary investigators recognise that doctoral students will require an impressive publication record in order to compete for further research positions. Papers in high impact journals make a post-doctoral position following graduation more likely, and are needed for the set-up grants required to become an independent researcher in academia. The priority on output is one that students themselves may accept where they see their goal as completing their projects, especially where the PhD project is part of a larger research undertaking. Students may worry, too, about failing where for them the aim of the science PhD has become the output of the lab: 'The experiments aren't working, I'll never get my PhD, I'm a failure'. Thus both students and supervisors may share these assumptions, and even demonstrating the ability to 'do good science' can be seen as a matter of completing projects.

The press to completions within shorter timeframes determined by institutional regulation and funding regimes makes it extremely difficult to gain a broad-based knowledge of fields that are multidisciplinary such as neuroscience and immunology. In neuroscience, students come from diverse backgrounds such as computation, life sciences, engineering, and psychology. In addition, in immunology, research is driven by technological breakthroughs allowing new questions to be asked. In such rapidly changing fields, acquisition of certain knowledge, skills and techniques may not leave the graduate with guaranteed employment (because new technical competencies and new knowledge are considered more valuable). These factors increase the importance of acquiring a broad-based knowledge of the field, yet in a climate (dictated by policy and economic factors) within which the students can feel obliged to adopt a pragmatic approach to complete a PhD on a discrete piece of work within a short timeframe. Significantly too, in this scenario, a comparable interest in nurturing a scientific mind-set and the skills of scientific analysis required for becoming an independent and adaptable researcher in the longer term is in danger of being underplayed.

Working with the tensions: supervisor and student expectations and priorities

While the pressures to complete projects, and on time, are intense, expectations as to the scope of a PhD, and priorities for the candidacy at the discipline and individual level can vary. A more nuanced view comes from seeing the way in which tensions are reflected in the responses of a group of biomedical science researchers (from neuroscience, immunology, biochemistry and molecular biology) who participated in a short survey exercise carried out by one of the authors. The views of students and supervisors (22 supervisors and 18 students; response rate ≈ 20 per cent) were gathered with a short questionnaire. Thirteen questions relating to the planning of the scope of the PhD project, the importance of generic skills and the relevance of the students' career plans were asked. The respondents were requested to rate the importance of each of these issues on a scale of 1 (low priority) to 5 (high priority). See Table 8.1.

The ratings of the items, and the ranking of items, indicate broad agreement on the scope of research training but variation in the detail of practice. Both supervisors and students agree, and give their highest priority to the notion, that a student should be creative and independent in their thinking (Q9), and high priority to the PhD as an original and significant contribution to the field (Q10), despite the fact that students have serious economic and time pressures that must influence aspects of their

Table 8.1 Student and supervisor expectations: ratings and ranking of questionnaire items

		Supervisors	R	Students	R
1‡	A student should be assisted in developing academic writing skills.	4.7	11	4.2	11
2*	A student should be assisted in developing good oral communication skills.	4.8	12	4.1	9
3‡	A student should be assisted in developing time management skills.	3.8	5	3.2	1
4	A student should be assisted in developing efficient information literacy/ library research skills.	3.9	7	3.4	2
5	A student should develop a broad-based knowledge on a wide area of research.	3.9	7	3.8	5
6	The research field is technically demanding and it is important that the student is an expert in specific techniques.	3.8	5	3.5	3
7	The research field is changing rapidly and it is important for the student to be able to adapt to change rather than be expert in current techniques.	4.1	9	3.9	6
8	A student should develop a focused and detailed expertise on a specific area of research.	3.5	3	4.0	7
9	A student should be creative and independent in their thinking.	4.9	13	4.6	13
10	The thesis should provide an original and significant contribution to the field.	4.1	9	4.5	12
11*	A student's future career plans (academic/ non-academic) are an important consideration during the planning and course of the PhD project.	2.6	1	4.1	9
12	A supervisor should introduce the student to scholarly networks.	4.4	10	4.2	11
13	A supervisor should encourage the student to become interested in areas outside their specific research topic.	3.3	2	3.7	4

Notes
* Significant difference between the two groups on individual items at $p < 0.05$, ‡ $p = 0.1$; SD ranging from 0.1–0.4.

postgraduate plan.[1] Another item rated and ranked highly is introducing students to scholarly networks (Q12). However differences on priorities are evident even where both groups agree overall, as for example the acquisition of generic skills (Q1–4), the need for which supervisors rate more highly than do the students. On the other hand, both support the provision of assistance in these areas, especially writing and communications skills, which are prioritised over time management and information literacy skills. On the issues concerning the depth and breadth of knowledge and expertise

(Q5–8) there is variation, with both groups agreeing on the need for adaptability in changing fields, expertise in specific techniques, and detailed expertise on a specific area of research.

Together the responses do not support a picture where students are totally task-focused in the short term on completions, nor where supervisors are very narrowly outcome-oriented. There are instead indications that supervisors are alert to broader issues and that students have longer-term career goals in mind. Most significantly students, in contrast to the supervisors, in response to Q11 ('A student's future career plans (academic/non-academic) are an important consideration during the planning and course of the PhD project'), rate this as having a very high priority, whereas the supervisors rate and rank it as the lowest priority of all the questions. A number of factors could be involved in this discrepancy, including the fact that the supervisors surveyed are, on the whole, in relatively secure academic positions and thus to some extent 'out of touch' with the career pressures on the current generation of post-graduate students. However, an argument against this idea is that the relatively junior, inexperienced supervisors were no more likely to consider this to have a high priority than older, established academics. The fact that supervisors have chosen a uniform career path (academia) may also be influential: they do not feel the need to consider other options for their students.

Another way to interpret this result is to look at the more positive responses by supervisors to Q5 and 7, as evidence that they appreciate the need for fostering breadth, creativity and adaptability, but do not see the need for explicit career planning or counselling in addition to what is already in place, such as the introduction to scholarly networks, which they rate highly. Whatever the reason, their responses indicate that many supervisors do not appreciate the importance placed on career planning during candidacy by students, and the need for more than enculturation into the disciplinary community.

Overall, the survey responses show broad agreement on the scope of doctoral education, but enough difference to establish the need for constant negotiation in individual circumstances. It is in this interface that we can expect a difference between what is agreed in general, and what is practised on the ground in the face of the usual contingencies of a high-pressured research environment. It is in these situations that students and supervisors face issues of major concern for both pedagogy and the scope of a doctoral curriculum that will develop research capacity and prepare students for diverse career outcomes. Is learning research as a hands-on activity sufficient? Will participating in actual research projects develop a scientific mindset and the scientific skills of analysis? Will this also develop capacities that open other employment opportunities outside science research? Do we need more generic components? How is career guidance to be provided?

Working with the tensions in practice – doing science

A complementary approach to our quantitative analysis came from the reflections of two of the authors on their own recent experience as students, and interviews by one author with colleagues who were currently post-doctoral fellows or early principal investigators supervising doctoral students in immunology and biochemistry. Five interviewees were asked two open questions, and encouraged to elaborate on this theme in their answers:

1   During your PhD how did your supervisor aid you in your development as a scientist, beyond the direct experimental supervision? How do you think you managed to develop a scientific mindset? Can you think of anything else that would have been helpful to you?
2   When you supervise research students, what techniques do you use to aid them in becoming more scientific in their analysis of data and planning of experiments? How do you help them out in their career?

Interviewees gave a range of views based on their experience as students and as supervisors in various institutions within and outside Australia. To ensure anonymity, as agreed as part of the process of gaining their permission for this material to be published, we give limited details on the interviewees. We use fictitious names for ease of reference in the text.

Four interviewees regarded their own doctoral supervision as being purely project-based in nature, with three interviewees specifically raising the importance of the scientific environment for their own development. Such an environment was seen as one that was full of people thinking scientifically, though this was understood as not sufficient for many students, who need to be actively supported by the supervisor. The attitudes on the role of the supervisor in fostering the ability of the student to develop a scientific mindset varied considerably, from those who thought 'it is impossible for a supervisor to help their student become scientific', and that the role of the PhD project was solely to give the student a chance to demonstrate their own innate capacity; to those whose supervisors had used deliberate techniques to develop the skills in students for thinking like a scientist.

The following vignettes, based on notes taken during these interviews, and from author reflection on their experience, give illustrative examples of a range of pedagogical practices, some of which are situated in a workplace or laboratory group setting, and some supervisor-led.

Thinking like an independent scientist – Anthea (Biochemistry)

[My supervisor] was really good at helping me think more like an independent scientist. We used to have these problem-solving sessions on a whiteboard. I would go to him with data and he would ask me what I saw, and what I thought it meant. We would then spend an hour going through it on a whiteboard, and he would punch holes in my logic where there were holes, and he would give me information that I was missing to make more coherent theories. I try to do that with my students. I really liked the approach so I have adopted it as my own. If they come in with data, I ask them what they think, I guide them into telling me where that conclusion would lead, and then I force them to think through the logic themselves, rather than telling them if I thought it was right or wrong, so that they had to come up with the conclusions themselves. I sometimes give them data they are missing, but when they are just being lazy I play dumb and ask them what the literature says on a particular point, so they have to go away and look it up themselves.

Critiquing analysis – Bob (Immunology)

In another manner [my supervisor] heightened my experience with data interpretation through external analysis. When I brought particular papers to his attention, he would sit down with me and go through the raw data within, and would discuss the particular strengths and weaknesses of the data before looking at the interpretations that the authors reached. When the data was still open to alternatives we often discussed various experimental designs that could be used to test the alternatives, and he would give me good feedback on those ideas that I had which were plausible, often elaborating them further as a thought-experiment. From relatively early on in my PhD, he also sent me manuscripts which he had been asked to review, and asked me to review them with him. At the start he gave me general advice on how to review a paper . . . and following that we would independently review the paper, discuss it at length together, and then he would usually modify my review of the paper (saying why he was modifying it) and send it in. This process made me quite confident in my ability to referee the first paper I was asked to independently review, so it was very successful as a professional development tool.

Journal clubs – Cath (Immunology)

The way in which I developed scientific skills was through the environment I was working in, and by following example. At the start I simply did what I was told, and over enough time I started to see what I was doing. By being in a really vibrant scientific community I was able to see other people being actively involved in science and was able to learn from that. Journal club and data club (divisional seminars) were the most useful experiences for me, because I was able to listen to the professionals create hypotheses, interpret data, and then be critiqued on this interpretation by others. In particular, during journal club, I was able to see people define the question, and the way in which they were testing it. I didn't actively participate, but it was very useful for me to watch the process, and over time I started to pick it up. The group I was in was very intense, and we had our own highly interactive journal club.

Publishing as a learning experience – Don (Immunology)

The concentration, even at PhD level, on publications does not necessarily limit the development of interpretation/critical thinking/creativity skills. During the meeting time [my supervisor] and I usually discussed the data that I had generated over the previous fortnight. He always liked to see the data in the raw format before seeing the processed data, and constantly emphasised the importance of having a thorough realisation of the reliability of the data, taking into account the nuances of the experimental process involved in the generation (which can affect the interpretation of the data). We always discussed future experiments stemming from the data in terms of figures required to turn the data into a manuscript and backup data required to ensure that we have the correct overview of the field. . . . We also discussed at length the best tactics for publishing a series of data, talking about whether it is best to publish a series of smaller papers, or a single large paper. . . . These conversations on the tactics of publication are of immense value to me now, when I am making these choices in a more independent manner.

Career advice – Edward (Biochemistry)

I think one of the things that I do that is helpful for my students' career progression is for me to be open about the career moves I am making myself. I am at the stage that is often the chief blockade in science, the transition from senior post-doc to permanent faculty member. When I am socialising with my students I am honest with them about the points in their careers that are relatively easy, such as the transition from PhD student to junior post-doc, and the points that are difficult, and then talk about the ways that I am currently trying to overcome my difficulties, such as organising school events, being on committees, and organising conferences. For a post-doc to become a permanent faculty member it is not sufficient just to have an excellent publication record and a good scientific grounding, there is also a sense that you must 'put in your time' in the institute you are in, by doing a lot of the undesirable administrative workload of the department.

At the end of their PhD I give my students advice on what topic they could work on, who they could work with, and what fellowships they should go for. I help them to plan their future steps, and people that they could go to for their second post-doc even. I am responsible for inviting guest speakers to the School, so sometimes I specifically invite speakers that I want my students to meet, as a possibility for future work. I like to guide them into thinking about their future and keep them from getting too narrow a focus. They have to get into the scientific community, talk to everyone and get their name known.

Lab meetings – Flora (Immunology)

In the lab we attempt to cultivate a very critical analysis of each other's work during lab meetings. Everyone takes a turn in presenting their data and interpreting it in front of the group, who then proceed to find any flaws that are present, or to provide alternative explanations. The students are able to observe this normal process of scientific critique happening to those around them, and then have the chance to present themselves and experience the process from the other side. The lab meeting gives good ideas and technical advice to students, but also demonstrates the method of scientific analysis.

A learning curriculum in the biomedical sciences

Usually the term 'curriculum' in any discussion of doctoral education with supervisors can be a barrier to productive discussion as many think that this term refers to taught courses. Most supervisors see 'learning how to do research by doing it' as the way to proceed and fear talk of curriculum as leading to structured teaching. For this reason it is helpful in addressing the curricular and pedagogical issues raised by the vignettes and the responses to our survey, to consider the distinction made by Lave and Wenger (1991) between a 'learning curriculum' and a 'teaching curriculum'. They argue that learning comes through participation in a practice, as is the case for apprentices, and we would argue for novice researchers (Pearson, 2005). A learning curriculum, Lave and Wenger explain, is 'essentially situated . . . and a characteristic of a community'. It consists of 'situated learning opportunities . . . for the improvisational development of new practice' and '. . . learning resources in everyday practice *from the perspective of learners*' (their emphasis is). In contrast they argue a 'teaching curriculum' involves direct instruction shaped '. . . by an external view of what knowing is about' (Lave and Wenger, 1991: 97).

In the light of this distinction, the vignettes are describing a learning curriculum situated in the practice of science where the students and their supervisors create learning opportunities from the ongoing business of doing science. They illustrate opportunities and strategies for nurturing a scientific mindset and providing career advice during a candidacy as requested by the students in the study on expectations and priorities.

Situated learning opportunities in the research environment

The vignettes include two examples of situated learning opportunities provided in the research environment. Cath describes a journal club and Flora a lab meeting. Journal clubs are a common occurrence in many science departments, as are lab meetings. As described by Cath, journal clubs can consist of the introduction of a recently published paper, usually of significance in the relevant field, for discussion. These presentations can be by a single person or by several students, they can be departmental-wide or laboratory-wide, and the style of presentation and interaction can vary. Lab meetings are within the work site and focus on the research that is taking place in that lab.

In relation to the journal club, there are potentially two main advantages to the involvement of research students. The first is the most visible to students, and involves 'keeping up to date' – the transmission of the latest knowledge in the field, state-of-the-art techniques, and hints on the direction the field is taking. The second advantage, explained by Cath, but often overlooked by many students, is arguably of even greater importance – exposure to the process of science. One of the key difficulties in the transition from an undergraduate student to a research student is the shift from being taught about science as a body of knowledge, to being taught how to contribute to that body. As a 'how to', this side of science is often accepted by academics as simply the natural thought process it has become to them, such that they rarely expose students to the method by which they reached a particular conclusion.

A journal club is a key opportunity to 'open up the scientific mind', and allow research students to directly observe academics in the act of analysing and debating technical aspects of the work and weighing up the conceptual worth to the field. Students will be able to observe, or better yet, participate in, debates over the best way to test a hypothesis, whether the results in the paper really support the conclusion that is being made, what the key result is, and how this addition to the field will relate to a huge body of partially contradicting data – is this the paper that integrates separate threads? Is the approach superior to that of other papers that have reached opposite conclusions? These thought processes, essential for science, are usually internal, or in private academic discussion and thus unobservable. The key advantage of a journal club is thus the externalisation of the process in an open session, as is the case for lab meetings such as that described by Flora where the research site is one for work and learning.

As in any learning environment, journal clubs can be more or less effective as a tool for aiding the development of research students in their scientific mindset, depending on the design and conduct. They can be constructive, educational and collegial, or conversely, destructive and demoralising. To be effective they need to be 'highly interactive', as described by Cath, and take place in an informal atmosphere allowing academics and students alike to be comfortable voicing a thought and disputing a position during the presentation as well as at the general discussion at the end.

Enhancing pedagogical practices

As well as being in the research environment, as one of the interviewed postdoctoral researchers commented, many students need to be 'actively supported' by their supervisor. This pedagogical support is crucially not direct instruction. Instead, the vignettes illustrate how in varying ways supervisor(s) can capitalise, in their interactions with their students, on learning opportunities arising from specific research activities being undertaken, acting as coaches and mentors.

In the vignettes of Anthea, Bob and Don, we see the supervisor providing active support for learning with the articulation, through verbalisation and discussion, of the processes being undertaken to analyse data, develop theories and develop how to think through to publishing the data. This type of support is a form of coaching that involves modelling and scaffolding, as with practice in reviews for Bob. The intent is to assist the student to learn the art of framing problems as well as solving them and evaluating their progress. For example, Ann now gets her students to evaluate their conclusions first before telling them her conclusions. It is through such externalisation of the learning processes and the ability to reflect on performance, as demonstrated in the vignettes, that expertise is acquired (Pearson, 2001; Pearson and Brew, 2002). Coaching in the doing of science can be provided by the formal supervisor or others in a lab or research group. Some may be postdoctoral fellows in the lab (Delamont et al., 1997), or even students nearer completion who are involved in using cutting-edge techniques.

Whereas coaching is about learning how to do science, and to do it with awareness, mentoring involves nurturing students' intellectual and personal development. In a study that sought to unpack 'supervision', Pearson and Kayrooz (2004) identify mentoring as a significant factor for student satisfaction where it offers enculturation into the academic/disciplinary domain, through both intellectual challenge, and emotional and personal support in the context of a student's evolving career goals. Not all students begin with a clear or fixed view on where they are headed. It is important that students can progress their candidacy in the context of their career goals, however tentative, if they are to choose wisely what learning opportunities they undertake. And it is in interaction with their supervisors and others that students develop their intellectual and research interests, and expectations for the future. Edward, for example, put considerable effort into both explicit guidance on how to further a career and modelling through discussion of his experience and strategic approach to his postdoctoral appointment. It is of interest that, in the Pearson and Kayrooz study, mentoring was distinguished from sponsoring students into disciplinary/professional networks, which in the survey supervisors rated more highly than considering students' career plans, indicating that this aspect of mentoring is not well recognised.

Conclusion

The strategies for enhancing pedagogic practices and enriching the curriculum illustrated in the vignettes are not exhaustive. The challenge for programs in a multidisciplinary field is to maintain quality, diversity and integration and, at the same time, depth and breadth (Hall, 2006; Hyman, 2006). This may suggest the need for other learning opportunities such as course work to extend specialist disciplinary knowledge. There is also the question as to whether it is sufficient for a student in multidisciplinary fields to work in only one subfield or one lab, as the majority do in Australia, unlike the lab rotation practice in the USA. What remains essential however is that students make these choices in negotiation with their supervisors to suit their individual needs.

Additionally, addressing the scope of the 'curriculum' for doctoral students is an issue that demands attention from the research group or academic unit in which the student is located, rather than being something left entirely to the individual supervisor(s). It may mean a collective change in priorities. It is of interest that in the survey both students and supervisors rated highly the need for creative and independent thinking (Q9), but rated encouraging students to become interested in areas outside their specific research topic (Q13) lower priority. Students will not benefit from being compartmentalised within their own speciality area, whether they expect to be career research scientists or look to other alternatives such as business, management or the public service. Whatever their career destination, they need to be open to intellectual and policy developments in the wider academic community if they are to be able to communicate to research-granting agencies and to the public at large, or draw on their scientific training in non-academic arenas.

In this chapter we have raised issues of major concern for both pedagogy and the scope of a doctoral curriculum in science, focusing on the importance students and supervisors place on developing research capacity and preparing students for diverse career outcomes, and on strategies used by supervisors to drive this outcome. Advocating more curriculum content in a context where pressure is on efficiency in the use of resources and time, and on increasing tangible outputs of research, appears to create an impossible situation. However, from the perspective of a learning curriculum situated in research practice, it is possible to reframe this apparent curriculum dilemma. The curriculum is extended by a critical enhancement of pedagogical practices in science doctoral education that produce an enriched learning curriculum: a curriculum that provides access to a range of learning opportunities where students develop a scientific mindset with a capacity for independence, adaptability and creativity in the context of their own research program.

References

Adams, F. and Mathieu, E. (1999) Towards a closer integration of PhD training to industrial and societal needs, *Analytica Chimica Acta*, 393: 147–155.

Delamont, S., Atkinson, P. and Parry, O. (1997) Critical mass and doctoral research: reflections on the Harris Report, *Studies in Higher Education*, 22(3): 319–331.

Denholm, C. and Evans, T. (2007) Introduction, in C. Denholm and T. Evans (eds), *Supervising Doctorates Downunder: Keys to Effective Supervision in Australia and New Zealand.* Camberwell, VT: ACER.

Enders, J. (2004) Research training and careers in transition: a European perspective on the many faces of the PhD, *Studies in Continuing Education*, 26(3): 419–429.

Gilbert, R., Balatti, J., Turner, P. and Whitehouse, H. (2004) The generic skills debate in research higher degrees, *Higher Education Research and Development*, 23(3): 375–388.

Hall, Z.W. (2006) Graduate education in neuroscience: maintaining vitality through change, in C. Golde and G. Walker (eds), *Envisioning the Future of Doctoral Education: Preparing Stewards of the Discipline–Carnegie Essays on the Doctorate*, San Francisco, CA: Jossey-Bass.

Hyman, S.E. (2006) Neurosciences and the doctorate: the challenges of multidisciplinarity, in C. Golde and G. Walker (eds), *Envisioning the Future of Doctoral Education: Preparing Stewards of the Discipline*, San Francisco, CA: Jossey-Bass.

Lave, J. and Wenger, E. (1991) *Situated Learning: Legitimate Peripheral Participation,* Cambridge: Cambridge University Press.

Osborn, M.J. (1997) A note on reshaping the graduate education of scientists and engineers, in R.G. Burgess (ed.), *Beyond the First Degree*, Buckingham: Open University/SRHE.

Pearson, M. (2001) Research supervision – mystery and mastery, in J. Higgs and A. Titchen (eds), *Practice, Knowledge and Expertise in the Health Professions*, Oxford: Butterworth-Heinemann.

Pearson, M. (2005) Changing contexts for research education: implications for supervisor development, in P. Green (ed.), *Supervising Postgraduate Research: Contexts and Processes, Theories and Practices*, Melbourne: RMIT University Press, pp. 11–29.

Pearson, M. and Brew, A. (2002) Research training and supervision development, *Studies in Higher Education*, 27(2): 135–150.

Pearson, M. and Kayrooz, C. (2004) Enabling critical reflection on research supervisory practice, *International Journal for Academic Development*, 9(1): 99–116.

Thompson, J., Pearson, M., Akerlind, G., Hooper, J. and Mazur, N. (2001) *Postdoctoral Training and Employment Outcomes,* Canberra: Department of Education, Employment, Training and Youth Affairs, Commonwealth of Australia.

Chapter 9

Representing doctoral practice in the laboratory sciences

Jim Cumming

A significant gap in the literature is acknowledged internationally with regard to what goes on in doctoral degree programs. A litany of complaints has been recorded over time that include inadequate probing into candidates' learning experiences (Haworth, 1996), the 'stubbornly invisible' nature of their work and training (Delamont et al., 2000), and the limited extent to which their perspectives are included in published research (Leonard et al., 2006). Not unexpectedly, such criticism has been accompanied by calls for more 'fine grained analysis' (Pearson, 2005) and 'careful empirical investigation' (Boud and Lee, 2005) of doctoral activities and environments.

At the same time, an inherent bias in the current literature has been identified. For example, Pearson (2005: 125) has argued that 'much of the recent scholarship on doctoral education is focused on social sciences, humanities and professional fields'. More recently, a review of the literature conducted in the United Kingdom found that 'there is little qualitative research evidence available on the doctoral student experience in science' (Leonard et al., 2006). Another finding was that the majority of studies were not based on any discernible theoretical framework. A study of doctoral practice in the laboratory sciences is thus an important and timely contribution to the literature. The objective of this chapter is to investigate the representation of doctoral practice with a particular focus on pedagogy.

The contents draw on research implemented in Australia as part of a large nationally-funded research project during the period 2004–2007.[1] The data were derived from three semi-structured interviews conducted in 2005, namely, an in-depth interview with one female candidate in the laboratory sciences, plus subsequent interviews with two individuals whom that candidate identified as playing a significant role in her learning and research. The next step in the research process was to construct a 'case narrative' that integrated these perspectives, but which contained no direct commentary on my part as narrator.[2] It should be noted that this data set is part of a larger collection of material that has been used to construct ten case studies across different disciplinary fields. Each of those studies incorporates a reflexive interpretation (Alvesson and Skoldberg, 2000), as well as a case narrative.

The argument I wish to advance here is that more effective ways of representing and conceptualising doctoral work in the sciences – and by implication the humanities – are needed. A major reason is the level of stereotypical imagery and under-theorised interpretation that pervades the literature at present. All too frequently the doctoral student experience is reduced or simplified to such an extent that its representational value is questionable. To employ a metaphor used in a related context, this is 'to change the art form from portraiture to caricature' (Becher and Trowler, 2001). After reviewing the literature on the doctoral experience in the sciences I have identified what appear to be a set of commonly held assumptions (Cumming, 2007). For example, doctoral candidates participate as a member of a research group; work on problems common to the group; and access the shared knowledge, resources and expertise of the group. My purpose is not to denounce these beliefs, but to question whether they constitute an accurate representation of doctoral practice in the sciences in the first decade of the twenty-first century.

The chapter is structured in four sections, the first of which locates this study in the literature on doctoral practice in the laboratory sciences. The second is a case narrative of doctoral practice in the field of molecular biology. This incorporates the perspectives of Jane – a doctoral candidate, Trish – her principal supervisor, and Scott – a peer who is about to submit his thesis. The third is a discussion about the extent to which this narrative validates or challenges the orthodox view of doctoral practice in the laboratory sciences. The last section contains some reflections on issues pertaining to representation.

What do we know about doctoral practice in the laboratory sciences?

The purpose of this section is to construct a conceptual framework that will inform, as well as assist, in the interpretation of the case narrative that follows. The framework is developed from a review of literature from Australia, the USA and the UK that reflects differing levels of specificity in the scientific domain. These range from the natural and physical sciences generally (Becher and Trowler, 2001; Parry and Hayden, 1994; Pole et al., 1997); to the laboratory sciences (Delamont et al., 1997, 2000; Hacking, 1992); to the biological sciences in particular (Bard, 1994; Gumport, 1993; Knorr-Cetina, 1999). When drawing on such broadly-based research, it is important to acknowledge that differences exist between systems in relation to coursework, supervision and examination, as well as breadth of disciplinary field.

Despite these differences, a common theme to emerge from this literature review is the significance of laboratory culture. Considerable emphasis is placed on social and relational aspects, whereby members of the lab interact on a regular – often daily – basis in the pursuit of shared goals and approaches. Each member is seen to be responsible for their own projects and tasks, but contributing to the collective output of the facility at the same time. Bard (1994: 529) describes this in terms of 'balancing the demands' of student and laboratory interests.

Although there is frequent reference to the collaborative, co-operative and mutually supportive ethos of the lab (Gumport, 1993: 269; Pole et al., 1997: 57; Delamont et al., 2000: 66–67), competitive and even aggressive behaviour is also mentioned (Knorr-Cetina, 1999). Knorr-Cetina explains this tension in relation to an internal 'logic of exchange', whereby each member of the research group expects something in return for a 'service' they offer (p. 236). For example, a doctoral candidate may run extensive tests or trials, the results of which might be made available to some or all members of the group. Given the unpredictable nature of much laboratory-based research, however, difficulties can arise when experiments fail or intended outcomes do not materialise. One study portrays a worst-case scenario for doctoral candidates, where 'students were equally aware how three years' work, in their own words, "could easily go down the toilet"' (Delamont et al., 2000: 58). It is not difficult to understand how a lab member might become disgruntled if his or her capacity to offer a service were to be impeded, or if others were unduly opportunistic with regard to services they did offer.

Another dominant theme is concerned with career development. A key feature is the sense of a destiny when commencing as an honours or masters degree student. Higher rungs on this vocational ladder include doctoral candidate, postdoc, researcher, senior researcher and ultimately laboratory leader. Knorr-Cetina (1999: 225) refers to the lab as a 'setting that they [scientists] pass through'. This is where budding research scientists are seen as having the opportunity to make their mark, albeit as soon as possible. Her phrase 'the ever-changing wave of students and postdocs' (p. 227) reflects the high rate of staff turnover in many labs associated with unstable funding regimes and changing priorities.

In order to focus more specifically on pedagogical practice, a collection of specified activities, illustrative extracts and theoretical constructs drawn from the literature is shown in Table 9.1. The critical role played by the lab leader is demonstrated in a number of ways. One is to determine the candidate's research topic and methodology with a view to embedding them in the lab's research priorities. Another is as a conduit through which candidates establish valuable contacts and avail themselves of opportunities beyond the laboratory. Members of the research group are also important – especially postdocs – given their capacity to pass on the tricks of the trade around the laboratory bench. A significant pedagogical characteristic is the taking on trust of pre-established knowledge by candidates at the beginning of their research projects.

Hacking (1992) employs a theory of scientific stability to help explain the continuous reproduction of scientific principles and procedures in the laboratory sciences. Using the analogy of a rope, he depicts scientific work as the intertwining of material, social and conceptual strands. Building on this foundation, Delamont et al., (1997, 2000) have built on this theory to create one of pedagogic continuity, where the emphasis is on 'enculturation' and academic socialisation. In this model, candidates are seen to develop expertise primarily by working alongside experts, rather than through extensive participation in specific skills training.

What follows in the next section is a case narrative that seeks to illuminate contemporary doctoral practice in molecular biology at one research intensive university in Australia. With pedagogical practice in the foreground, it integrates three perspectives – candidate, supervisor and peer – in order to create a holistic account. Select quotations are included as part of the text – rather than indented or italicised – to reduce the potential for privileging either the researcher or the researched.

Table 9.1 Aspects of pedagogical practice in the laboratory sciences identified in the literature

Specified activities	Illustrative extracts	Theoretical constructs
• Acceptance of pre-established scientific knowledge • Selection of research topic and methodology by the lab leader • Provision of guidance and support by postdocs • Interaction around lab benches • Holding of internal lab meetings on a regular basis • Emphasis on tacit skills development rather than specific skills training • Working long hours in the lab	• 'In the sciences students are apprentices . . . it's a full-time job . . . as many as 60–80 hours per week in laboratories' (Gumport, 1993). • 'Skills are grasped and intuited as much as they are caught and taught' (Delamont et al., 2000). • 'The supervisor provided the main link not only with the university, but also with the discipline in which the research was located' (Pole et al., 1997). • '[Lab] leaders held a near monopoly over interacting with the field' (Knorr-Cetina, 1999).	• Scientific stability (Hacking, 1992). • Pedagogic continuity (Delamont, et al., 1997, 2000). • Academic tribes (Becher and Trowler, 2001).

A case narrative about doctoral practice in molecular biology

As a third-year doctoral candidate at Tinternvale University, Jane is conducting research on a type of parasite with a view to limiting its negative impact on poultry in the longer term.[3] She knows the molecular science laboratory on campus like the back of her hand given that's where she completed her honours year, and then worked for 12 months subsequently as a research assistant. Awarded a 'junior research fellowship' by the Chicken Consortium at the end of 2002, Jane receives an annual stipend of $25,000 and a technical budget of $6,000 per annum for the triennium 2003–2006.

Trish is Jane's principal supervisor and heads up the lab where Jane is conducting her doctoral research. Trish has been at Tinternvale for around 30 years, during which time she has traversed the fields of zoology, biochemistry and genetics on her way to becoming an acknowledged expert in the field of parasitology. The advent of gene technology in the 1990s inspired her to undertake a five-year period of self-directed professional development in order to learn about this technology and apply it to her research on parasites. With a string of research grants, publications and a commercial patent to her credit, Trish's laboratory is recognised internationally as a site of best practice. One of her current research projects is funded jointly by the Fowl Foundation and the Chicken Consortium to the value of $450,000 over three years.

Another member of the lab with whom Jane interacts on a regular basis is Scott, a PhD candidate who is employed as a research assistant for 12 months while he completes his dissertation.[4] Prior to this Scott was an off-campus student located at the Trentham Institute – an external research agency – for four years. With Trish as his principal supervisor, Scott was co-supervised by a researcher at Trentham for most of his time there. He maintained contact with Jane by attending lab meetings at Tinternvale, and assumed a mentoring role given that she had followed up an aspect of his honours thesis on joining the lab. Like Trish and Jane, Scott's research has been in the field of parasitology, and although he specialises in a different aspect of biology, many of the approaches, methods and techniques used are very similar.

Trish has been collaborating with industry for most of her career. Her involvement began in the early 1980s when she was negotiating a patent for a new drug to be used on parasites. Recalling the episode with a smile she says, 'we managed to get a large pharmaceutical company interested in our research – we met with them over breakfast at a conference – this is how things work.' Many research projects have followed over the years, invariably commissioned and funded by an external agency. She describes the arrangement associated with one of her current projects in the following statement: 'They [Chicken Consortium and the Fowl Foundation] told us that they were prepared to invest so much money in our project, and requested us to determine a process to achieve the objectives we had identified'.

One of Trish's strategies is to establish as many links as possible between the research that is conducted under the auspices of her lab. She works from the premise that 'all lab members need to work together to solve problems'. Even though the lab's research has 'an applied focus', in her view it also 'contributes to biological knowledge'. In this context, Trish frames the topic and general approach to Jane's doctoral research based on the outcomes of prior lab-based projects. She also negotiates an arrangement whereby the outcomes of Jane's research will feed directly into the larger co-funded industry project. By the time Jane starts on her research project, a set of targets and milestones reflecting these arrangements has been endorsed by the university and the industry partners in various forms of contractual agreement.

A set of benches variously adorned with scientific apparatus occupies a central position in the lab, with refrigeration units, random pieces of equipment, shelves and cupboards jostling for space around the walled edges. The benches are where most of the action takes place – experiments, trials, record-keeping, analysis and so on – and where researchers, students (PhD, Masters and honours) and technical staff work in close proximity to each other. All up the lab houses seven full-time members. Trish has an 'office', although this is squeezed into one corner of the lab with barely enough room to house her desk, computer and visitors' chair.

Like many other members of the lab, Jane puts in the hard yards in terms of time on task. As she explains, 'I normally work from about 8.00am to 6.00pm during the week, and then most weekends I'll come in and do a few hours and . . . for example, continue with an experiment or something like that and then leave.' Her research involves screening around 20 genes initially with a view to identifying a set of validated targets – possibly two or three – that ideally will form a launching pad for the next stage of an ongoing process. The objective is to find molecules that will interact with these targets and possibly inhibit them, so that strategies for developing treatments for drug-resistant parasites might be developed subsequently.

Together with Trish, two advisers from related departments at Tinternvale constitute a supervisory panel designed to monitor Jane's progress and provide support. She also attends meetings and seminars with the Chicken Consortium periodically, to present progress reports and exchange information. The level of collegiality in the lab is such that she is able to pick the brains of lab members on the spot, or discuss an innovative technique she might be using. As Jane reveals, 'Scott is a really good person to talk to and I am really glad he has moved into this lab. I now talk to him about my project and some ideas that I have had, and he usually has some good ideas too'. Although he has not yet submitted his thesis, Scott perceives himself to be 'doing the work of a postdoc'. For example, he includes in his list of current tasks 'supervising students, writing papers, thinking about the research that is needed and driving that'.

There are times when Scott utilises his external contacts to help resolve an issue Jane is wrestling with, often getting his own hands dirty in the process. He recounts an instance when he co-opted a colleague at Trentham with expertise in microscopy to provide such input: 'Sometimes, I have actually gone and done the work with Jane, in a collaborative way. So there is hands-on methodology help, and there's also general concepts and ideas, and that's just on a day-to-day discussion basis.' Jane is highly competent at the bench, so many of her discussions with Scott, Trish and others in the lab tend to be about theorising. As she explains, 'in my [doctoral] project, I have been one of the first to do some of the technical things, so it has been more a case of talking to other people elsewhere who have been working in this area and trying to adapt their experiences to what I am trying to do. So it's definitely not technical, but more conceptual and to do with ideas.'

Gradually aspects of Jane's project begin to permeate the lab with the result that other members become involved in what is considered to be part of the lab's ongoing work. After Jane's initial screening and selection, the remaining genes are then 'farmed out' to other students to work on. For example, Scott is analysing five, while others will be offered to honours students to investigate as they come on stream. Scott describes the situation in the following way: 'Everyone knows the names of the genes; where people are up to; and everyone is making a contribution. . . . It's nice to have everyone on the same page with a common interest.'

A number of structured opportunities exist for lab members to exchange information on current research – both within and beyond Tinternvale. One is a fortnightly lab meeting organised by Trish, who encourages candidates 'to make a presentation on a paper they have read – not necessarily on what they are working on, but what they think might be of interest.' Another is a weekly 'progress seminar between labs', where candidates present and discuss aspects of their doctoral research. Given the international standing of the lab, Trish actively supports regular participation in conferences and seminars as a means of keeping up to date with the latest developments in the field.

After presenting a number of poster sessions in the early stages of her candidature, Jane is invited in 2005 to speak at an international audience of 120 experienced scientists. She admits to being 'a bit apprehensive about it at first' and 'a bit intimidated'. However, continuing more assertively she adds, 'but then you go along to these things and you meet and interact with them and you think, well they have just got a lot more experience than I have. . . . Once you realise that, then you feel a bit better about interacting with them, and are not as intimidated as you normally would be.'

Jane is also building up a personal network of academics and specialists who work in a diverse range of settings and contexts. In her words, 'I will read a paper and see that they have used a particular technique and then write and ask them about it, and see if I could use strains or things that they have used. Generally, I have found in my area that people are really friendly and happy to help out, and give you things for your project. . . . A lot are university-based researchers, but also people who are associated with hospitals, as well as industry too. Other students, too, of course.' This strategy is strongly supported by Trish, who encourages all of her students to assume a proactive role in the networking process. 'When I don't know an answer I tell them to find out who might know, and then email them. In other words, they need to make the contacts – and most of them do. Especially in this day and age, with communications the way they are, and the level of competition as high as it is in this country, you really need people who can get out there and fend for themselves'.

Jane works as a part-time tutor in the lab and decides to undertake a registered teacher training program offered free of charge at Tinternvale, with a view to enhancing her skills in this area. Typically she is responsible for two courses each semester, which involve around six hours per week, plus marking. One is with first-years, where 'basically you look after a bench in the lab', while the other involves group projects in which third-year students are engaged, where 'it's more of a supervisory role'. As Jane elaborates, 'I think it is a worthwhile experience to do as a student. It keeps you up to date with the things that undergraduates are learning and refreshes things that you tend to forget. If you want to go on later and do some teaching, then it gives you some really good experience in terms of how to interact with students. You learn certain skills that you wouldn't otherwise do, if you locked yourself away in your lab for, like, 24 hours a day, so to speak.'

Even though Scott is closer to submitting his thesis than Jane, both view their initial career trajectories in terms of postdocs – hopefully at Tinternvale – although the opportunity to work in a prestigious lab overseas is considered an ideal outcome. Jane's general strategy involves 'taking steps towards my own future by being proactive in teaching, going to conferences and putting myself out there to meet other local and international researchers.' Scott, however, sees his future in terms of 'know[ing] exactly what I want to do – it's a question of whether I can. I want to go overseas for a few years, to one of the serious . . . big-time labs. . . . Cementing my position as an academic is my objective.' While neither has ruled out the possibility of working in industry, the prospect does not appear to be high on their personal agendas.

Jane, Scott and Trish have some personal reflections on the doctoral practices being implemented in their lab at Tinternvale. Jane sums up her situation as follows: 'for the most part, my experience has been really positive, and there have been no negatives associated with my project.' However, she acknowledges that despite her achievements to date, gaining acceptance as a fully-fledged researcher is still some distance away. As she confides, 'I am still a student . . . I don't really feel like I'm part of that community yet.' Comparing the Trentham and Tinternvale labs, Scott highlights a major difference regarding the role and status of doctoral candidates. In the former, students are 'expendable . . . and not really core business or that important', whereas in the latter they are 'valued and an important part of the working of the school'. He is adamant that in the case of Tinternvale, 'without the students, no [research] work would be done at all.'

Trish's extensive experience as a supervisor provides her with an opportunity to reflect critically on the issue of doctoral pedagogy: 'Twenty years ago a student may have taken five years to tackle a particularly ambitious problem; this is no longer possible. Today, we make sure that a PhD student has a problem that we know will generate sufficient material for their thesis. We probably go for slightly less ambitious projects, and certainly supervise them much more closely than we used to, in order to make sure things are going in the right direction.' By the same token, Trish is averse to 'mollycoddling them all the time', especially given her assessment that 'science is now moving much faster than it used to – at least in the area of molecular biology'.

As a postscript to this narrative, Jane completed her research and submitted her thesis in March 2007. She took up a postdoc position later in the year as part of a new three-year project to be funded by the Chicken Consortium and the Fowl Foundation that will involve two laboratories in addition to the one at Tinternvale. The genes that Jane investigated as part of her doctoral research will not be followed up as targets; however, the new project will pursue a target uncovered in a similar screening process. Scott is in a similar position in the lab and investigating future overseas positions in the UK and Western Europe.

To what extent does the case narrative validate or challenge the orthodox view of doctoral practice in the laboratory sciences?

The case narrative confirms the essential characteristics of doctoral practice identified in the first Part of this paper. For example, Trish's influence in relation to Jane's topic and approach, along with Scott's mentoring and supporting role as de facto postdoc are clearly in evidence. The concepts of scientific stability and pedagogic continuity help to explain the way in which Jane is learning how to perform as a research scientist in a laboratory context. Elements of typical lab culture and staged career planning are well illustrated.

At the same time, however, this case challenges and extends stereotypical images of doctoral practice. Overall, the narrative reflects much greater openness and flexibility. The narrow confines of the lab and the domineering role of the leader have been replaced by a wider stage, a larger cast and an expanded repertoire. When the spotlight is beamed towards pedagogical practice, additional aspects are revealed (see Table 9.2).

Table 9.2 Additional aspects of pedagogical practice revealed in the case narrative

Specified activities	Illustrative extracts	Theoretical constructs

• Supervisory panel meetings
• Industry partner meetings and seminars
• Conceptual rather than technical learning is paramount
• Pro-active roles in
  – lab meetings
  – inter-lab meetings
  – international conferences
• Personal networks of
  – academic researchers
  – external researchers (eg hospitals, industry, vets)
  – doctoral candidates
• Teacher training course
• Tutoring
  – first years: bench work
  – third years: 'supervisory'
	JANE–candidate
	• 'Talk to other people elsewhere' and 'adapt their experiences to what I am trying to do.'
	• 'Learn skills that you wouldn't otherwise do.'
	• 'Put myself out there.'
	
	TRISH–supervisor
	• 'Go for slightly less ambitious projects.'
	• 'Supervise them much more closely.'
	• 'Avoid mollycoddling them all the time.'
	• [Encourage them to] 'fend for themselves.'
	
	SCOTT–peer
	• 'Hands-on methodology.'
	• 'Everyone on the same page.'
		• Becoming and belonging (Lee and Roth, 2003).
		• Workplace learning (Hager, 2004).
		• Peer learning (Boud and Lee, 2005).
		
		• 'Skilful performer' (Pearson and Brew, 2002).
		• 'Enterprising self' (Tennant, 2004).
		• 'Self-organising agent' (Boud and Lee, 2005).

These can then be analysed subsequently in terms of subtle variation or significant points of departure.

First, pedagogy is not confined to the lab. While the university laboratory remains a focal point, there are strategic connections with other labs – at Tinternvale, in other universities, and in the private sector. There are also links with industry, hospitals and veterinary clinics. Jane exchanges scientific information and ideas at conferences and in other settings. Second, guidance or instruction is not restricted to experienced members of the lab. While the principal supervisor and the de facto postdoc remain key figures in Jane's learning and research, other significant individuals are actively involved. Examples include researchers located in the academy and in industry, as well as students. Jane interacts with members of her supervisory panel and engages with the industry partner on a regular basis. Third, pedagogy is not limited to supervision and thesis production. Learning, teaching, mentoring, facilitating and related pedagogical activities are evident in many aspects of Jane's candidature. For example, there is a great deal of experiential learning and critical reflection that occurs while Jane is researching, tutoring, presenting and so on. In addition, Jane participates in a teacher training course at her university with postgraduate students from other fields of study.

Of even greater significance, however, are the connections that exist, not only among pedagogical practices, but also with other elements of doctoral work. To continue with the example of Jane's teacher training, it is noteworthy that she undertakes this course while employed as a tutor. This suggests a 'just-in-time' approach to learning as distinct from the conventional 'front-end' model of training. Moreover, by working part time as a tutor she is augmenting her generic as well as her specialist skill base. As Jane acknowledges, the learning of certain skills wouldn't be possible if 'you locked yourself away in your lab'. There is also a link with the development of career trajectories, given that this experience of academic teaching has the capacity to broaden her postdoctoral employment options beyond scientific research. A related factor is Jane's increasing confidence with regard to raising awareness of herself and her research by developing personal networks and actively contributing to meetings, seminars and conferences. However, Jane's status as a molecular biologist remains liminal. Jane is a legitimate participant engaged in a complex process of coming in and belonging to a professional scientific research community (Lave and Wenger, 1991; Lee and Roth, 2003; Wenger, 1998).

Another aspect of pedagogical practice worth highlighting is Trish's changing approach to supervision over the past 20 years. There is clearly a degree of tension around providing sufficient direction and control in relation to candidates, on the one hand, and building their capacity to act as independent researchers, on the other. While it is beyond the scope of this chapter to provide a detailed explanation of the theoretical constructs listed in Table 9.2, when viewed collectively they help to inform this pedagogic tension. A common element is the emphasis placed on the continual enhancement of expertise in authentic settings. Rather than develop expert knowledge and technical skill independently or in isolation, these theoretical constructs suggest an integrated approach whereby individuals strive to achieve practical understanding. For example, Pearson and Brew (2002: 137) defines a 'skilful performer' as someone who not only knows about what to do, but also knows how to apply that in practice.

It is also worth drawing attention to a number of nuanced elements associated with the case narrative. While the idea of regular internal lab meetings is common to both, Trish encourages members to make a presentation on a topical paper not necessarily related to their research. This reflects a desire to expand horizons rather than remain focused on the inner workings of the lab. Another is Scott's role in identifying expertise beyond the lab, and then working with Jane in a hands-on capacity to utilise specialist input. This suggests a level of peer learning that is above and beyond the showing of ropes to a neophyte. The concept of continuous professional learning is seen to apply to all members of the lab – not just candidates – as demonstrated by Trish's extensive upskilling in the 1990s.

Reflections on the representation of doctoral practice in the laboratory sciences

The purpose of this final section is to offer some critical reflections on the representation of doctoral practice in the laboratory sciences in this chapter. On the one hand is the orthodox model derived from the literature that endeavours to reduce practice to a set of common and agreed characteristics. On the other is the case narrative that strives to probe practice in greater depth in order to 'ferret out the unapparent import of things' (Geertz, 1973: 26). At issue is not whether one representation is better than the other, but their combined capacity to inform discussion on changing practices in doctoral education.

The value of the orthodox model is a capacity to generalise about doctoral practice by drawing on select studies in different contexts. The strength of the narrative is the illumination of doctoral practice through the provision of 'insider' perspectives on contemporary development. My argument has been that representation as narrative provides an effective means of illustrating the complexity and particularity of doctoral practice that is invariably masked by reductionist approaches. My intention has been to demonstrate that this case in molecular biology extends the orthodox model considerably. Given that my objective is to deepen understanding about doctoral practice, questions of potential blank spots or blind spots in my research need to be considered (Gough, 2002; Wagner, 1993). In other words, have I chosen to omit or downplay certain aspects, or ignored others inadvertently?

In reference to potential blank spots, while pedagogical practice constitutes a major theme of the narrative, there are several sub-themes. Examples include links with industry and differences between laboratories in universities and the private sector, as well as broader issues concerned with power, gender and so on. There is value in considering the issue of industry links briefly, given that it opens a window on changing doctoral practices. The role of the Chicken Consortium and the Fowl Foundation constitutes a conventional approach to industry involvement in scientific research. These industry bodies have high impact given the level of external funding provided, but relatively low impact in relation to pedagogical and research practices. Rather than a changing doctoral practice, the industry link in this case is part of an established pattern that began over 20 years ago. One nuanced element of the narrative worth noting, however, is that the funding is allocated directly to the candidate rather than the lab. Another is that two industry bodies are acting cooperatively as reflected in the joint funding of projects.

Further evidence of the conventional model of industry funding in this case can be seen in relation to two other schemes operating in Australia from the early 1990s – Australian Postgraduate Awards – Industry (APAIs) and Cooperative Research Centres (CRCs). Initiated by the Australian government, both are designed to promote collaboration and cooperation between the academy and industry, with the specific objective of promoting research careers in industry for postgraduate students. Reviews of APAIs (Powles, 1996) and CRCs (Harman, 2002), together with one of my other cases in the scientific domain (Cumming, 2007), suggest a different type of model in which industry partners play a more proactive role in doctoral research and pedagogy.

It is also possible that some of the theoretical constructs used to interpret the case narrative (see Table 9.2) may have blinded me to other possibilities in my role as researcher. For example, my predisposition to social theories of learning and communities of practice may well have averted my gaze from any divisive elements.

On reading an earlier draft of this chapter, a reviewer remarked on an 'eerie level of symmetry' around the perspectives of Jane, Trish and Scott. Although the reviewer was not questioning the veracity of my data, this comment challenged me to think about my lack of probing in that respect during the interviews. There was nothing recorded during the interviews to suggest any lack of collaboration, but this should not have precluded my testing for that possibility. Another potential blind spot is the potential for exploitation of doctoral candidates by their supervisors. While Scott referred to the 'expendable' nature of candidates at Trentham, and there is the occasional comment in the literature about 'slave labour' (Bard, 1994: 529), I did not raise this issue with my three informants. One reason was that during my initial dialogue with Jane, she had volunteered that while familiar with this scenario, it did not apply in her situation. In retrospect there would have been value in interrogating my informants a little further. Perhaps this is a topic for future research?

Conclusion

While the narrative representation of doctoral practice in molecular biology in this chapter reflects many aspects of the orthodox model derived from the literature, it also challenges that model in fundamental ways. By illuminating contemporary activity using insider perspectives that are then set in a conceptual framework, higher levels of complexity and particularity have been revealed. At the same time, however, it is important to remain vigilant with regard to potential blank spots and blind spots in qualitative research of this nature. Hopefully, the empirical research reported here is not only 'fine grained' and 'careful', but also sufficiently theorised to facilitate the development of new insights and deeper understandings.

Acknowledgements

This research has been funded through the Australian Research Council's Linkage Grant Program. The cooperation of the informants in this case is acknowledged. I am also grateful to the reviewers who commented on an earlier version of this chapter.

References

Alvesson, M. and Skoldberg, K. (2000) *Reflexive Methodology*, London, Sage.

Bard, J. (1994) How should we train PhD students in the biosciences?, *BioEssays,* 16(8): 529–530.

Becher, T. and Trowler, P.R. (2001) *Academic Tribes and Territories: Intellectual Enquiry and the Culture of the Disciplines*, second edition, Buckingham: Open University Press.

Boud, D. and Lee, A. (2005) 'Peer learning' as pedagogic discourse for research education, *Studies in Higher Education,* 30(5): 501–516.

Cumming, J. (2007) *The doctoral experience in science: challenging the current orthodoxy*, paper presented at the annual conference of the British Educational Research Association, London.

Delamont, S., Atkinson, P. and Parry, O. (1997) Critical mass and doctoral research: reflections on the Harris Report, *Studies in Higher Education,* 22(3): 319.

Delamont, S., Atkinson, P. and Parry, O. (2000) *The Doctoral Experience: Success and Failure in Graduate School*, London: Falmer Press.

Geertz, C. (1973) *The Interpretation of Cultures*, New York: Basic Books.

Gough, N. (2002) Blank spots, blind spots, and methodological questions in postgraduate research, keynote address presented at the Postgraduate Research Conference, Deakin University. at: http://www.latrobe.edu.au/oent/Staff/gough_papers/noelg_DUSA_2002.pdf.

Gumport, P. (1993) Graduate education and research imperatives: views from American campuses, in B. Clark (ed.), *The Research Foundations of Graduate Education: Germany, Britain, France, United States, Japan*, Berkeley: University of California Press, pp. 261–293.

Hacking, I. (1992) The self-vindication of the laboratory sciences, in A. Pickering (ed.), *Science as Practice and Culture*, Chicago, IL: Chicago University Press, pp. 29–64.

Hager, P. (2004) Conceptions of learning and understanding learning at work, *Studies in Continuing Education*, 26(1): 3–17.

Harman, K. (2002) The research training experiences of doctoral students linked to Australian cooperative research centres, *Higher Education*, 44(3): 469–492.

Haworth, J.G. (1996) Doctoral programs in American higher education, in J.C. Smart (ed.), *Higher Education: Handbook of Theory and Research*, New York: Agathon Press, pp. XI, 372–422.

Knorr-Cetina, K. (1999) *Epistemic Cultures*, Cambridge, MA: Harvard University Press.

Lave, J. and Wenger, E. (1991) *Situated Learning: Legitimate Peripheral Participation*, Cambridge: Cambridge University Press.

Lee, S. and Roth, W. (2003) Becoming and belonging: learning qualitative research through legitimate peripheral participation, *Forum: Qualitative Social Research*, 4(2), at: www.qualitative-research.net/fqs/impressum/roth-e.htm.

Leonard, D., Metcalfe, J., Becker, R. and Evans, J. (2006) *Review of Literature on the Impact of Working Context and Support on the Postgraduate Research Student Learning Experience*, London and Cambridge: Institute of Education and UK GRAD Programme.

Parry, S. and Hayden, M. (1994) *Supervising Higher Degree Research Students*, Canberra: Australian Government Publishing Service.

Pearson, M. (2005) Framing research on doctoral education in Australia in a global context, *Higher Education Research and Development*, 24(2): 119–134.

Pearson, M. and Brew, A. (2002) Research training and supervision development, *Studies in Higher Education*, 27(2): 136–150.

Pole, C., Sprokkereef, A., Burgess, R. and Lakin, E. (1997) Supervision of doctoral students in the natural sciences: expectations and experiences, *Assessment and Evaluation in Higher Education*, 22(1): 49–63.

Powles, M. (1996) *A longitudinal study of participants in the Australian Postgraduate Research Awards (Industry) Scheme*, Melbourne: Centre for the Study of Higher Education, University of Melbourne.

Stenhouse, L. (1978) Case study and case records: towards a contemporary history of education, *British Educational Research Journal*, 6(1): 1–6.

Tennant, M. (2004) Doctoring the knowledge worker, *Studies in Continuing Education*, 26(3): 431–441.

Wagner, J. (1993) Ignorance in educational research: or, how can you not know that?, *Educational Researcher*, 22(5): 15–23.

Wenger, E. (1998) *Communities of Practice: Learning, Meaning and Identity*, Cambridge: Cambridge University Press.

Chapter 10

Supervision development and recognition in a reflexive space

Angela Brew and Tai Peseta

In recent years, models and practices of doctoral education have come under increasing scrutiny world-wide. There is a growing view that changes to research education are needed in order to cope with reforms to the higher education sector and in response to new kinds of knowledge generation and production. This critical questioning of doctoral education is not only evident within the academic and scholarly literature but is also reflected in the policies of governments and universities. As a result, it is not only the forms and provisions of doctoral education that are being critically questioned but also the associated pedagogy itself. It might be said that doctoral education now occupies an increasingly contested and reflexive space – a space operating at a number of different levels:

- *At the government level*, for example in relation to gaining value for money and providing for the needs of what has been termed the knowledge economy.
- *At the institutional level* in terms of the ways in which doctoral degrees are defined and managed.
- *At the faculty, school or department level* in terms of the research climate and facilities to be made available for doctoral candidates.
- *At the supervisor level* in terms of the kind of supervision pedagogy to be provided.
- *At the level of the student* in terms of their motivations and the anticipated rewards of candidature.

Yet these levels do not operate in isolation. They each impact on and shape the others. For example, academics cannot consider their supervision and students cannot consider the course of their candidature without some engagement with the government or institutional policy terrain. The practices that constitute doctoral education then result in sometimes conflicting challenges and dilemmas, as different agendas are played out in particular contexts.

In this chapter, we draw on the idea of doctoral education as a reflexive space in order to explore the practice, positioning and recognition of research supervision development. Changes to the provision of research education may mean changes to the way academics are prepared for their roles and responsibilities as supervisors. It may mean further support is required to assist in the development of certain supervisory skills; it may also mean that increasing resources will need to be made available to support supervisors in their decision making.

For the past ten years, we have been responsible for implementing a Development Program for Research Higher Degree Supervision at a large research-intensive university in Australia. The focus of our program has been to work with supervisors to articulate a theorised conception of their pedagogical practice in order to improve the research student learning experience. At its heart, it is a model of critical reflection (Boud et al., 1985) organised around an inter-relationship between supervision practice, reflection and writing. In this chapter, we describe the program of supervision development and then illustrate some of the challenges and dilemmas that can result when contested ideas of supervision development and recognition are played out in this reflexive space. In doing so, we seek to raise further questions about the ideas of pedagogy that are driving new forms of research education.

An institutional program for supervision development

The Development Program for Research Higher Degree Supervision offers academics a set of resources to support their work as supervisors. In the main, the resources are housed online and are supported by a series of workshops. The program makes supervision resources available in two ways: first, as a set of discrete or stand-alone resources able to be downloaded as the need arises and, second, as a systematic program of independent study. The Independent Study Program comprises seven online study modules, in which the first six are focused on the typical stages of a research student's candidature. Each of the first six modules contains a set of learning outcomes. In supporting supervisors to achieve those outcomes, the modules include: background scholarly literature, links to university policies, reflective triggers, practical activities, a discussion forum, an opportunity for self-assessment and a mechanism for the provision of feedback (see Figure 10.1).

The seventh and final module differs in structure and in function. Called the Recognition Module, supervisors are invited to write a case account of their supervision learning bearing in mind the university's criteria for good supervision practice. The Recognition Module is completed in three stages: a Reflective Account, Descriptive Account and then the Case Study itself (see Figure 10.2).

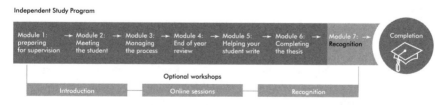

Figure 10.1 Structure of the Independent Study Program.

Stages in writing your case

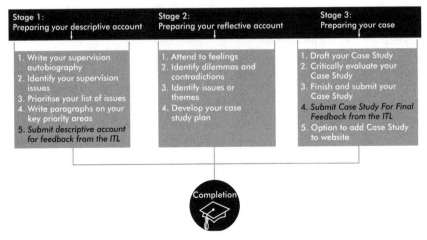

Figure 10.2 Stages of the Recognition Module.

The Recognition Module is intended to help supervisors bring together their learning about supervision in a way that returns their focus to a number of challenges in their own supervision practice and to consider how they might proceed in addressing them. They are free to choose the topic of their case study and, at specific points along the way, we provide supervisors with extensive feedback on the progress of their case study. We have reported elsewhere on the importance of feedback for shifting supervisors' conceptions of supervision (Brew and Peseta, 2004). At the end of the program, supervisors have the beginnings of a written account, which documents their learning and ideas about the pedagogy of supervision practice.

Supervisors who complete the program (which takes about 28 hours of study time, i.e. equivalent to one subject in a Masters in Education) receive a certificate. Since 2002 (when the Recognition Module was introduced), 97 supervisors have completed the program, while overall, a total of 572 supervisors have engaged with the program in some way since its introduction in 1997. In 2004, program completion was made part of the university's process for registering new supervisors (University of Sydney, 2004). This imperative puts a new pressure on the program.

Program participants come from a wide range of disciplines and exhibit a broad range of views on supervision. Some are experienced supervisors and some are new to supervision. Some study the program voluntarily and others do it because it is a requirement for their registration. Through its emphasis on starting from supervisors' own experiences, the program has been able to accommodate a variety of responses and to move each supervisor along the path of critical reflection. Participants' responses on the extent to which each module has met its objectives, together with a systematic analysis of Recognition Module outcomes published earlier (Brew and Peseta, 2004), show clear evidence of changes in supervisors' conceptions as a consequence of engaging in the program. Further, there is now emerging evidence of a link between the number of modules per full-time equivalent member of staff studied in a faculty and improvements in supervision as measured on the university's Student Research Experience Questionnaire (SREQ).

In our work to implement the program, we have been reflexively engaged with questions about doctoral education at a very practical level: how to improve it through improved supervision. This has caused us to reflect on the nature of supervision pedagogy and the tensions that arise through competing agendas of the different stakeholders. These and similar challenges are at the heart of any program designed to develop the expertise of academics but they are brought into stark relief when they become related to the improvement of doctoral education through the improvement of supervision. This is particularly so in the reflexive space that doctoral education currently occupies. A focus on these issues highlights the ways in which particular reflexive discourses dominate. These underscore questions of training versus education; questions about the relevance of particular kinds of education for supervisors; the ways in which supervisors think about supervision, and about teaching or research. Taken together, these challenges derive from competing agendas for supervision and their translation to supervision development and practice. Within this scenario, the ways in which we, as developers of such programs, are positioned become complex and problematic.

Why reflexivity? Setting the theoretical framework

We have been influenced in our work by sociological writers, such as Pierre Bourdieu, who have drawn attention to the underlying cultural assumptions that shape our experiences and our responses to the situations in which we find ourselves. Bourdieu refers to these as the 'habitus'; which he describes as the distinctions we make about what is good or what is bad, what is appropriate and what is inappropriate behaviour (Bourdieu, 1988). These assumptions generally go without question. Bourdieu's concept of reflexivity refers, first, to the fact that people have awareness of their own social and cultural background. Second, it refers to the fact that people become aware of their particular standpoint and how it is derived from the social position they occupy. Third, reflexivity refers to the capacity that people have to stand back from abstract practices in different contexts and think about them intellectually (Schirato and Webb, 2003). What is important for Bourdieu is what he calls the 'systematic exploration' of these 'unthought categories of thought' (Bourdieu, 1990). Such categories of thought drive what can be thought. They limit the ways we think about the issues, ideas and theories on any particular topic.

Shifting supervisors' ideas of supervision

It is only through engaging supervisors in the kind of systematic exploration described in Bourdieu's work that we have been able to break through our supervisors' basic assumptions about the nature of supervision. Here is an example of how, in providing feedback on the ideas of one supervisor, we laid the groundwork for this supervisor to think in new ways about their supervision:

> One thing that really struck us in reading your descriptive account, Peter, was the importance you attach to creating a good environment in the lab. We were wondering whether you might think in terms of framing your supervision as creating the right environment, not just in the lab, but in other aspects of the supervisory relationship. This would include attending to the kind of relationship you establish with your student(s); the ways in which you interact with them right from the outset, taking account of their views of the supervision as you proceed. It is the quality of the relationship that you establish at the outset which will determine whether the student feels able to raise any concerns about the supervisory relationship in addition to questions about the content and process of the research.
>
> We hope that you are able to move beyond a reaction to/against your own supervisory experiences as a student. Remember that students will not only often have a sense of the relationship but also that each student's experience and expectations are different and that will mean you will need to develop a repertoire of responses. We think that you have begun to recognise the importance of not assuming one style of supervision for every student. However, there is some ambiguity in your descriptive account because you appear to be seeking some recipes for success. For us, a crucial aspect of a student-focused approach to supervision is setting up an environment where different student needs, desires and approaches can be accommodated as they arise. We think that the scholarly literature can provide you with clues, ideas and a way of testing the ideas which underpin your practice. Like many of our academic practices, we don't often turn to the literature to inform what we do as supervisors. So we encourage you to return to some of the work cited in the Modules to inform your understanding of what it means to engage in student-focused supervision more fully. You may wish to dip into Prosser & Trigwell, (1999) to inform your understanding.
>
> (Extract from our feedback on a supervisor's descriptive account,
> 27 May 2007 – pseudonym used)

In a climate where the performative agendas of governments or institutions are becoming increasingly dominant, one of the challenges we face, as people with a responsibility to develop teaching and curricula in higher education, is to hold on to notions of *meaningful* learning or development for academics/faculty. In the above extract, we do this through starting with where the supervisor is coming from and encouraging them to extend their ideas beyond the contexts of current application, e.g. extending their ideas of creating a good climate in the laboratory, to thinking of this as framing the supervision more generally; by encouraging them to reflect on the quality of the relationship they establish with students as a basis for supervision; by challenging the supervisor to reflect on the differences in students and to develop a repertoire of approaches to supervision; and, importantly, by encouraging a scholarly approach through the reading of the literature that would inform their practice.

In studying the independent study program online, supervisors come to terms with techniques and strategies that may be new to them, but they also come into contact with scholarly readings that challenge them to think about their approaches to supervision. After devising the process for supervisors to write about their experiences and ideas about supervision, and after reading what they had written, we found that the supervisors were utilising some of the suggested techniques but were still mainly guided in their supervision by what they had experienced when they themselves were research students. We evaluated the effects of providing feedback and we now know that it is this feedback which moves supervisors into new ways of thinking and acting (Brew and Peseta, 2004). As a result, many supervisors have changed their conceptions of supervision. For example, in response to the question: 'What was the most helpful aspect(s) of this module for your learning?' asked at the end of the reflective process, one supervisor wrote:

> This module provided the literature (and discussions) that encouraged me to think deeply about areas of supervision that I may not have attended to. It clarified my thinking on the ways my own experience had been excellent and supported my learning, but it also showed me where the deficiencies in my own supervision had been which I may not have thought about so deeply (or maybe not even have recognised as issues as they were non-existent for me). It also spurred me to think of tasks I can do, that will ensure my future students do not have the same issues to contend with, so that their experience will be the best I can provide in relationships with them.
>
> (Anonymous feedback on Module 7, 2006)

There is, however, implicit in our feedback, a critical stance on other agendas. Not assuming one style of supervision for every student, for example, is implicitly critical to government agendas, which imply one particular model of supervision. In Australia, following the publication of the federal government's report on research and research training (Department of Education, Science and Training, 2004) and the implementation of funding strategies where the bulk of resources for supervision follow thesis submission, many universities have been concerned to provide supervision training that would guarantee effective supervision and timely completions – just as the government hoped. The subsequent introduction of the Postgraduate Research Student Questionnaire (PREQ) at a national level in 2002 has underscored the government's determination to ensure quality. All of these measures arise from the critical scrutiny that research higher degree education has attracted from sources outside the university, as mentioned above. For institutions, this raises a number of important questions as, in turn, they too engage in the process of critical questioning of doctoral education themselves. Universities have funding imperatives to meet the demands of governments. They also have responsibilities to ensure high quality learning experiences and outcomes for their students. In this context, questions universities are likely to ask about supervision include:

1   How can universities ensure that supervisors develop their supervision?
2   What is an appropriate mechanism for initial supervision?
3   How can we ensure initial education/training, as well as ongoing professional development?
4   How can supervision training be assessed?
5   How can a university ensure that a supervision training program is effective? What are the measures and indicators of effectiveness?
6   Does developing supervision improve students' experiences of research higher degrees?

Shifting institutional ideas on supervision development

These are all questions that we have engaged with too, as we manage our program of supervision development. Our focus has been on establishing a program that provides in-depth, flexible, online supervision development aimed at providing, in the first instance, a set of useful skills and knowledge of strategies for effective supervision. However, as mentioned above, our aim goes beyond discourses of effective practice to support supervisors in developing the ability to critically reflect on their practice in the light of the literature on supervision pedagogy and to develop an informed pedagogical rationale for their supervision. Our university has also come to engage with these questions but for very different reasons and with a different logic. Its strategy of requiring new supervisors to undertake our program as a requirement for registration as a supervisor has been successful, as demonstrated by the improvements in supervision that have taken place since this requirement was introduced (Behnia, 2006). Further, we now know that there is a statistically significant relationship between engagement in our program and improvements in students' experiences of the supervision they receive and their experiences of the research climate of their departments (Brew and Peseta, 2007). However, the orientations and motivations of the university in general and specific faculties more particularly, are often very different to our orientations and motivations, which again, may be different to those of individual supervisors who study the program.

This also raises the question of whether what we are doing is education or 'training'? The Australian government, for example, has chosen to use the language of 'training' and this is the discourse that has been adopted in institutions. For example, in our university the language of 'postgraduate education' and 'graduate studies' has given way to the language of 'research higher degree candidates' and 'research training'. Yet we have consistently wanted to go beyond narrow notions of training because using the language of training appears to us to embody pedagogical practices that diminish the complexity of the processes which support students' learning in a research higher degree. For example, as mentioned above, we know that the main way in which supervisors supervise is related to the way in which they themselves were supervised as research students; either in ways that emulate good supervision or as a reaction against poor supervision they experienced (Kandlbinder and Peseta, 2001). This leads to the adoption of what might be considered an amateur approach to supervision, where, based on their past experience of being supervised, a supervisor is only able to use a single approach/strategy to meet the needs of all students. We also know that training supervisors in a range of skills and techniques can go some way to providing a beginning groundwork for the candidature, but this 'training' does little to change supervisors' basic orientations with regard to supervision. It does not encourage the 'systematic exploration of the 'unthought categories of thought' that Bourdieu (1990: 15) talks about. It does not lead to reflexive engagement with the complexity of doctoral education. Our experiences and our knowledge of the literature on supervision pedagogy show us that supervision is a professional pursuit that requires education as a professional, so that supervisors are able to utilise a variety of proactive strategies to meet the needs of different students. Training supervisors to use good practice skills and techniques does not tend to challenge or change their conceptions of supervision and it does not provide opportunities for them to understand and critically evaluate the approaches they adopt (Brew and Peseta, 2004).

In other words, in order for these realisations to surface, supervision development has to go beyond 'training'. In order for supervision to improve, supervisors' learning needs to be guided by an educational program which may include some elements of training but which goes much deeper and encourages critical engagement with the complex and problematic nature of doctoral education.

Yet, our commitment to education rather than training (a view that can include training) raises another dilemma: how to communicate this process to decision makers and senior personnel. In response to the government agendas outlined above, our university's committee responsible for supervision of research higher degree students decided to require faculties to implement a system of supervisor registration. A good deal of critical reflection and discussion went into what should be the requirements for registration with the result that our program became the centre-piece of research supervision development. The decision was made in the context of a number of senior staff on the committee engaging with the program online. So on the committee, by and large, it was known what was being asked of supervisors. Yet the program takes time. Since 2002, the throughput of people completing the program increased from 3 per year to approximately 50 per year and the numbers continue to grow.

The nature of the clientele also changed. No longer were we dealing solely with supervisors committed to development. Now we are dealing with conscripts; people who have a limited or no concept of either the governmental imperatives, or the university's need to improve supervision but who simply want to get on with the job of supervising. A key challenge for us, then, has become how to communicate the importance of developing a scholarly and considered critically reflexive approach to supervision to people who do not want to engage in any form of professional development, let alone a lengthy period of it. Judging by the quality of work we assess, and evaluations of the program conducted, we know that we have made more friends than enemies and that once supervisors have engaged with the program they tend to be 'won over'. Given that many supervisors now are required to complete the program, supervisors respond remarkably well to it. At the end of each of the seven modules of the program they have an opportunity to provide feedback. Over 90 per cent of supervisors who responded agreed that the learning outcomes of each module had been achieved.

Another dilemma for us is that, because the program is now a requirement for registration, it means that many of the people studying it are doing so before they supervise, so the experience they bring to the program is that of being a student, not a supervisor. There are some benefits in this. However, it means that a program that was intended for in-service professional development is now being used as initial training. Ideally participants on the program will have had some experience of supervision. Yet both experienced senior academics and those with no previous experience of supervision have successfully completed it. This is made possible by the program's focus on encouraging critical reflection on experience, both as a supervisor and a student. Yet the institutional requirements mean that we cannot control who engages with the program or when supervisors complete it.

Moving towards a more theorised position

A fundamental aspect of the education we provide for supervisors is to assist them in developing a coherent rationale or theory of supervision; a unified account of their supervision practice. We argue that this can provide the basis for decision-making. However, when supervision is seen in an institutional context as something that simply requires tweaking with a few tips and techniques, and in general ignorance of the literature on supervision, it is sometimes difficult for us to make a case for this kind of considered pedagogy. Yet we know that it is a key to developing a confident and proactive approach to supervision.

Developing ideas of supervision as teaching or research

One issue that we think is critical to how supervisors think about what they are doing when they supervise is whether they think of supervision as teaching or as research. This affects how they supervise: which issues they choose to focus on in supervision and which issues they tend to ignore. It is an issue on which there is ambivalence in the literature (see, for example, Connell, 1985; Green and Lee, 1995; Johnson et al., 2000). Kyvik and Smeby (1994), for example, suggest that there are disciplinary differences related to whether supervisors considered their supervision as teaching (which they suggest is more common in the humanities and social sciences), or as research (which they argue is more common in science, medicine and technology). Clearly many supervisors consider both of these approaches at different times during a student's candidature, but more often than not supervisors do so without awareness that there may be other ways to approach supervision. In encouraging supervisors to critically reflect on their orientation to supervision, we have found that it is not so much whether supervision is thought of as teaching or as research that is important, but rather the particular conceptions of teaching and of research that influence how they think about supervision and ultimately what they do as a supervisor (Pearson and Brew, 2002). What is vital is that supervisors are aware of the particular conception they favour and are able to put that in the context of other views that, for example, their students may have.

So, for example, if supervisors think of supervision as teaching and approach it from what Prosser and Trigwell (1999) describe as a 'teacher-focused information transmission' view of teaching, then they will tend to focus on telling, on treating all students in a similar way and asserting a view of supervision that makes central the supervisor's responsibility to set deadlines and manage the process of completion. On the other hand, a 'student-focused conceptual change' view of supervision will tend to lead to a view of supervision as negotiation, where the student's views of the supervision and how it should proceed as well as their orientation to the subject-matter are fully taken into account. Learning in a research higher degree is seen as a process of changing the student's conceptions and the supervision is tailored to meet the needs of differing students. This supervisor, for example, when asked at the end of completing the program what aspects were most helpful, illustrated the process of changing conceptions in this way:

> The student-focused aspect vs teacher-focused. 1. My approach in the past has been teacher-focused which was not very helpful as I realise. 2. My approach to supervision are(sic) now better understood based on pedagogical theory and practices as contained in literature. 3. Critical reflection of my approach to supervision has been enhanced by articulating my case study.
>
> (Anonymous feedback on Module 7, 2006)

Different conceptions of research will similarly lead to different foci for supervision (Pearson and Brew, 2002). This is particularly so where the supervisor has a conception of supervision as research. Where the supervisor has an 'externally' focused view of research (see, for example, Brew 2001) they may focus on the integration of the student into the research community and the development of appropriate scholarly networks. Where the supervisor's view of research is predominantly 'inward' looking (ibid.), the focus will tend to be on the development of particular techniques or methodology, or on understanding data. If the view of research is that the person of the researcher is an important aspect of the research process, then the supervisor is likely to take account of the student as a whole person. However, if their view of research is that the person of the researcher is incidental to it (as if absent from awareness), then personal issues are likely to be ignored. An awareness of different approaches provides a basis for developing a more substantial repertoire of approaches to supervision to meet the varied needs of different students at different times during their candidature. We have considered it important to extend supervisors' awareness. We do not suggest that any one of these approaches is preferable. They each on their own have their limitations. However, it is clear that an understanding of the research that has delineated different conceptions of teaching and of research is likely to extend supervisors' understanding of what they are doing when they supervise. It provides a basis for a more theorised understanding of practice and brings with it an extended repertoire of responses.

Developing a repertoire of approaches to supervision fits with our basic assumption that a student-focused approach (which, according to Prosser and Trigwell, 1999, encompasses a teacher-focused approach) is preferable to a teacher-focused approach which tends to ignore the student's perspective and their experiences. So our approach is inevitably normative. Our values are inevitably enshrined in the program and how we run it. This is no different to any other pedagogy. However, these values are often at variance with those who insist that supervisors study the program – particularly when the drivers of institutional quality assurance processes rely on a logic that is largely technical, mechanistic and instrumental in value.

Articulating a theoretical approach to supervision: the importance of critical reflection

In encouraging supervisors to develop an overarching theoretical approach to supervision, we argue that this provides a basis for decision making so that responses to particular challenges in the supervision relationship are seen as instances of a wider theoretical approach. When supervisors engage with our feedback, they appear to be able to make sense of their supervision as a whole, to come to terms with the limitations and ad hoc nature of their original approach. Understanding the rationale for why they supervise in the way they do, we argue that they are able to make decisions in a more proactive way than they were able to when they were simply reacting either to the particular situation that presented itself or to the way they were supervised.

In this context, the role of critical reflection is vital. In encouraging supervisors to articulate a rationale for their supervision, to articulate their assumptions, we believe we open up the possibility of change. That this change happens is illustrated in the writing of a supervisor who describes the changes in thinking that have taken place through engagement with the program. The discussion is quite lengthy, so we include some extracts:

> At the beginning of the Supervision Program I thought being qualified to supervise mainly meant being an expert in one's discipline area. Although a principal supervisor must have integrated and abstract knowledge in a field of study appropriate to a student's research topic, I understand now that supervisory practice is much more than 'knowing what' or having declarative knowledge (Biggs, 2003). Indeed it is more about having functioning knowledge (Biggs, 2003) and empowering my students so that they too can use their knowledge to function successfully or 'stand on their own feet'. As Grant (2003) argues, 'supervision is not only concerned with the production of a good thesis, but also with the transformation of the student into an independent researcher' (p. 175). For Pearson and Brew (2002), the goal of supervision is to 'facilitate the student becoming an independent professional researcher and scholar in their field, capable of adapting to various research arenas' (p. 139).

> Thus one of the key learning outcomes for me from the Supervision Program has been my realisation that good supervision starts with opening a dialogue with my

students about our individual values and views about learning, research and supervision. I must create a comfortable atmosphere for my students to reveal their
visions of their project and expectations of my role. Perhaps the best way is
simply to acknowledge their expertise and say, 'You know more than me where
you would like to go with your research project. What are your preferences for
how you would like me to supervise you?'. . .

In this extract, this supervisor is utilising the literature on supervision pedagogy to make
sense of and extend their ideas of, supervision. Rowland (2000) argues that, when teachers begin to inquire into aspects of their teaching, they sooner or later have to confront
their values which underpin what they are doing. In this supervisor's case study, we see
the way in which he comes to terms with the way power operates in the supervision relationship and confronts his own values in considering the implications of the way power
operates. Again, he draws on the scholarly literature in developing his critical awareness
of the dynamics of the complex relationships between supervisor and student.

> The other key realisation that I have experienced in the Program is the idea that
> students can have power over me (Grant, 2003). We can constantly alter the
> power balance as we travel together through the supervision landscape. Inviting
> students, for example, to express their preferences and visions is giving them
> greater power in the student–supervisor relationship.
>
> The term 'power' commonly has a negative connotation, but in supervision I
> think it can imply positivity. Power has been defined as 'whatever it takes to get
> others to do what you want and not do what you don't want' (Richards, 2004: 3).
> Richards argues that, 'one important aspect of power that is often overlooked is
> that of empowerment—gaining power by giving it away, strategically . . . in acad-
> eme giving control and credit (power) away is the mark of a successful leader of
> change' (p. 4). Perhaps giving power to a student is the mark of a successful super-
> visor. Students also come to the supervisory relationship with their own power,
> and allowing them to exercise this power strategically may be another indicator of
> good supervisory practice. As Russell (2000) argues, 'what a student needs in
> defining the thesis is . . . confidence and a sense of power' (p. 15). These tentative
> ideas or hypotheses could be explored in an inquiry project which I will outline at
> the end of my case study. . . .
>
> Grant (2003) argues that in most tertiary institutions the power of supervisors and
> students is not equally constructed. Typically, the supervisor is seen as "an experi-
> enced and successful researcher, an established authority in some area of her/his
> discipline, as 'finished', as an overseer of the student . . . On the other hand, the
> student is positioned as not knowing, insecure, inexperienced . . . needy, con-
> sumed by the project" (p. 181). I think to be a successful supervisor I have to
> continue reconstructing my ideas of how power is distributed in the student–
> supervisor relationship.
>
> (Extracts from Graham Hendry's case study)

Graham's case study illustrates the complex way in which a supervisor comes to terms with the literature on supervision and the importance of developing a nuanced and scholarly approach to understand supervision. These extracts illustrate the process of critical reflection embedded in practice.

Yet at the same time as we see such work amongst the supervisors who have engaged with the program, the institutional structures in which we are situated position us as the gatekeepers. In a sense we are. We are the people who decide whether each supervisor has met the criteria for good practice in supervision which underpin the program and against which each supervisor's work is judged. We take this responsibility very seriously but this means that occasionally we have had to judge that a particular supervisor's work is not yet ready to meet the requirements because it does not engage with the criteria. We are often asked by supervisors whether they have to do the program. We are not the makers of the policy, nor do we have an institutional responsibility to implement the policy. We provide a program that is the focus of the policy. It is up to each faculty to monitor the implementation of the policy and some faculties are more assiduous than others. In doing this, we have to recognise that we are in a powerful position; one which is not overtly acknowledged in the institution. However, it does behoove us to ensure that the quality of the program is appropriate to meet the needs of supervisors, and that they find it valuable and learn from it. For the university, it is important that the program works to improve supervision in the university. For us, it is important that a reflexive approach to supervision is embedded in practice.

Conclusion

In this chapter, we have explored some of the dilemmas that we have encountered as we implement for supervisors an educational program that has pedagogical integrity and at the same time meets the performative requirements of a large research-intensive university. We have explored some of the challenges in encouraging supervisors to take a reflexive approach to their supervision of research higher degree students. We have located those challenges in the context of the reflexive space that, we argue, now characterises the field of doctoral education. We have shown how we have steered a course through different discourses surrounding doctoral education, how we have held on to notions of professionalism in supervision in the face of compulsory requirements for supervisors to complete our program, and how we have moved supervisors to theorised and nuanced understandings of the nature of supervision and their role in doctoral education suited to the differing needs of students.

It is to be hoped that informed awareness of supervision pedagogy on the part of supervisors will, in turn, inform debates surrounding doctoral education more generally. It should lead to more nuanced awareness at the level of faculties, schools and departments, and in turn, at the level of institutions. Engaging students in also reflecting on their experiences and understandings of supervision will feed into their critical awareness of issues involved in doctoral education. Ultimately, this all which, hopefully, inform policy debates even at the governmental level.

References

Behnia, M. (2006) *Analysis of Student Research Experience Questionnaire (SCEQ): Areas of Best Practice and Suggested Improvements*, Sydney, NSW: Office of the Dean of Graduate Studies, University of Sydney.

Boud, D., Keogh, R. and Walker, D. (eds) (1985) *Reflection: Turning Experience into Learning*, London: Kogan Page.

Bourdieu, P. (1988) *Homo Academicus*, translated from the French by P. Collier, Cambridge: Polity Press.

Bourdieu, P. (1990) *The Logic of Practice*, Cambridge: Polity Press.

Brew, A. (2001) Conceptions of research: a phenomenographic study, *Studies in Higher Education*, 26(2): 271–285.

Brew, A. and Peseta, T. (2004) Changing supervision practice: a program to encourage learning through feedback and reflection. *Innovations in Education and Teaching International*, 41(1): 5–22.

Brew, A. and Peseta, T. (2007) *Report on Research Higher Degree Supervision Development Program*, prepared for University of Sydney Research and Research Training Committee of Academic Board, at: http://www.usyd.edu.au/ab/committees/rrtc/agendas/Research_Higher_Degree_Supervision_Program.pdf.

Connell, R. (1985) How to supervise a PhD, *Vestes*, 28(2): 38–42.

Department of Education, Science and Training (2004) *Backing Australia's Ability: Building our Future through Science and Innovation*, Canberra, ACT: DEST.

Green, B. and Lee A. (1995) Theorising postgraduate pedagogy, *Australian Universities' Review*, 38(2): 40–45.

Johnson, L., Lee, A. and Green, B. (2000) The PhD and the autonomous self: gender, rationality and postgraduate pedagogy, *Studies in Higher Education*, 25(2): 135–147.

Kandlbinder, P. and Peseta, T. (2001) *In Supervisors' Words: An Insider's View of Postgraduate Supervision*, Sydney, NSW: Institute for Teaching and Learning, University of Sydney, at: http://www.itl.usyd.edu.au/supervision/casestudies/book.pdf.

Kyvik, S. and Smeby, J.-C. (1994) Teaching and research: the relationship between the supervision of graduate students and faculty research performance, *Higher Education*, 28(2): 227–239.

Pearson, M. and Brew, A. (2002) Research training and supervision development, *Studies in Higher Education*, 27(1): 135–150.

Prosser, M. and Trigwell, K. (1999) *Understanding Learning and Teaching: The Experience in Higher Education*, Buckingham: Society for Research in Higher Education and Open University Press.

Rowland, S. (2000) *The Enquiring University Teacher*, Buckingham: Open University Press and Society for Research in Higher Education.

Schirato, T. and Webb, J. (2003). Bourdieu's concept of reflexivity as metaliteracy, *Cultural Studies*, 17(3/4): 539–552.

University of Sydney (2004) *Postgraduate research higher degree training at the University of Sydney*, Academic Board Policy, at: http://www.usyd.edu.au/ab/policies/PG_Rsch_Hghr_Dgree_Train_Sprvsn.pdf.

Part III

New forms of doctorate

Chapter 11

Specialised knowledge in UK professions

Relations between the state, the university and the workplace

David Scott, Andrew Brown, Ingrid Lunt and Lucy Thorne

An ideal typical model of a profession requires a specialised body of knowledge and skills, a division of labour within the workplace of the profession, training credentials for entry and mobility within the profession and training programmes which result in this credentialising, usually based in institutes of higher education (Etzioni, 1969; Freidson, 2001; Millerson, 1964; Saks, 1995). In addition, the profession should have some independence from the state in determining the specialised body of knowledge and the way practitioners acquire it. Whitty (2001) describes this degree of autonomy from the state as a 'professional mandate', which is a bargain with the state that determines the degree of independence and autonomy it can claim. This has been referred to as a 'special relationship' with society (Skrtic, 1991: 87), the essence of which is

> that professions are given greater autonomy than other social groups. [They] set their own standards . . . operate with fewer restraints than the arts, trades or business. In return the professions are expected to serve the public good and enforce high standards of conduct and discipline.

The professional mandate or 'special relationship' is shaped in three distinct ways. First, the degree of autonomy negotiated between the profession and the state is subject to renegotiation at different times and in different ways. Second, the professional body may fragment so that a profession develops alternative forms of professionalism, which consequently have different relations with the state (Whitty, 2001). Third, the profession's ideological base may change. As Hanlon (1998) suggests, professions were characterised by an ideal of beneficence in which the professional expert was trusted to work in the best interests of the clientele body. This, he argues, has been partly replaced by a 'commercialised professionalism', where the search for profitability has meant that some clients are privileged over others.

This, however, has not exhausted the currency of professionalism, or even of attempts by specific occupations to engage in processes of professionalisation (Whitty, 2001), where the occupation seeks professional status and influence and the rewards that accompany it. Professionalisation may therefore be understood as a move by members of occupations to extend their power and influence, to support their particular epistemology of practice, and to secure in place the means for their contin-ued existence. One part of this strategy is the development of a professional doctorate so that recognition of achievement by a university both accredits learning for the indi-vidual, and bestows status on the profession to which the individual belongs, with the intention of creating stronger forms of insulation within the occupational division of labour. However, this means that the profession is subject to a form of regulation by an external body (the university), which is in its turn regulated by the state.

This chapter will focus on professional study at doctorate level in two occupational fields: education and engineering. In particular, it will draw on evidence from two pro-fessional doctorate programmes in the United Kingdom: the EdD and the EngD. It will address the tensions between three sites of knowledge production (research, ped-agogic and workplace) in relation to professional doctorates, and show how knowl-edge is reconfigured in response to internal and external pressures at each site. In particular, it will show how the resolution of these conflicts has implications for the development of a specialised body of knowledge for the occupation. By specialist knowledge production, we take as axiomatic that this refers to the content, skill devel-opment, means of acquisition and potentiality for identity formation implicit in a body of knowledge, insulated from other specialised bodies of knowledge.

Professional doctorates are offered in other countries in the world as well as the UK; indeed, the first Doctor of Education (EdD) was introduced at Harvard University in 1921. Professional doctorates in the USA are generally pre-service rather than in-service awards. In Australia, where they have been established since the 1980s, two generations of professional doctorates have been identified (cf. Maxwell, 2003). The first conforms to a model of coursework plus thesis and is dominated by academic interests. The second is characterised by a shift in orientation of both the site and nature of knowledge production (Seddon, 2000), so that academic interests coexist with workplace concerns. Although the focus of this chapter is on two UK profes-sional doctorates and their relations with their respective workplaces and the state, these issues have resonances with the development of professional doctorates in other parts of the world.

In the UK and elsewhere recently there have been moves to provide national stan-dards and formal procedures for doctoral completion (Quality Assurance Agency, 1999), with pressure placed on providers to improve completion rates, with some suc-cess. However, the result is, as Cowan (1997: 196) suggests, 'an increasing bureaucrati-sation within doctoral programmes; of pedagogic sequence; of pedagogic relations; through memoranda; and of knowledge, into training methods.' Alongside this increasing bureaucratisation, and thus transfer of power from universities to the state, there has been an increased emphasis on the creation of instrumental forms of knowl-edge, and a desire to make doctoral programmes and doctoral completion more rele-vant to the perceived needs of the economy and in particular professional practice. This has been driven both by universities operating within the market and thus competing for a limited number of potential students (developing a vocational element for doctoral study widens the potential pool of applicants), the desire by the professions to give higher status (endorsement by universities) to both their forms of professional development and in some cases licensing-to-practice arrangements, and by governments determined to establish close connections between disciplinary forms of knowledge and economic productivity. These drivers have led to more diversity in doctoral study, as well as closer control by quasi-governmental bodies of procedure, if not output.

It would, however, be misleading to suggest that developments in doctoral study around the world have coalesced into the creation of professional doctorates alone. Alongside the rapid growth in this new form of doctoral study have gone the reinvention and reconfiguration of the PhD (Allen et al., 2002). Indeed, PhD study has now begun to embrace a significant taught element (for example, the New Route PhD), and is thus coming to resemble in its pedagogic form the type of doctoral study (the professional doctorate) that it gave rise to. But even then, it is possible to distinguish between the UK professional doctorate and PhD study, in terms of the requirement for the student to take a series of assessed courses, which constitute a programme of study, focused on both the development of research skills and their substantive area of concern. The student's subsequent thesis is shorter than the PhD, with the average length being 50,000 words.

The study adopted a multi-site case study design and consisted of two phases. In the first phase, in-depth case studies of 12 professional doctorate programmes based in universities were made to collect evidence about the experiences of staff and students. In addition to interviewing students and staff in Phase 1, in Phase 2 a number of students and graduates were selected to explore the relationship between the professional doctorate programme and their own professional practice. This also comprised interviews with students' and graduates' employers and professional colleagues in order to obtain their perceptions of the programmes and the contribution made to professional practice. Extracts from these interviews will be used in the text which follows as evidence of the way each programme was constructed, the impact of each programme and its contribution to the development of a specialised body of knowledge within each occupational group. The intention was to document both why and in what way institutions have developed professional doctorates (in order to be able to understand the features that characterise them), and the relationship between these programmes and the professional practice and development of students. However, our contention is that knowledge development, and, indeed, relationships between the different sites are regionalised (Bernstein, 1997), which suggests that within different occupations, different types of knowledge are being developed; and furthermore that the professional mandate operates in a different way for these different occupations.

Freidson (2001) refers to three types of specialised training: craft, technician and professional. Professional doctorates are of the last type, and he suggests that this professional training inevitably takes place in specialised schools or university faculties. He goes on to argue that the university faculty, as a part of the profession,

> do not merely recruit, train and certify students. What gives them and their profession of which they are a part the capacity to preserve and even expand their

jurisdiction is the fact that in addition to teaching, their faculties can devote themselves to systematizing, refining, and expanding the body of knowledge and skill over which the profession claims jurisdiction.

(Ibid.: 96)

This model of advanced professional training in specialised schools or university faculties still leaves a number of problems in relation to professional doctorates. We have already suggested that the type of knowledge developed on professional doctorate courses is different in different occupations. Further to this, the capacity of the faculty to erect a labour market shelter around their professional doctorate through controlling the supply of recruits to higher levels of the profession is limited in the two fields discussed in this chapter. The promotional and status benefits of higher professional degrees, such as professional doctorates, are complex and differ considerably between different professional groups. On the one hand, a profession such as clinical psychology in the UK (and increasingly other types of psychology professions) requires a professional doctorate qualification for entry, and increasingly rewards senior practitioners who have undertaken professional doctorates; on the other hand, in the field of education the acquisition of a higher professional degree such as the EdD rarely has direct promotional or status benefits. Indeed with regards to some professions governments have sought to bypass university-accredited professional qualifications and create their own. This is exemplified in the UK by head teachers in schools who are now required to gain a qualification which is accredited and taught outside the university sector. Finally, professional training is both pre-service and in-service, and though Freidson's model fits better with the former rather than the latter, it is still misconceived in that it implies a servicing arrangement by universities for the profession. University academics certainly at doctoral level have their own agendas, which cannot be subsumed into a jurisdictional claim by the profession.

Three interdependent sites of knowledge-construction are identified here: the research site where knowledge is initially developed; the pedagogic site at which members of the profession acquire that knowledge; and the workplace site in which this knowledge is applied, though knowledge development, acquisition and application are not exclusively located at these sites. These sites are interdependent in that workplace knowledge provides the context in which particular forms of pedagogy are enacted and influences what those forms might be; and in turn feeds back into the research site. In a similar way, the pedagogic site has a dialectical relationship with the research site, which is always evolving in response to the development of new knowledge or the development of new pedagogic forms or the development of new workplace practices. However, the state intervenes to a greater or lesser extent at all three sites, and this determines the degree of autonomy allowed for that profession. Furthermore, because these sites operate in different ways in different professions or occupations, then it is possible to designate knowledge development as regional to indicate the different forms of knowledge that are developed as they impact on the workplace.

Sites of knowledge

Three sites of knowledge construction, then, are identified in relation to professional doctorates. The first of these constitutes the research site of knowledge formation. Though usually located within the university, in recent times this has become attenuated and now includes external agencies to the university and state-sponsored agencies that operate by giving expression to the interests of the state (cf. Gibbons et al., 1994). In the two different fields of knowledge that we are concerned with here, education and engineering, these research sites are constituted in different ways. Bernstein (1996) developed a set of categories to delineate different types of symbolic systems. He distinguished between horizontal and vertical forms of discourse, and then added a further distinction within the latter between hierarchical and horizontal knowledge forms. Horizontal forms of discourse are described by Bernstein (1996: 170–171) as:

> the form of knowledge usually typified as everyday, oral or common-sense knowledge [which] has a group of features: local, segmental, context dependent, tacit, multi-layered, often contradictory across contexts but not within contexts.

Vertical discourses, by contrast, are defined in terms of two characteristics: verticality and grammaticality. Verticality denotes the way theory is developed and it can take two forms. The first of these is hierarchical, where the constructs that form the mode of knowledge can be arranged in a hierarchical fashion, starting at the base of the pyramidal structure with more concrete propositions and moving upwards to more general and abstract principles, which are effectively integrated within a hierarchical structure. However, some knowledge bases have a horizontal structure which consists of the proliferation of more and more specialised forms or languages which are incommensurable with each other. An example of this might be the field of education.

Whereas this type of knowledge form is concerned with internality – the relations between the parts of the discourse that are internal to itself – Bernstein develops a further relation which attempts to connect it to the empirical world – grammaticality. Some knowledge bases, then, have a weak capacity to 'generate empirical correlates' (Moore and Muller, 2002) and therefore a weak capacity to progress as a form of knowledge; whereas others have a strong relationship with the empirical world, have developed a strong language for confirming or disconfirming theory, and therefore have a greater capacity for progression.

Though knowledge may be formed in a particular way at the research site and influences the messages delivered at the pedagogic site, in turn, knowledge reconfiguration at this site also occurs as a result of internal and external factors which include interventions by the state. A knowledge base of a profession may therefore comprise a weak horizontal structure, with a proliferation of languages; however, interventions by the state may mean that one of those languages is given a privileged status over the other. For example, Scott et al. (2004) identified four modes of knowledge developed on professional doctorate courses. The first of these is disciplinarity, where the practice setting is understood as the source for reflection, but not the arena in which that theorising takes place. Technical rationality, on the other hand, prioritises outsider knowledge over practice-based knowledge, with the result that the practitioner is required to implement protocols and practices developed elsewhere. Dispositionality comprises the teaching of certain skills and dispositions, such as a capacity to reflect and in turn meta-reflect on practice, which allows the practitioner to develop their understanding of what they do in the workplace. The fourth mode of knowledge is criticality, and here the student-practitioner reflects critically on the discourses, mores and ways of working of the institution of which they are a member, with the intention of changing the way it works.

The state has in recent times redefined its role in relation to the professions, and in certain circumstances will channel its considerable power to favour forms of technical rationality at the expense of disciplinary, dispositional or critical forms of knowledge. For example, the state in the UK has reallocated government funds for in-service training from universities (through HEFCE grant arrangements) to the Teacher Development Agency and placed strict limits on the type of course that can be accredited for professional development. This further blurs the distinction between discretionary and mechanical specialisation, where these are understood as work being organised in the first case to enhance and in the second case to limit the degree to which discretion is appropriate if the task is to be performed successfully.

Tensions between the three sites means that in practice these modes of knowledge are compromised in various ways. This is achieved through processes of adaptation and colonisation, so that hybrid forms of knowledge are developed. For example, a discipline may have evolved so that it is understood as a practical activity with clear and explicit relations to the practice setting. One of the consequences of this is that weak boundaries are established between the academy and the practice setting. The EngD more closely aligns itself with this model. On the other hand, some forms of integration are more problematic, and tensions exist between these different modes of knowledge. A particular mode of knowledge may be so powerful, and may be supported by the state, that it subsumes other modes of knowledge. By examining the development of professional doctorates as influential, though not exclusively so, in the formation of specialised bodies of knowledge in two occupational groups, it then becomes possible to understand both the different ways such formative processes take place and the nature of those specialised bodies of knowledge which are the end result. The first of these is the engineering doctorate.

Engineering doctorates

The move by some occupations to gain or enhance professional status requires that occupation to better secure a monopoly over a defined set of tasks, and a body of knowledge. Engineering is commonly described as an applied discipline, though it draws from a basic or pure knowledge base, which in Bernstein's (1996) terms can be described as having a hierarchical form. Furthermore, the relationship between the research site and the workplace is weakly framed.

Members of the faculties teaching on the EngD programmes generally had industrial experience, and indeed arrangements for tutoring and mentoring students blurred the distinction between industry and academia, as one EngD coordinator noted:

> All the research that I'm involved with is with companies anyway, so I'm effectively working as part of a team in industry. I just happen to be based at the university. How we define who is an industrial mentor and who is an academic mentor is very simple. If they are a university employee, they are an academic mentor; if they are a company employee, they are an industrial mentor. We look at each particular scheme to make sure that they are there, but we have some industrial mentors who are more academic than your average academic. And we have some academic mentors who are extremely good industrial mentors in setting the commercial direction.

Furthermore, they understood their discipline as a practical activity, with the end product as outputs that were able to compete in the market place. Monopoly claims over the type of knowledge that characterised the engineering profession were more easily sustained, as epistemological fragmentation was less in evidence. Indeed, one marker of a monopoly claim to knowledge, the ideological core of professionalism (Freidson, 2001), is weak boundaries between academic and practice contexts. In engineering, these weak boundaries are exemplified by the way that the knowledge delivered on the professional doctorate course was barely contested by other academics and practitioners, and the close relationships established between academics and practitioners evidenced in part by the examination arrangements that required academic and industrial assessors. An EngD tutor explains this relationship, and suggests that it is best illustrated by the way the EngD student is described as a research engineer:

> So we're looking to develop engineers to produce innovation. The EngD came about because of a big feeling in the industry that they were going to have to retrain a lot of the PhDs that they were accepting. And generally the people were very good at coming up with new ideas but implementing them in a real environment was something they just hadn't done before. So we tried to get that combination of the creativity and the implementation within the programme. And one of the main requirements of the EngD is that the candidate has to demonstrate innovation in the application of knowledge to the engineering business. We tend to call them research engineers rather than students.

In Bernstein's terms, engineering can be characterised as having a strong hierarchical knowledge structure, but paradoxically a weak infrastructural position in the market. This has developed as a result of the variety of tasks that engineers perform in different industries, the differently formed divisions of labour within the various workplaces, and the relatively fluid distinction between technician and engineer, so that in the workplace maintaining a labour shield around a specialised cadre of skilled and professional workers is difficult to maintain (cf. Freidson, 2001).

Furthermore, in engineering, the programmes were driven by professionally and academically identified competences that were well defined and agreed with the appropriate professional body. McWilliam et al. (2002) distinguish between shallow and deep linkages between the state, the profession, the university and the workplace. In the former case, where links are shallow, a particular workplace is the site from which students come and to which they return at the end of their studies. There is a limited and ad hoc utilisation of workplace practitioners in the development, delivery and assessment of the programme; and marketing is focused on the targeted individual and their professional development. In the latter case, where links are deep, the development of the professional doctorate is driven by the workplace and the profession, and this includes defining the type of training to be undertaken and the particular skills and attributes that the student is expected to acquire. The profession and workplace practitioners are partners in the delivery, supervision and examination of the programme, and funding arrangements exist between universities, workplaces and external bodies, including the state. Finally, the potential benefits of the programme are agreed and specified by all the partners, with clear and agreed understandings about the type of knowledge that is developed on the programme. In these terms, the Engineering doctorate can be described as having deep links with the state, the university and the workplace.

The UK EngD was initiated by the Engineering and Physical Sciences Research Council (EPSRC) in 1992, a quasi-governmental body set up to allocate government funds to bodies engaged in activities within their remit. As a result of the recommendations of the Parnaby (1992) and Finniston (1979) Reports, the EPSRC funded five 'Centres' as hubs 'of interaction between different schools within the university and between the university and participating companies' (EPSRC website, Winter 2002–3). Following a review in 1997, a further ten centres were set up in 1999 and 2001, making 15 in total, the majority of which are located within aerospace, transport knowledge and systems engineering, environmental technology, steel technology and manufacturing systems engineering. Funding these centres and providing financial support through them for research engineers indicates a shared purpose and common epistemology, and suggests a deep linkage between the state, the university provider and the profession.

The pedagogic approach taken by deliverers of the EngD programme was strongly framed, tightly regulated and supported by high levels of confidence in the relationship between engineering and both professional and disciplinary academic knowledge. This instrumental approach also allowed successful collaboration with other regions of knowledge, in this case management and business administration. Here a tutor of an EngD programme argues that disciplinary eclecticism is a distinctive feature:

> Broader based in the sense that the projects had to be done with a much broader perspective of not only science and engineering, but also its application, commercially and looking at the cosmetics, sort of economics of it, and so there is a wider context, to represent much more the nature of most industrial research.

The EngD programme was seen as making a contribution at a variety of levels: the career development and advancement of the research engineer, the development of the profession through the creation of a cadre of skilled engineering managers, practical applications of knowledge developed in universities, and economic regeneration both regionally and nationally. Furthermore, the delivery of a product that has practical applications in the workplace was considered to be of prime importance, as this EngD tutor suggests:

> But even if the student's main technical idea were to turn out to be a failure, it's very unlikely that the student would have been unsuccessful from an industrial point of view, because in the process of doing all that work, they probably produced a lot of improvements and change, new ideas and new concepts, new ways of working into their parent/host company in any case. I think we need to be much more aware of the industry that we're working with than say a chemist would be of chemical manufacturing, if it were a chemistry PhD. We have to be aware of the technological limitations, which you wouldn't have to be if you were developing a new variation on a particular molecule where it doesn't matter if you're irrelevant.

Here, an academic tutor on the programme argues that the development of performative knowledge is the end-point for both the academy and the workplace. Input from the university produces a better product:

> Generally, what most people say is that the improvement they get, whether that's made in the loop, reduction in price, improvement in performance or whatever, is generally about half as much again what they would expect they would have got if they simply were doing it as a part of their day to day work. And that's quite a consistent figure, isn't it?

The research engineer learns certain skills, and acquires specific attributes on the programmes of study that enable him or her to perform better at the practice site. As we have suggested, the EngD displayed a closer relationship between the disciplinary and practice settings than the EdD, and thus was more likely to adopt a technicist mode of knowledge. Furthermore, this fits better with the imperatives of the state, and contributes to its recognition and sponsorship by government, whereas the EdD has not attracted this same level of recognition, either with the state or as a marker for advancement within the profession.

Education doctorates

The teaching profession in the UK since 1988, when the Education Reform Act was passed, provides an example of an occupation which has experienced changing relations with the state, professional fragmentation and a reconceptualisation of its ideological ethos. Before 1988 the occupational group had a degree of autonomy from the state, and this meant that it was able to shape its future direction. This referred to the particular ideal of service it subscribed to, the degree and extent to which it focused on common activities, the specific nature of the discourse community that was established, the distinctive epistemology of practice to which it worked, and the control it exercised over the development and maintenance of its specialised body of knowledge. If these five infrastructural elements are formed in response to the needs of the state and through the policy cycle in which the state takes a dominant role, then this constitutes a diminution of control that the occupational group can exercise over its core business. Indeed, the decline of the professional authority of the teaching profession in England since 1988 has been extensively documented (Bottery, 1997; Bottery and Wright, 2000; Helsby, 1999; Smyth, 2001; Troman, 1996). This would suggest in turn that the teaching body in England should be characterised as a state-regulated rather than a licensed occupation.

However, the present UK government has allowed the teaching body a limited form of licence through the setting up of the General Teaching Council in England. This degree of licence has been granted only so long as the work of the profession does not conflict with the overall strategic driving by the state. This has been achieved by restricting the remit of the Council; so, for example, the new General Teaching Council has discretion about matters to do with sexual behaviour, relations between staff and pupils and matters of professional conduct. Professional competence, however, is now determined and enforced by the state through processes of financial, discursive and structural control, and through inspection of practice and outcome.

The second fundamental change to the teaching profession in the UK over the last 15 years has been the fragmentation of its professional remit. This is best exemplified by the way head teachers and teachers are increasingly being understood as different types of professionals, with different sets of competences, different relations with the state and quasi-governmental bodies, and indeed changing relations with each other. New head teachers are now required to have gained a national qualification, delivered and accredited by the recently established National College for School Leadership, before they can be appointed.

The net effect of these changes has been to managerialise the head teacher role. From a situation where the head teacher was understood as a leading teacher, the role has now changed to one of managing teacher performance or 'productive autonomous performativity' (Gunther and Ribbins, 2002). As a result different lists of competences have been developed for head teachers and teachers, with a consequent fragmentation of the profession and a distancing in professional terms of teachers from managers. Further to this, schools are now seen as cost centres in a quasi-market system, which compete for pupils and results with each other, and understand the direction of their accountability relations as being to governments, quasi-governmental bodies and parents, rather than to the profession as a whole.

A third significant change to the professional mandate of teachers in England relates to the way pre-service and in-service training is now regulated both by governments and by universities, with the latter in turn granted a license to deliver these courses by the state. At the pre-service level, university deliverers are required to conform to a code as to what they can teach and how they teach it, and this is formally inspected by the national inspection body, OFSTED, which has the power to withdraw that license from the providers. Regulation by the state therefore operates both at the site of practice, and more importantly for our purposes at hand, at the site of professional training.

The profession, the workplace and the university, as we have suggested, are weakly linked (McWilliam et al., 2002) in relation to the development of the Education doctorate. Furthermore, the knowledge base for the EdD may be characterized as having a horizontal structure, with a proliferation of specialized languages (Bernstein, 1996). It is therefore to be expected that the forms of knowledge developed by the different university providers of EdDs would reflect this epistemological fragmentation, with some university providers embracing technical rationality as their preferred mode of knowledge and others adopting more dispositional and critical forms of knowledge. An example of a critical approach is provided here:

> I would say that they, throughout the three years, must develop the confidence in which to stand back and look at things critically, and develop a more sophisticated analytical framework in which to make sense of the world they're in.
>
> (EdD Tutor)

In like fashion, an EdD student reflects on what she has learnt from her period of study:

> It makes it very difficult when you deconstruct the notion of special educational needs, and you're going round having to take part in assessments using terminology you feel is oppressive. Most of the time, you learn to forget it and compartmentalise your kind of knowledge. That's what I mean about this whole thing. It's not simple putting together theory and practice. I think that there are loads of people who pretend that it's a nice smooth continuum and it's not.

This can be contrasted with the approach taken by an EdD programme director, who argued that:

> Our knowledge base is about best practice in teaching and learning and giving the students the best way to develop their own practice.

He is suggesting that it is possible to identify a body of specialised knowledge which can then be used in an unmediated way to reshape the workplace. Such a clear specification of purpose was rare. Indeed, individual personal and intellectual development was generally foregrounded; and consequently, the benefits of participation in a professional doctorate programme in Education were located at the level of the individual. An EdD tutor describes these benefits in the following way:

> The students that I am supervising are very much motivated by the notion of personal development, and there's a lot of person stuff tied up with their reasons for beginning this kind of programme, personal investment in terms of the project,

and also, since the research is based within their workplace, their personal identity and professional identity is a key part of what they are working on. So confidence or personal integrity is an important part of what they bring to the experience.

This has implications for the extent to which the EdD can make a monopoly claim for a specialised body of knowledge. Though there were benefits to the EdD students at an individual level, this rarely extended to institutional or professional levels. This ambiguity as to the nature of the benefits of the EdD is illustrated by this comment from an EdD tutor:

> There are all sorts and types of research within our field. I wouldn't want to say that education research is necessarily about improving practice. It's much more complex than that, and our students are likely to have conflicting opinions about its worth.
>
> (EdD tutor)

Such claims that were made about the benefits of completing an EdD programme focused on personal reflection and the development of the individual as an autonomous and self-directed person. Furthermore, the EdD student was expected to conform to a set of practices developed in and regulated by the university. Professional practice was objectified through a focus on textual production that in many cases had little direct influence on workplace practices. For example, a student on an EdD programme suggested that there were few benefits from completion, in relation to her own career, her status within the workplace and her own professional practice:

> This [the EdD] didn't enhance my career prospects. In fact, it produced a certain amount of resentment amongst senior managers that I was doing this. It came to light when we were Ofsteded in the school where I was and you had to put down what you were doing. You had to fill this big form in, and you had to put down what you were doing. And senior people who looked at it said 'Well, we know you're doing a doctorate but you don't have to write it down.'

This was underpinned by a seemingly insecure relationship between education as a region of knowledge and both professional practice and academic disciplines. As a result, only shallow linkages have been established between the state, the university and the workplace, and this is in contrast to the deep linkages developed by EngD programmes, which in turn has direct implications for, and is in part a result of, the types of professional status granted to and claimed by the two different occupational groups.

Conclusion

The emergence and expansion of professional doctorates in the UK over the past decade is linked to a wider agenda within the professions and a wider project of professionalisation. However this link is complex and multi-faceted. The two professional doctorates which are the subject of this chapter were the first to be established in the UK, though for different reasons, and for very different occupational groups. One aspect of professionalisation is a claim to specialisation and specialised knowledge. For the EngD, the development of specialised professional knowledge was a clear goal, with an instrumental focus based on a synergy between the academy and industry; this synergy has its roots in the history of and reasons for the development of EngDs by the Engineering and Physical Sciences Research Council. By contrast, EdD programmes made limited claims to the development of specialised knowledge, and the relationship between the university and the workplace was often more tenuous and was mediated through individual professional development.

We have further argued that knowledge development for an occupational group is regionalised, and thus a generic model is untenable. The extent therefore to which an occupational group can claim professional status and a monopoly over a body of knowledge is determined by a range of factors which operate at the three sites of knowledge development and is a consequence of the special relationship which that occupational group has with the state. This mandate has been shown to operate differently for two occupational groups: engineering and education. As a consequence, that body of specialised knowledge is either strongly or weakly framed, and if the latter, this impacts on the capacity of the occupational group to maintain both a labour market shield around a cadre of trained and accredited workers and a strong insulation between the different levels or layers of the division of labour within their occupation. However, we have further suggested that this is only one factor, and that structural issues within the specified occupation may also be influential. Finally, we are not suggesting that professional doctorates in themselves exclusively determine the degree of control an occupational group exercises over a specialised body of knowledge, only that they can constitute one factor in the development or otherwise of this monopoly control.

References

Allen, C., Smyth, E. and Wahlstrom, M. (2002) Responding to the field and to the academy: Ontario's evolving PhD, *Higher Education Research and Development*, 21(2): 203–214.
Bernstein, B. (1996) *Pedagogy, Symbolic Control and Identity*, London: Taylor and Francis.
Bernstein, B. (1997) *Class, Codes and Control*, Volume 3, London: Routledge.
Bottery, M. (1997) Teacher professionalism through action research – possibility or pipe dream, *Teachers and Teaching: Theory and Practice*, 29(1): 273–292.
Bottery, M. and Wright, N. (2000) *Teachers and the State: Towards a Directed Profession*, London and New York: Routledge.
Cowan, R. (1997) Comparative perspectives on the British PhD, in N. Graves and V. Varma (eds), *Working for a Doctorate: A Guide for the Humanities and Social Sciences*, London: Routledge.
Etzioni, A. (ed.) (1969) *The Semi-professions and their Organization: Teachers, Nurses, Social Workers*, London: Collier-Macmillan.
Finniston Report (1979) *Committee of Enquiry into British Engineering*, London: HMSO.
Freidson, E. (2001) *Professionalism: The Third Logic*, Chicago: University of Chicago Press.
Gibbons, M., Limoges, C., Nowotny, H., Schwartzman, S., Scott, P. and Trow, M. (1994) *The*

New Production of Knowledge: The Dynamics of Science and Research in Contemporary Societies, London: Sage.

Gunter, H. and Ribbins, P. (2002) Leadership studies in education: towards a map of the field, *Educational Management and Administration*, 30(4): 387–416.

Hanlon, G. (1998) Professionalism as enterprise: service class politics and the redefinition of professionalism, *Sociology*, 32(1): 43–63.

Helsby, G. (1999) *Changing Teachers' Work: The Reform of Secondary Schooling*, Buckingham: Open University Press.

McWilliam, E., Taylor, P., Thomson, P., Green, B., Maxwell, T., Wildy, H. and Simons, D. (eds) (2002) *Research Training in Doctoral Programs: What Can be Learned from Professional Doctorates?*, Canberra: ACT: DCITA.

Maxwell, T. (2003) From first to second generation professional doctorate, *Studies in Higher Education*, 28(3): 279–292.

Millerson, G. (1964) *The Qualifying Associations: A Study in Professionalisation*, London: Routledge.

Moore, R. and Muller, J. (2002) The growth of knowledge and the discursive gap, *British Journal of Sociology of Education*, 23(4): 627–637.

Parnaby Report (1992) *Working Party Report*, London: HMSO.

Quality Assurance Agency (1999) *Code of Practice for the Assurance of Academic Quality and Standards in Higher Education*: Postgraduate Research Programmes (updated 2004), London: QAA.

Saks, M. (1995) *Professions and the Public Interest: Medical Power, Altruism and Alternative Medicine*, London: Routledge.

Scott, D., Lunt, I., Brown, A. and Thorne, L. (2004) *Professional Doctorates: Integrating Professional and Academic Knowledge*, London: Open University Press.

Seddon, T. (2000) What is doctoral in doctoral education?, paper presented at the 3rd International Professional Doctorates Conference, Doctoral Education and Professional Practice: The Next Generation?, Armidale, 10–12 September.

Skrtic, T.M. (1991) The special education paradox: equity as the way to excellence, *Harvard Educational Review*, E(12): 148–206.

Smyth, J. (2001) A culture of teaching 'under new management', in D. Gleeson and C. Husbands (eds), *The Performing School: Managing, Teaching and Learning in a Performance Culture*, London and New York: RoutledgeFalmer.

Troman, G. (1996) The rise of the new professionals? The restructuring of primary teachers' work and professionalism, *British Journal of Sociology of Education*, 14(4): 472–487.

Whitty, G. (2001) Teacher professionalism in new times, in D. Gleeson and C. Husbands (eds), *The Performing School: Managing, Teaching and Learning in a Performance Culture*, London and New York: RoutledgeFalmer.

Chapter 12

Projecting the PhD

Architectural design research by and through projects

Brent Allpress and Robyn Barnacle

This chapter addresses the opportunities and obstacles presented by the PhD by project model. Understanding what the PhD by project is and what it has to offer requires attending to the specificity of research education practice within its disciplinary context. As a case study, we examine the framework for undertaking architectural design research offered by the Architecture Discipline at the Royal Melbourne Institute of Technology (RMIT) in Australia (see: http://architecture.rmit.edu.au).

Our discussion raises issues of relevance to other design disciplines and to creative practice research in general through focusing on the role of disciplinary ways of knowing in the research process. By addressing the key question of how to account for research embodied through projects, we sketch out the issues and concepts necessary for understanding and situating project-based research within creative disciplines.

Doing a PhD immerses and acculturates the candidate in modes of knowing specific to a research community, its technologies and practices. The PhD by project offers an alternative to the traditional written thesis model. While we specifically examine the RMIT Architecture model for undertaking postgraduate project-based design research, this does not restrict the import of our discussion to the design disciplines. It is the very specificity of our case study that enables the issues concerning PhD by project to be opened up. Our discussion raises insights and questions of relevance, not only to other design disciplines, but also to inquiry more broadly. Questioning conventions in research education raises broader issues concerning the role of different ways of knowing in knowledge generation. Consideration of alternative knowledge generation practices casts light on the limitations of conventional models, limitations that are not always evident from the inside. This raises opportunities for re-thinking and innovating research education across the disciplines.

Research education context

Conceptions of research education in recent years have been increasingly informed by perceived social and economic imperatives. The emergence of so-called 'knowledge economies', in particular, has led to an increasing emphasis on the role of research education in contributing to economic prosperity and innovation – the UK's 'creative industries' model is a case in point (see Department for Culture, Media and Sport, UK:

http://www.culture.gov.uk/what_we_do/Creative_industries/). As other commentators have noted (Drummond, 2003), it seems that the work we must now perform on ourselves is aimed more at society's economic solvency than one's own moral betterment or wisdom. In such a context, the specialisation involved in the pursuit of in-depth knowledge, once so prized about research degrees, has transformed into a liability. In a knowledge economy, knowledge is only valuable if it is useful and utility does not reside in depth but application. Doing something with what you know, or better still, doing something with what you don't know, is the end game. This is why research degree candidate generic capabilities development has gained such currency in universities within Australia, the UK and elsewhere. Generic capabilities, or the broad range of research skills, qualities and dispositions developed or honed through undertaking research, hold the promise of transferability: of being deployed in relation to topics and contexts beyond the scope of the particular research project that comprises a PhD. Armed with transferable research skills, a PhD graduate is arguably a potent source of innovation.

In some respects the project-based PhD could be seen as ideally placed within such a context. The model brings with it a potential workplace orientation of immediate appeal to the instrumentality evident within current trends in higher education policy. But it would be a mistake to assume that project-based research, even if it is workplace-related, is necessarily useful in the sense of being directly applicable and relevant. Indeed, as research degree candidates from the School of Architecture and Design at RMIT have commented, it is the difference between research work and workplace work that can make the former so worthwhile:

> [We are] coming to university for the research experience and the connection with ideas. So then it's silly to try and model the research experience more on workplace skills because that's what we're trying to get away from. . . . The university provides something that the workplace doesn't. So the more you make the university like the workplace, maybe the less attraction the university would have.
>
> (Barnacle and Usher, 2003: 351)

In some disciplines, specifically education and business, research degrees by project tend to be workplace-based in the sense that the research is based on the candidates' current professional work and intended to have direct benefit to workplace practice, understanding of workplace issues, etc. In other disciplines, notably architecture and fine art, this is not necessarily the case.

In this chapter we are addressing a broader definition of research by project that encompasses, but is not restricted to, professional practice undertaken in an industry context. Our main focus is the model of research undertaken through the activity of project-based design investigation, or in other words, through knowledge-generation practices specific to the discipline of architecture. Such research may occur in the context of a candidate's professional work or it may occur through selectively framed design investigations undertaken within the academy. These latter investigations may be entirely speculative and therefore lack any direct industry benefit. This is not to say, however, that there will be no benefit at all. There is a wider debate to be had about the social and economic role of research education and the supposed transferability of research knowledge and skills that we will not go into here. Instead, what we want to emphasise is that project-based research may lack a direct industry focus and therefore have more in common with the traditional 'blue sky' or speculative research that occurs within disciplines such as philosophy or theoretical physics. Such research is typified by the search for knowledge for its own sake, a pursuit that is dangerously undervalued when the instrumental value of knowledge becomes paramount, as it has today. Of interest within project-based research is that this search for knowledge is centred on and through disciplinary ways of knowing and, as such, is crucial to the understanding and advancement of disciplinary knowledge.

There is one final point that needs to be made here regarding the relationship between research by project and the workplace. It is useful to think of doctoral candidates as already engaged in labour: as doing work. There is a need to challenge the idea that doctoral candidates are merely preparing for a legitimate form of labour or production that would occur upon entering the labour market and workforce on completion. As others have argued, notably Pearson (2005) and Evans et al. (2003), doctoral candidates in all fields of study should be thought of as undertaking a form of professional education in that during their course of study they are already practising researchers, actively contributing to knowledge societies and economies.

This has particular resonance for project-based research degrees, as many candidates are of a mature age and are already practising professionals. Moreover, as RMIT Innovation Professor of Architecture Leon van Schaik (2005) has argued, practitioners within the design disciplines can only become better designers through designing. Project-based research degrees are uniquely placed to offer practitioners such opportunities.

On the differences between research by project and thesis

Perhaps the most obvious point of differentiation between PhD by thesis and project is in the way in which the thesis is conveyed. To have a thesis means taking a position: putting something forward. While the thesis is conveyed largely theoretically in a conventional PhD by thesis, it is conveyed largely empirically in a PhD by project (we emphasise largely because a PhD by project usually also involves a theoretical component and conventional PhDs often also utilise different types of media). In a thesis, a position is put forward theoretically through argument. The argument depends on evidence, which may be obtained either empirically, through case studies or experimentation, or theoretically, through conceptual analysis. Either way, the thesis represents or refers to the evidence through theoretical description and analysis. In a project-based PhD, on the other hand, a position is put forward empirically through the creation of some kind of work, which itself embodies the research. Such work could take the form, for example, of a three-dimensional prototype or model, a film, drawings or paintings, or a piece of creative writing.

A further distinction is that in the PhD by project the research activity is often not as delimited as in the conventional thesis approach. This distinction is evident in the etymology of the words thesis and project. The former is derived from ancient Greek and means 'setting down'. The latter is derived from Latin and means 'throwing forth'. Both involve conveying or communicating ideas but they do so differently. An argument aims at singularity of meaning: laying it down as it is, if you like. When research is embodied within works that do not communicate through argument, the meaning may be less defined and more open to multiple interpretations.

Importantly, however, this is not always the case. A thesis conveyed through written argument is at least legible to any educated reader. For disciplines whose primary mode of knowing is not linguistically based, legibility beyond the discipline can be limited. The meaning, therefore, may be considered indefinite to anyone lacking literacy in the particular form of expression utilised. This can cause misunderstanding concerning the status of research within the creative disciplines broadly.

Disciplinary ways of knowing

How we understand the world, our ways of learning and knowing, are oriented and shaped by historical, cultural, social and personal forces. As a vehicle of these forces, one's discipline provides a framework, both codified and tacit, through which engagement with the world occurs. These frameworks tend to become so effective, so natural, that they are obscured and we no longer recognise how completely they inform our ways of thinking and acting.

The significance of ways of thinking is evident in the concept of the thesis itself, which reveals apparently subtle historical changes in meaning that involve easily overlooked ontological implications. According to the German philosopher Martin Heidegger, the meaning of thesis to the ancient Greeks as 'laying down' meant 'letting lie forth', in the sense of making an oblation, or 'bringing something forth into what is present', such as letting a statue be set up (see Heidegger, 1993: 207–209). In the modern conception of thesis, however, it has come to be understood, instead, as commandeering and 'fixing in place'. While the former involves a 'letting happen', the latter suggests securing or holding down. The significance of this difference concerns the nature of truth: whether truth is conceived in terms of an 'account to be rendered' or as an 'unconcealing'. These two alternatives involve vastly different assumptions concerning the nature of knowledge and the relation of thought to world, the former rationalistic and the latter poetic.

Putting aside the question of the relative merits of either, the significance of such a difference, in this context, is the extent to which different modes of disciplinary practice lend themselves more readily to either model. More broadly, this leads to the issue of the status and performance of the various disciplines within the current political economy of research, in which the techno-sciences, privileging, as they do, utility over wonder, continue to thrive. More specifically, however, how truth is conceived has implications for the question of how research by project can be accounted for as an alternative mode of knowledge generation.

The account of thesis as a 'letting happen' offers an important model for understanding the PhD by project on its own terms. Through the notion of 'letting truth happen in the work' it becomes possible to account for a mode of knowing operative within the PhD by project that does not rely on argument and, indeed, makes a virtue of the lack of argument. We are not suggesting that all PhDs by project necessarily embody this model (nor that conventional PhDs cannot). It is rather that they have a particular potential to do so due to the processes of their production.

Architectural research by project

The issues discussed above concerning the nature of the thesis are played out in the history of the PhD in the discipline of architecture. Traditionally, postgraduate research within architecture has involved a thesis dissertation, often employing research methodologies drawn from the adjacent disciplines of art history, building science and sociology. Such theses have usually conformed to the common definition of an extended, logically constructed, coherent and integrated argument that answers a specific research question or questions, with arguments presented through the established conventions and methodologies of the sciences or humanities. While this approach can be effective in research *for* design and *about* design, it effectively precludes and marginalises the possibility of engaging with research *through* design.

Peter Downton (2003) defines research *for* design as facilitative research to enable design, such as, for example, through the provision of information and data analysis. Research *about* design usually involves situating design precedent or issues historically and theoretically. By contrast, candidates who are primarily undertaking research *through* design typically engage in a series of project-based design investigations and speculations. Research *through* design is conducted by employing disciplinary design practices and techniques such as architectural drawings, diagrams and models. This research activity does not readily follow the hypothesis-testing model of the sciences. It involves, but is not simply reducible to, problem solving. Design research is necessarily exploratory and iterative. It occurs through cycles of performative creative investigation in response to a selective framework of focusing concerns or problematics. Key architectural relationships embodied within integrative contexts are framed and brought to the fore. Productive design responses to particular situations or concerns are trialled. Research questions are usefully revised and refined during the candidacy through reflection on the provisional outcomes of the designing. Disciplinary and design knowledge is advanced through cycles of creative application and critical reflection. In this way, the postgraduate project-based research model offers a far greater capacity for an engagement with methodologies and processes involving relevant disciplinary design and communication practices.

RMIT Architecture was the first architecture program internationally to offer a postgraduate research by project model. Under the leadership of Leon van Schaik, the Master of Architecture (research by project) degree was inaugurated in 1987 with the first cohort of graduates completing in 1990. The PhD in Architecture (research by project) degree was subsequently developed in the mid-1990s, with the first candidates graduating in 2000. Historical precedent for this model can be found in the project-based PhD in Fine Arts offered at RMIT and elsewhere.

This model of research by project has subsequently been adopted across RMIT and is now the dominant mode for postgraduate research in the design and professional disciplines, with both Masters and PhD by project degrees offered in Interior Design, Industrial Design, Landscape Architecture, Fashion and Communication Design. The model is also being utilised within Engineering. RMIT Fine Arts has a slightly different model for the Masters of Fine Arts (by project), with less emphasis on written exegesis. In other professional disciplines such as Education, the differences in approach have been primarily in the contextual setting of the research projects, with workplace research being the most common model for research by project, often employing an action research methodology. In RMIT Architecture, candidates may undertake research through projects situated in industry contexts, but they may also engage in research through speculative unbuilt works.

As with the traditional thesis, the duration of the PhD by project degree is normally over the equivalent of four years full-time candidature, often completed part time. This is spent primarily undertaking a supervised program of original research through design investigations in close dialogue with a senior and second supervisor. In the RMIT PhD by project, the creative, design or professional practice project is accompanied by a framing exegesis that is between 20,000 and 40,000 words. The primary project-based component of the research involves a scale and scope that is more difficult to prescribe, but it is recommended that the heuristic and productive scope of research by project be comparable in scale of endeavour to a traditional dissertation. The scope and duration of the PhD lends itself to a series of project investigations rather than a singular design project or building, but this would depend on the scale and complexity of the project. One of the dangers for candidates undertaking the PhD by project is that they can tend to attempt to do two PhDs by giving the written component of the exegesis a greater role as a quasi-dissertation.

Common and established models of research undertaken *for* design or *about* design can be readily accommodated within the traditional thesis dissertation format. For candidates weighing up whether to undertake research in a traditional thesis mode or by project, a simple test of the value of the project-based approach is to consider whether this mode of working would enable investigations to occur that could not be readily undertaken otherwise.

Reflective practice

The RMIT Architecture research by project programs are conducted in a number of parallel streams that include urban architectural research undertaken in the Urban Architecture Laboratory (Murray and Bertram, 2005) and design research involving digital technologies within the Spatial Information Architecture Laboratory (see: http://www.sial.rmit.edu.au). The founding stream for architectural research by project at RMIT is the Reflective Practice Invited Stream, directed by van Schaik. Exemplary practitioners who have already demonstrated professional mastery in their design practice and have received peer acclaim are invited back into the academy to reflect on their body of work and the implicit research embodied within their practice. Candidates then extend this mastery in a research context through new projects undertaken during their candidacy, in dialogue with the community of supervisors and other candidates within the program. One of the most common reasons given anecdotally by practitioners for re-entering the academy is the opportunity provided to participate in a dialogue with a supportive critical community to deepen design thinking and develop innovative and effective practices.

The Invited Stream began as a Master of Architecture (by project) research degree and has more recently been extended and developed as a PhD (by project) stream. This in part recognises the potential downgrading of the status of the Master of Architecture by research with the move across Australia towards a variant of the European Union Bologna Protocol model, with five-year undergraduate professional architecture degrees becoming three-year undergraduate pre-professional degrees followed by a two-year professional Master of Architecture by coursework. The RMIT move towards the PhD in Architecture (research by project) as the primary postgraduate qualification acknowledges the demand latent within existing architecture school staff cohorts internationally from academics who are active practitioners. These candidates, who often have a Masters degree, have hit a glass ceiling of promotion and professional advancement and are seeking to undertake a PhD to develop and capture the original contribution to knowledge they are making through their practice and project-based research.

One of the key operational innovations in the running of project-based postgraduate programs at RMIT is the interdisciplinary Graduate Research Conferences held twice a year by the School of Architecture and Design. Candidates present work in progress to visiting international and local critics and supervisory staff and are exposed to the work and endeavours of other candidates, in addition to the outcomes of completing candidates who are examined through public exhibition in concurrent events. A community of practice is forged at these events by the critical dialogue that develops between practitioners and academic peers. This is a key ongoing benefit of the invited model at both the Masters and PhD levels, and reconfigures the relationship between the academy and the profession by fostering the innovative leadership of key exemplary practitioners, who have in a number of cases gone on to maintain adjunct professoriate roles with the institution.

The role of exegesis

Any architectural design project is an integrative undertaking that responds to, and engages with, a complex set of competing contextual conditions and constraints. Project vehicles located outside the academy in the realms of professional practice and other industry economies present particular difficulties for candidates who are negotiating competing professional and research responsibilities. Candidates employing actual built projects as vehicles are encouraged to selectively distill and foreground the design research embodied within the integrative project that makes an original contribution to knowledge in the discipline. This embodied research and often implicit knowing is selectively framed, and made available to a broader disciplinary community through exegetical text, documentation and other disciplinary modes of representation such as drawing, modelling and diagramming that serve a framing exegetical role. The issue of the role of architectural representation in a research context presents complexities for candidates, as architectural modes of representation have usually played other professional and promotional communication roles. A key responsibility of architectural representation in a research context remains the requirement that it have the capacity to make new knowledge available to the field of architectural design and to other design researchers and practitioners.

An exegesis is a framing exposition that situates the research project and the processes by which it has been formed. One danger here is the potential fall into the prescriptive delusions of design methods and other variants of design science. This somewhat discredited methodology had its heyday in the 1970s. It sought to provide a coherent and rational account of design processes. In practice, it was an overly instrumental account of the complexities of designing that relied on an overdetermined, linear narrative of design process in the service of logical criteria. This rationalist methodology is not adequate to account for the complexities of the integrative act of designing. The assumed linear progression of design process pays little heed to the non-linear, recursive and cyclical nature of creative project investigations and design development.

Examination

The research by project model demands a relevant mode of disciplinary documentation that makes the embodied research legible and available to others. This has implications for examination assessment, archival storage, and subsequent dissemination. Candidates in the RMIT School of Architecture and Design mount a public exhibition of their work. They are examined through a presentation and defence of the thesis in front of a panel of three examiners, with the event chaired by a senior member of the research staff. Examiners are not expected to take the role of critics, which is a common mode of discourse for design assessments at undergraduate levels. Rather, they ask clarifying questions that seek to elicit further exposition of the research from the candidate. Final assessment takes into account the candidates' exhibition, their verbal defence of the work and their framing exegesis. This mode of assessment differs from the sciences in that it focuses primarily on qualitative criteria. The chair's role is to ensure that examinations are conducted in accordance with the candidates' specific research questions and the relevant assessment criteria.

Following the examination, the candidates submit a final Durable Visual Record (DVR) of the research project that is the equivalent of a bound thesis but captured in a format and in media relevant to disciplinary practices and conventions that ensure the project research is legible and accessible. The DVR includes the exegesis and permanent documentation of the exhibition. The RMIT Architecture program also resources the video-recording of the examination defence as a permanent archival record of the event.

The PhD by project model meets the same demands of the traditional PhD for the demonstration of an original contribution to knowledge within the field of architectural design. The discovery primarily occurs through applied research. Design research seeks to foster innovations through the development of emerging practices and techniques, responding to selectively nominated design problematics and concerns in order to achieve qualitative improvement in outcomes.

Dissemination

Examiners are asked to assess whether the work achieves the standard required, that of making an original contribution to knowledge, by considering the extent to which the work is publishable, or a project is publicly presentable or able to be exhibited, at the highest level. The candidate would also be expected to demonstrate independent and critical thought and the capacity to work independently of supervision. Ultimately, the awarding of a PhD by project is, like other PhDs, an acknowledgement that a candidate shows promise as an independent scholar and researcher able to make an ongoing contribution to the disciplinary field and who can initiate and conduct independent research.

This raises the issue of what dissemination vehicles are available for candidates undertaking project-based design research. As the model of project-based research is a relatively new one, existing venues for publishing or exhibiting such research are minimal. RMIT Architecture has a long tradition of publishing postgraduate projects in a series of books through RMIT Press to aid the dissemination of design research and promote the program. However, there has been a dearth of wider dissemination opportunities for refereed project-based design research. There are ample journal and conference venues for research focused on architectural history and theory or technology. The term *design research* is often accounted for as design science, relying on empirical analytical methodologies drawn from outside the discipline. Designing is a core activity of the architectural discipline, and yet there are few academic refereed publications documenting and disseminating design-driven research.

Co-author Brent Allpress and Professor Michael Ostwald of the University of Newcastle, founded the *Architectural Design Research (ADR)* journal in 2005 to address this gap in the architectural discourse economy. *ADR* is a peer-reviewed, international journal that publishes project-based design research and associated discourse on design. Informed by the PhD by project model, it primarily aims to publish architectural research undertaken through the design of projects where the research is embodied within project-based design investigations and outcomes. The exegesis accompanying the published project-based research plays a role in situating, framing and clearly communicating the contribution that the project makes to knowledge within the field of architectural design. The exegesis may be text-based but it may also encompass other disciplinary modes of representation such as diagrams and drawings that also play a framing exegetical role. The journal also promotes discourse on architectural design, and includes scholarly design research essays addressing significant contemporary architectural design problematics, emerging design strategies and practices, scholarly critiques of contemporary design practice and projects, and extended essays by authors on their project-based design research. The journal also seeks to provoke a shift in the grant funding economies by providing a potential pathway to gaining a peer-reviewed track record for design researchers seeking project-based research grant funding.

The first issue featured the article 'Architectural Design and Discourse' by Shane Murray (2005), in which he reframed research undertaken through the RMIT PhD in Architecture (research by project) program. Murray critiques the relationship between architectural discourse and design practice internationally. He argues that architectural theory has increasingly been employed as a source of external authorisation of design, drawing on the authority of discourses outside the discipline to legitimate outcomes. He proposes other models for design discourse as a means to reflect on, frame and disseminate the disciplinary design processes and practices that architects undertake when doing design, particularly design development. Murray offers a clear account of the complexities involved in accounting for the contribution to knowledge in the field of architectural design by designers and practitioners. This essay raises issues of relevance to anyone engaging in the complex task of framing and accounting clearly for the research embodied within project-based architectural design investigations and outcomes.

Murray's PhD by project, completed in 2003, also offers an example of exemplary practice within this mode of research. In it he undertook three primary case study design projects. All were competition entries that lent themselves to being a vehicle for design speculation. His research consisted of a proposition and trial of a research method by which an individual design process could be investigated and described so as to develop a body of discourse able to contribute to the understanding of architectural design processes. This approach attends to a key responsibility of project-based design research, which is that it must be captured in a way that it can add to knowledge within the field and be drawn on by other researchers and practitioners to inform further project research.

Institutional economies

Distortions have been created historically by the dominance of the traditional thesis mode of postgraduate research. In the past, active practitioners who undertook postgraduate study had to abandon their primary, project-based practices of embodied disciplinary knowing and expertise, such as designing, drawing and making. In undertaking a traditional thesis, candidates have had to adopt discursive and empiricist research methods, largely borrowed from the adjacent disciplines of art history and building science. In the architecture discipline, relatively few active, exemplary practitioners internationally have undertaken PhD study and subsequently sought or gained tenure as architectural academics. As a result, academics with art history and building science backgrounds have been disproportionately represented on architecture school staff in many institutions around the world.

In addition, research in architecture programs funded through national competitive grant schemes, such as the Australian Research Council, also tends to be undertaken by academics employing building science or art history related methodologies, rather than in the professional discipline of architecture and rarely ever in design.

The impact of this distortion on the development of innovation in the areas of architectural design research, and the related lack of exemplary practitioners subsequently gaining tenured academic appointments, has led to a cultural schism between the academy and the profession in many institutions. This has also stifled innovation in the areas of architectural design teaching and research internationally. One key implication of the introduction of the PhD by project model is that it provides a career pathway for academics in the discipline of architecture whose primary expertise and focus is in architectural design and practice. Similar discipline-relevant research modes and pathways are an issue in the other related design disciplines across the creative industries and fine arts.

At RMIT, a number of respected and emerging international academics and institutions have been exposed to the research by project model through involvement as visiting international critics and examiners. Professor Colin Fournier and Professor Jonathan Hill were early visitors who went on to direct the MPhil Urban Design (by project) and the PhD (by project) programs, respectively, at the Bartlett School of Architecture, University College London.

Other schools that have adopted aspects of the RMIT approach and process through involvement in the program include Unitec School of Architecture in Auckland, New Zealand, which offers a Masters of Architecture and of Landscape Architecture by project under the directorship of Professor Mike Austin; and the University of Westminster, School of Architecture, in London, which offers a Masters and PhD by design project. Professor Jenny Lowe graduated with a PhD in Architecture (by project) from RMIT in 2002 and is now Head of School of Architecture, Brighton, UK and is developing a research by project program there.

Comparable programs have commenced at the University of Auckland, the University of Sheffield, London Metropolitan College and the Royal College of Art. The Centre of Architectural Research at Goldsmiths College, London offers an interesting variation on the model in an intermediate position where research is undertaken by project but not by design, with project-based disciplinary practices being deployed to address analytical and other research concerns. This approach has relevance across a range of disciplines, including architecture, where the creative endeavour may not always be the primary activity but, at a methodological level, project-based practices would be most appropriate to undertake certain forms of research or address certain categories of questions or problematics.

Literature on the field

As an emerging model, there is relatively scant literature and discourse on research by project in the architectural discipline. RMIT Architecture's professoriate have been actively documenting and disseminating the model through a series of publications and papers. Van Schaik has published a series of postgraduate Invited Stream books, featuring individual postgraduate candidate projects and framing essays on the model

(1993, 1995, 2000, 2003). He has consolidated his reflections on the first 20 odd years of this program with the book *Mastering Architecture* (2005), which draws on the research of 50 architects who have participated in this reflective practice-focused program.

This book also outlines a broader aspiration for the role of the institution in fostering innovation in practice through providing infrastructure for the establishment and maintenance of communities of practice that extend well beyond the candidacy of any particular student. One particularly provocative chapter entitled 'Thwarted Mastery' addresses the obstacles to this aspiration commonly encountered in local practice and institutional contexts. Van Schaik categorises these as: overshadowing by the establishment; technical over-refinement at the expense of other concerns; the forgetting of accumulated cultural capital; confusion of the knowledge base through excursions into realms outside the primary area of disciplinary expertise, and the failure to elevate innovations into a metropolitan discourse that engages with an international conversation around emerging ideas and practices.

Observations and reflections on interdisciplinary research methods for project-based candidates have been collated over a similar period of time by Peter Downton. In his book *Design Research* (2003), Downton provides a textbook account of research methods by project for postgraduate candidates across the creative industries and design professions. It offers a framework for considering the complexities involved in capturing and sharing embodied knowledge and practices and promoting innovation through cycles of critical reflection and production, avoiding the design science and design methods trap of oversimplifying process and assuming some instrumental causality between constraint and outcome.

A philosophical account of the theory and practice of creative research across art and design disciplines has been put forward by Paul Carter, a University of Melbourne based Visiting Professor to the RMIT program, in his book *Material Thinking* (2004). Carter focuses particularly on collaborative practice between and across disciplines as a key site of innovation. Van Schaik and Carter co-supervise a cohort of RMIT PhD by project candidates who work across architecture and public art, grouped through their shared sensibility for ephemerality as a temporal and contextual condition.

Conclusion

Governments and institutions internationally have begun to heed Richard Florida's (2002) economic argument that the creative industries are an increasingly significant component of the economy in the shift from heavy industry to an emerging consolidation of creative capital in key urban centres such as Dublin, Boston or Melbourne. A key criticism of Florida's position is that his modelling privileges quantitative economic activity in the creative industries regardless of the inherent value of the outcomes of that activity (Rossiter, 2006). Criteria are needed for assessing qualitative outcomes and the development of strategies for investing in and supporting innovation in this area.

Lessons can be learnt from the institutional structures and cultural practices that have been developing around the PhD in Architecture (research by project) model at

RMIT and elsewhere. It offers procedures and practices for enhancing and extending the capacity of design professionals to develop and transform their disciplinary practices and achieve genuine innovations in responding to complex contemporary urban situations and emerging technologies. The research by project model adopted at RMIT fosters, and is in turn supported by, an exemplary community of practice that bridges between the academy and industry, maintaining a constructive critical dialogue between practitioners, researchers and an emerging elite of leading practitioner researchers. Policy makers, both within government and universities, could benefit by recognising the role that research education can play in fostering a productive dialogue between industry and the academy. The research by project model challenges the standard, one-directional conception of the transferability of research knowledge and skills between academy and workplace by demonstrating that the movement can go both ways. A focus on 'generic skills' development is also of limited value within a context in which doctoral candidates are already successful professionals who are more than adept at communication skills and the like. Of far more interest is the candidates' potential for innovation and leadership that arises through the development of new knowledge and practices. The key lesson here is that research within a creative discipline must progress on its own terms, utilising and renewing its own disciplinary ways of knowing. This in turn has the potential to promote genuine innovation within broader professional practice.

References

Barnacle, R. and Usher, R. (2003) Assessing the quality of research training: the case of part-time candidates in full-time professional work, *Higher Education Research and Development*, 22(3): 345–358.

Carter, P. (2004) *Material Thinking*, Melbourne: Melbourne University Press.

Downton, P. (2003) *Design Research*, Melbourne: RMIT University Press.

Drummond, J. (2003) Care of the self in a knowledge economy: higher education, vocation and the ethics of Michel Foucault, *Educational Philosophy and Theory*, 35: 57–69.

Evans, T., Macauley, P., Pearson, M. and Tregenza, K. (2003) A brief review of PhDs in creative and performing arts in Australia, paper presented at the Australian Association for Research in Education mini-conference, 'Defining the Doctorate', Newcastle, at: http://www.aare.edu.au/conf03nc/ev03007z.pdf.

Florida, R. (2002) *The Rise of the Creative Class*, New York: Basic Books.

Heidegger, M. (1993) *Basic Writings*, edited by D. Farrell Krell, New York: Harper Collins.

Murray, S. (2005) Architectural design and discourse, *Architectural Design Research*, edited by B. Allpress and M. Ostwald, 1(1): 83–102.

Murray, S. and Bertram, N. (eds) (2005) *38South Vol 3: Urban Architecture Laboratory, 2002–2004*, Melbourne: RMIT University Press, at: http://gallery.tce.rmit.edu.au/131/38south/.

Pearson, M. (2005) Framing research on doctoral education in Australia in a global context, *Higher Education Research and Development*, 24(2): 119–134.

Rossiter, N. (2006) *Organized Networks: Media Theory, Creative Labour, New Institutions*, Rotterdam: NAi Publishers.

van Schaik, L. (ed.) (1993) *Fin de Siecle? and the Twenty first Century: Architectures of Melbourne, RMIT Masters of Architecture by Project*. Melbourne: 38South Publications.

van Schaik, L. (ed.) (1995) *Transfiguring the Ordinary: RMIT Masters by Project*, Melbourne: 38South Publications.

van Schaik, L. (ed.) (2000) *Interstitial Modernism*, Melbourne: RMIT School of Architecture and Design.

van Schaik, L. (ed.) (2003) *The Practice of Practice: Research in the Medium of Design*, Melbourne: RMIT University Press.

van Schaik, L. (2005) *Mastering Architecture: Becoming a Creative Innovator in Practice*, Chichester: Wiley-Academy.

Chapter 13

Building doctorates around individual candidates' professional experience

Carol Costley and John Stephenson

The doctorate in professional studies (DProf, sometimes called Prof D) illustrates a different kind of approach to doctoral education than one focused on research training or contributing to professional development within a particular profession. It is aimed at developing professionals to the highest level of academic ability within their own contexts through building on generic high level abilities, and making a significant contribution to practice acknowledged as such by peers in the same field. Though significantly different in kind to the PhD and other professional doctorates, it seeks to give capable individuals, who are usually full-time workers, opportunity to gain doctorate status through achievements based primarily on research and development and demonstrating doctoral capability in professional practice. DProf programmes are designed to impact in any professional field where influence is achieved via individuals and their organisations, networks, etc. in key areas of professional life. This chapter shows how the particular practices of this doctorate emerged from work-based learning and how, through case example, the programme is constructed, implemented and assessed.

The DProf is firmly located in the paradigm of work-based learning, which is consistent with the UK's online Learning Through Work (LTW) programme launched in 2000 (Learning Through Work, 2007). LTW carries out what Billett (2006) refers to as the 'central role of the dualities comprising the affordances of social practices, particularly workplaces, on the one hand, and individuals' engagement on the other as a basis to understand how learning proceeds.' It gives the learner the central role in linking university and employer in support of practitioner development. A UK Council for Graduate Education report shows that 'a small number of universities offer generic professional doctorate programmes, typically with the content being negotiable by the student in order to meet his/her professional needs' (UKCGE, 2002: 34). A later report related that 'the case for using the title DProf is well illustrated' (UKCGE, 2005: 37) and records growing numbers of DProf programmes in the UK UKCGE, 2005: 95–99).

The work-based learning approach adopted by the DProf requires learners to define the scope and focus of their programmes, in which they are able to make changes through advanced learning and knowledge production to the practice of their organisations or professional areas. The DProf, modelled on work-based learning (Boud and

Solomon, 2001), holds a position relating to knowledge that is practice-based and draws on practitioner-led enquiry as a principle for research and development. It has not emerged from an existing academic discipline that had operated within a particular paradigm with an existing pedagogy. It is designed to develop the practice of people at work and does not borrow from subject-based curricula but focuses on giving individual practitioners the opportunity to develop and demonstrate doctoral level learning in their professional/personal context. The DProf or Prof D often uses a learning agreement to plan study that embraces progress to date, current professional initiatives, proposed impact in the candidates' fields and longer-term development (Glasgow Caledonian University, 2007).

Current debates about the range of professional doctorates distinguish between generations one and two (see Chapter 11). The DProf is not easily identified as being an example of either generation. Lester, a holder of the DProf who transferred from a PhD, describes first-generation professional doctorates as seeking to approach professional practice 'with the perspective of the researcher working on a practice situation, rather than that of the practitioner working within it' (Lester, 2004). The second generation, Lester continues, 'takes a more situated view of the research process and the centrality of the practitioner within it', but nevertheless could still manifest how 'the student undertaking professional doctorate study is required to put to one side their ways of working and assume those that characterise another mode of knowledge. Disciplinary practice sometimes acts in this way so that the student is required to conform to the rules that underpin it, regardless of their current orientation' (Scott et al., 2004: 54). Lester describes the difference between his experience as a PhD student and the DProf as follows: on the former he was seen as a part-time student; on the latter he was seen as a full-time professional.

The DProf is built around individual professional profiles by the practitioners themselves and has been designed specifically to engender high level performance in a professional context, and to fit structurally and operationally into the nature of the professional context in which it is demonstrated even when they do not map on to established professional forms. The emergence of publicly available generic criteria endorsed by the UK's Quality Assurance Agency for achievements at all HE levels, including doctorate, provides the opportunity for professional excellence in 'non-traditional' contexts to be judged in terms of comparability of level though different in structure, content and style with other doctorates (Thorne, 2001).

An example of a DProf programme

Participants

We illustrate the DProf through the example of the Middlesex University version (Middlesex University, 2007) that was launched in 1998 and has grown rapidly. At the time of writing (August 2007) there have been 72 successful completions, with 251 'live' ongoing doctorate enrolments. The programme is managed within the university's Institute for Work-based Learning, which has a pan-university remit and specialises in awards, research, and consultancy in work-based learning. Arrangements have also been made for specialist fields in the university – Health, Social Science and Business – to promote and manage their own versions of the programme. Some candidates prefer to work directly with a specialist field, gaining the advantage of working with other candidates and supervision in a subject discipline. To date, a further 60 candidates have been enrolled in these areas. Other candidates prefer to work in the generic DProf area, gaining advantage of working with others from a range of backgrounds and undertaking an approach that is different from the disciplinary paradigm with which they are already familiar.

A flavour of the range of candidates attracted to the scheme can be seen from the following brief profiles of some recent completions:

- A head teacher seeking to establish a new community-oriented learning culture in her school.
- A senior interment manager for a major city tackling problems of burial congestion, within major environmental, cultural and bureaucratic constraints.
- The administrative head of a major international religion, setting out an informed agenda for its future development based on a review of past and current practice and likely trends.
- An architect seeking to become established as an authority on mediation of disputes and to contribute to wider understanding and practice in that field.
- A physiotherapist seeking to raise the status of the profession via new in-service postgraduate opportunities.
- A vocational qualification consultant working on establishing the professional status of a specialist group currently lacking professional status.
- A psychotherapist, extending opportunities for experienced practitioners to advance themselves via a new practice-related higher level programme.
- A senior researcher for national assessments of school pupil developing systems, standards and procedures to meet current needs.
- A government advisor on special care services, developing audits of effectiveness of government services in that field.
- A university quality-assurance manager developing systems for a new faculty.

The above selection shows they already have sufficient authority and leadership in their work to undertake doctoral level research and development projects that can have a wide-ranging effect on their organisation, community or professional field, producing innovations commensurate with a high level contribution to knowledge. They are all seeking to use the DProf to contribute in some way to better practice in their specific fields. In some cases their field maps on to university disciplinary areas, but some do not. Employers (usually line managers) or a key person in the candidate's professional field are required to endorse the learning agreement, mainly for the purposes of verifying that the proposed project is a pertinent one for the field.

Structure

A credit-based modular programme is used to support work-based conceptions of research and scholarship through the way the curriculum is designed. Module descriptors and credits consistent with the university's and the Quality Assurance Agency's requirements for awards at doctorate level are allocated to the core generic processes (QAA, 2000). Five hundred and forty credits, of which 180 are at Master's level and 360 are at doctorate level, are needed for the award of a modular doctorate. Key modules are:

- Review of learning (20 credits at Master's level).
- Recognition and accreditation of learning (RAL) (up to 100 credits at Master's level and 160 credits at doctorate level depending on the standing and nature of current learning and ability to relate the learning appropriately to the DProf level descriptors and provide evidence).
- Planning and practitioner research (60 credits at Master's level).
- The main research and development project itself (between 160 and 360 credits, depending on successful RAL claims at doctorate level).

Each candidate can balance the relative size of RAL and the size of the final project according to their personal circumstances. For instance, a person with a large portfolio of extensive professional achievements might achieve up to 160 credits for RAL and aim to complete a smaller main project; whereas a less experienced professional would need a different balance between the two. The award of RAL credit is by no means a routine procedure. All candidates have to prepare a fully researched and authenticated review of their own work in the context of the generic criteria for the DProf award, a process typically described by one candidate as 'very stretching'. The length of doctoral study ranges from 7 semesters to 11 semesters, depending on whether doctorate level RAL claims have been successfully made.

The 60-credit Planning and Practitioner Research programme module introduces a range of research approaches and is compulsory for all candidates who are required to demonstrate high level abilities in a methodology appropriate to their proposed final project.

Assessment and quality assurance

The initial Master's level modules prepare candidates for the final Research and Development project by enabling them to go through an in-depth process of reflectively reviewing their personal and professional development to date, evaluating how and why they have reached their current position and level of expertise. The early modules also prepare the candidates, who are already practitioners with considerable expertise in their fields to understand research as a means by which they can enrich and inform their fields bringing a level of theoretical and informed thinking to their organisations and/or professional areas. Appropriate supervision and examiners for the programme entails finding colleagues who have the knowledge of doctoral education and who are also willing to approach this doctorate with the understanding that there should be an outcome that has the potential to make an original contribution to practice that is also underpinned by theoretical reasoning. In essence, this means that those with the appropriate experience have to have the will to undertake supervision and examining for this doctorate and the ability to view doctoral learning progressively. Not all experienced PhD supervisors are suited to this role.

Underpinning the university's work-based learning programmes are generic levels of performance that students have to demonstrate before an award can be made. The DProf scheme has generic level statements that are made available to all candidates at the beginning of their programme and are used as a guide and a measure of progress at crucial stages during the course and in the final assessments. When negotiating credit for experience, there has to be a match between evidence and explication of experience against specific doctorate level criteria, e.g. a senior government officer made a claim about his knowledge and abilities concerning issues surrounding the environmental management of the 94 miles of the tidal Thames; other examples include writing for publication, leadership and management in setting up various systems in professional work, leading on organisational or professional change, such as introducing sustainable development policies and setting up staff development initiatives for a particular professional area. The claim that is made must be directly relevant to the proposed project work. When planning and seeking approval for their major project they must demonstrate how it has potential to produce work that can be judged against those criteria. The initial modules are 'taught' and assessed within the university's modular curriculum, which has the long-established routines of assessment boards, hand-in dates, external examiners and so on. This process keeps candidates to time and ensures each stage of their work is assessed and feedback given on their progression.

As part of their final piece of work, they must demonstrate to external examiners how the project has professional impact that meets the generic criteria. By the end of their programme all successful candidates have a firm understanding of what constitutes doctoral level work. Engagement with those criteria at every stage ensures that their activities and abilities in their professional area are comparable in level with work produced by candidates operating within a conventional university subject area. As will be seen in the cases reported below, this process of constant engagement with criteria of good performance has a valuable outcome in terms of candidates' personal and professional development.

The generic level criteria are grouped under three general headings: cognitive, transferable and operational. As a brief illustration, the cognitive level criteria include knowledge, analysis, synthesis and evaluation. The criteria have descriptors for Master's and doctoral levels that correlate with the UK's Quality Assurance Agency's guidelines. Doctorate level knowledge, for instance, requires 'evidence that the candidate has great depth of knowledge of an inter-disciplinary nature in a complex area and is working at current limits of theoretical and/or research understanding' (QAA, 2005). Formal assessments of each candidate's plans and final projects include rigorous face-to-face interviews conducted by independent specialist internal and external examiners. Examiners are approved by the university's research degrees committee in the same way as all the university's doctorate examiners; they should have previously examined at least three doctorates and have experiential knowledge of the relevant field. In addition, the programme has a chief external examiner who reviews the early modules, reports on consistency and standards across the whole scheme, and is appointed through centralised university regulations with her/his field of expertise being doctorate learning.

Support and supervision

Effective tutorial support includes an additional challenge of helping candidates, whose experience, expertise and long-term interests lie in practice-based contexts, to embrace what for many is an unfamiliar culture or at best a culture they may have experienced in the past but which does not represent their ongoing interest and activity. The wide diversity of work situations and locations (some at great distance from the university) means that candidates mostly communicate remotely through online lectures and seminars, discussion boards and email. Topics concern common process issues and research approaches. These activities are conducted by academic staff, including many of the visiting professors linked to the Institute of Work-based Learning. The seminars are recorded and can be viewed live, followed by live debate or downloaded by candidates through the virtual learning environment. Examples of the seminar topics have been *Ethical Issues for Practitioner-Researcher projects*, *Phenomenology and Reflective Thinking* and *Producing Original Knowledge through Doctoral Projects*. The wide diversity of working situations means that peer groups form remotely. Most exchanges between tutors and candidates occur via telephone and email with face-to-face meetings arranged at mutual convenience.

The university allocates two personal supervisors, one from the Institute's core team (known as the academic advisor) who provides support with overall procedures. The other supervisor is usually from elsewhere in the university, with expertise appropriate to the field in which the programme is set. Because the specialist tutors work closely with the candidates' main projects, particular attention is given to their selection and appointment, based on their personal credibility working at doctorate level in the relevant field. As the candidates' programmes begin to take shape, an external consultant with established expertise in the relevant professional field may be added to the support team provided for each candidate. The advisor is well-placed to help the candidate understand the basic features and procedures of the doctorate programme as a whole. The advisor's main educational role is to help the candidate to develop self-critical and substantial reviews of their previous learning, compile and evaluate evidence of their professional experience when negotiating academic credit and articulate their professional aspirations into a major project proposal. The specialist supervisor and external consultant became more involved in supervision when the research project starts and help with specialist understanding in current contexts that are often influenced by socio-political factors, access to resources appropriate to the candidate's field of enquiry and other specialist support.

An ongoing research project analysing tutor–student on-line exchanges (Young and Stephenson 2007) found that advisers are most helpful when they:

- help candidates accept and exercise control of their own programmes.
- are sensitive to candidates' initial wariness and lack of familiarity with higher education culture in general and doctorate level work in particular.
- are available, by arrangement, at times consistent with workplace cycles of activity (not just during semesters), with just-in-time responses to candidate need.
- provide clarification on all aspects of university procedures relevant to the programme.
- build confidence in the candidate's ability to take on the challenge.
- provide reassurance, where appropriate, that candidates initiatives and outputs are 'on the right lines'.
- are prepared to give honest feedback on candidates' progress and performance, with negative feedback always accompanied by suggestions of how progress can be made.
- are willing to develop a mutually respectful relationship – tutor respecting candidates' prowess in their professional field and candidates respecting tutors' expertise in the culture and procedures of the university.

Specialist supervisors have familiar roles to those in conventional academic doctorates, i.e. challenging candidates' specialist understanding and providing access to ideas on sources and resources. The external consultants focus mainly on helping candidates achieve impact in the field.

Resources

Resources related to key processes in the DProf programme, particularly assessment, the generic criteria of doctorate level work and advice on claiming credit for prior experience are available as handbooks in booklet format and via the programme's intranet. The Institute provides specialist advice on research methods appropriate to different kinds of project, supplemented by research seminars on campus. All candidates have access to the specialist resources of the university but they tend to particularly use online library services.

The main focus of programmes is generally within the candidate's workplace or its wider professional context, or both. In each of the examples mentioned earlier, specialist material relevant to the project came mainly from routine sources such as professional bodies, wider communities of practice, ongoing research and development projects at work and colleagues with similar interests. Indeed, it is not unusual for workplace colleagues to associate themselves with the candidates' projects, supplying relevant materials and information. Projects, in situ, tap into seams of knowledge and understanding revealed through social and informal exchanges with professional colleagues (Eraut, 2004). Some candidates use their status as a doctorate candidate, especially in fields where 'doctor status' is rare and respected, to open doors and secure access to specialist materials that would not normally cross their desks. 'To help me with a doctoral project, can you let me see/have etc . . .' is a more effective approach to otherwise separate departments for information and advice than a routine request. Resources from the work context are, of course, supplemented by materials from the university library, augmented by reading rights in other university libraries using the joint universities scheme and, of course, the British Library.

Work-based candidates also make use of the internet as a resource. Some of those mentioned above published items relevant to their main field on sites that draw constructive responses from other professionals, thereby providing a larger knowledge base as well as valuable peer review. Indeed, such online exchanges can be used in the final assessment as part of candidates' evidence of achieving professional impact.

Ongoing research and evaluation

Academics working on the generic Middlesex DProf have researched and evaluated the programme consistently since its inception. In particular, in 2004 the university began a series of research activities investigating the experience of candidates who had completed the DProf generic programme. Because of the highly individual nature of candidates' experiences, this research focused on individual cases using course documents such as personal reviews of previous learning, claims for credit for professional experience, and major products submitted for final assessment. Valuable insights were also obtained via analyses of transcripts of one-to-one post-completion reflections, of how the programme impacted on them, both personally and professionally (Stephenson and Costley, 2007; Stephenson et al., 2006). This section draws on these sources, as well as experiences and observations of the authors who have key roles in managing the generic DProf scheme. Analysis of candidates' personal reflections on the experience as a whole suggests the personal benefits perceived by successful participants to be:

- Greater personal and professional credibility:
  as an individual: *'It's nice to know that you are, you're considered, the sort of expert, in this particular territory of the profession.'*
  and for the wider professional group: *'I also felt that the [professional community] deserved it and that it was probably going to enhance some sort of standing in terms of the various negotiations we continue to have.'*
- Enhanced personal and professional capability and belief in their power to perform:
  'The ability to see connections between different pieces of work and to draw lessons over and above that are greater than the sum of the parts'
  'I now know I can make a difference in what I am doing.'
- Strengthened commitment to continuing development:
  'Doing advanced work in the second half of one's professional life, that's very good, because the idea of continually learning in an academically credited context is very good for people in their fifties.'

'Once you finish the programme, it's meant to be only the start of the next phase or the next series of projects.'

Insights into particular components (modules) of the programme have been gained from the views of successful candidates and staff evaluation, as follows. The first module, *Review of Learning*, is a critical appraisal of previous educational and life experiences. It can initially be thought to be a digression from the specific project that candidates wish to develop but soon its value becomes widely appreciated. It enables them to anchor their enrolment onto the programme within the context of their own personal and professional history and aspirations. Typical reflective views on the experience were: 'cathartic', 'honest self-appraisal', 'revealing'. As a consequence, candidates are able to start the programme from their current position and develop a clearer understanding of their motivation to work for an academic award at this level (Doncaster and Lester, 2002; Stephenson et al., 2006).

Recognition and accreditation of learning (RAL) enables professional workers who already have expert knowledge to become familiar with the generic level criteria for doctorate level work. It introduces them to the complexities and conceptual differences between notions of quality and success in the academic and professional worlds and helps them to appreciate the quality and value, in academic terms, of their previous professional experiences ('It showed I was better than I thought'). The RAL process clarifies and confirms the direction of their intended project and its impact in their field (Armsby et al., 2006; Doncaster and Thorne, 2000).

Within *Programme planning and research methods*, candidates took a very pragmatic view of research methods, being frustrated by having to learn about research principles in general but committed to research methods likely to be relevant to their professional intentions. The programme approval procedures, which includes oral presentations to senior academic and professional figures in the field of study, provides a discipline for articulating their plans and exposing those plans to formal critical scrutiny. Academic approval of plans provides an increase in confidence that their work-based projects are 'on the right lines' and confirmation that they, as successful professionals in their own right, can succeed in academe as well (Costley and Armsby, 2007; Gibbs et al., 2007).

Final project assessment procedures require candidates to make a formal presentation to an assessment panel and engage in discussion about points raised by examiners. There is acceptance of a wide variety of final outcomes proposed by the candidates as part of the basis for final assessment, such as professional project reports, book, policy documents, sets of guidelines and regulations describing programmes of action designed to achieve significant impact in the professional context. The methodological approach, the ethical considerations and the specifics of the final outcomes that define how candidates have played a unique role in implementing change, developing innovative approaches and creating sustainable solutions to complex issues are all key issues that have been the subject of on-going research (Doncaster, 2000; Lester, 2004; Costley and Gibbs, 2006; Costley and Armsby, 2008).

Emerging propositions and implications

Many candidates enter the programme to develop themselves in new ways of thinking that extend 'beyond [their] current community of practice' (Doncaster and Lester, 2002). They are already experts within their own professional sphere and know how to access familiar, paradigmatic professional and subject-based knowledge. The DProf provides the opportunity to develop learning in ways that have been differently described as trans-disciplinary learning (Gibbons et al., 1994; Barnett, 2000), horizontal learning (Bernstein, 1999), inter-connectivity (Antonacopoulou et al., 2005) generic, multidimensional and inter-professional learning. Certain features of learning and of context such as learner autonomy, individual development and work as the main context for learning are shown to contribute significantly to achievements on the programme, over and above those which are gained from the specialist activities of the candidates' research projects. This concurs with Malfroy and Yates (2003), who found that context, supervision and pedagogy, and knowledge production were the three key aspects that link doctoral education to the workplace.

Antonacopoulou (2004), in a tribute to the work of Argyris, focuses on his research on scholarship and reflection at work, and how he concludes that ultimately scholarship is personal and at its core entails a journey of self discovery. Antonacopoulou finds that some people take learning very seriously and not only as a phenomenon to be studied, but as a way of living. She later expanded on this with others (Antonacopoulou et al., 2005) to show that learning becomes a part of working life and that working and learning are both integral parts of life's journey. This thinking is seen in the way the DProf projects, because they are located in real-time working situations and take place in organisations or professional communities, are able to impact positively and be meaningful to the candidates.

DeFillippi (2001) sets out four perspectives on what he terms 'project-based learning', and these are then defined by different authors. The DProf provides a further perspective, adding different insights from an epistemologic approach that is derived from work-based learning that in turn has its roots in independent learning, social science and experiential learning. De Fillippi also discusses Raelin's (1997) presentation on designing action projects for work-based learning and recognises the 'growing body of evidence that projects may prove immensely beneficial to the long-term success of companies'. Raelin's findings correspond with the intentions of the DProf research and development project to influence organisations and/or professional fields.

Criticisms of project-based learning can be made in relation to its use of practitioner-based enquiry that '. . . is rooted in nature/nurture and macro/micro debates in social and behavioural science and in arguments about the nature of knowledge' (Murray and Lawrence, 2000: 18). Gathering data as an insider needs careful attention especially concerning ethical considerations, questions about insider bias and validity. This doctorate approaches the learning of doctoral candidates and the epistemologies that are followed from the perspective of bringing about original contributions to practice that are informed by underpinning knowledge. The purpose of the projects, to make actual change either during or at the end of the research practice, places particular constraints on researchers because they are working within systems where there are limits to research practice and change. Their experience and situatedness within their area of professional expertise is a necessary prerequisite for this kind of doctoral study. They need to access particular insider information, inform and bring about significant changes to practice. Their situation is important because there is usually a right time and place for innovation to be introduced. Successful projects may be in some part due to the practitioner-researchers' ability to negotiate around normative constraints, i.e. how they balance systemic norms with their creativity and ingenuity.

Gibbons et al.'s (1994) distinction between Mode 1 and Mode 2 knowledge, Scott et al. (2004) argue, is limited; more important, they argue, is 'the way universities understand and in the process construct relationships between academic and professional knowledge' (p. 42). On the evidence gathered from the DProf, relationships between the professional context and the university are forged by candidates themselves within a planning framework established by the university to assure the level of the final academic award. The candidates are able to build such a relationship because they have to justify to and agree their individual programme with both the university and their organisation or professional group. Gustavs and Clegg (2005) demonstrate that on a work-based learning programme the three-way partnership between candidate, university and organisation can become problematic and that much of individual and organisational learning is concerned with the appearance of having particular capabilities. Returning to the points made by Antonacopoulou (2004) regarding scholarship, it appears that the DProf places more emphasis on the individual's role in planning their own scholarship, albeit within a setting that is not an academic one, but with some degree of freedom to decide what is considered appropriate learning for their work. Of the five modes of knowledge presented by Scott et al. (2004), the contribution to knowledge made by the DProf would appear to be through the dispositional and transdisciplinary model in that it is 'essentially concerned with the individual and their own practice' (p. 51). The DProf programme resists 'methodological imperialism' (p. 48) in that individual programmes are distinctive in field and method. There appears to be a difference in the way candidates theorise their work as they call upon both professional and academic sources. As with Scott et al.'s (2004) definition, credibility in the DProf model comes from recognition amongst professional colleagues as much as academe.

Reflection upon current practice, evaluation of previous experience against doctorate level criteria and the adoption of a reflexive approach to their work are crucial aspects of the DProf. Self-development requires candidates to understand their professional selves in relation to personal self-understanding. Tennant (2004) suggests that the conception of the 'autonomous student' is becoming more like the 'enterprising self' in contemporary doctoral education and the DProf provides some support for this assertion. Having to build effective working relationships between themselves, their professional area and the university and justify their work, achievements and intentions to critical audiences in work and academe, promotes greater self-belief, wider acceptance amongst peers, intellectual skills and a commitment to continuing self-development in the context of their work. The self-management of the programme itself is a prime means of inducing self-managed learning. Debate about the learning process itself is of particular importance because of the growing awareness of the role of high-level personal or 'soft' skills and qualities in professional work (Eraut, 2004).

The pivotal role of learner control could be an additional aspect in Scott et al.'s (2004) dispositional model because a clear benefit for the candidate derives from the exercise of the candidate's sense of agency within critical environments and this comes primarily from the structure of the programme that supports and tests the exercise and outcomes of that agency. This primacy of the learner in managing the relationship between the university and the workplace was envisaged by Stephenson and Foster (1998). Eraut et al. (2004) found the importance of having confidence for mid-career learners and that confidence arose from meeting challenges at work, while the confidence to take on challenges depended on the support that was received. In the case of the DProf, those challenges are set in the demanding context of having to justify achievement and progress to critical partners in the wider profession and the less familiar world of academe. Boud and Lee (2005), in relation to the PhD, question what explicit pedagogy provides the opportunity for peer learning and they construct 'becoming a peer' as meaning becoming a member of the research community. For the DProf, 'becoming a peer' means becoming regarded as an active and acknowledged contributor to the development of the professional area. The support framework provided for doctoral learning is therefore of great importance to enable candidates from a variety of professional backgrounds to bring doctoral level learning to their differing contexts.

A trans-disciplinary approach can attract criticism of this kind of academic programme. PhDs and most professional doctorates are centred round a subject specialism and this is in keeping with conventional structures of universities. The transdisciplinary DProf is based on generic assessment criteria that do not require in-depth knowledge of a particular subject or body of knowledge that is necessarily held in a discipline. The abilities of the DProf candidates are judged upon broad, generic criteria that are directly related to practical, real-world outcomes. This approach is not embedded in university practices; university staff have not had an education in this way of learning and how to assess across disciplines and across professional roles (Boud and Tennant, 2006). There is no standard stock of external examiners that can be called upon to judge the outcomes of such programmes and there is little specific theoretical background in this area to conceptualise the field of study. Many academics are sceptical about trans-disciplinarity and cannot find the depth of substantive knowledge to satisfy their expectation of a thesis that makes a contribution to knowledge. The complexities of knowledge in practice underpinned by theory that are claimed for the DProf as being the essence of a doctoral project are not always understood as having an equivalence to the thesis that can be judged by experts from the disciplines.

There is some evidence, however, that in doctoral study it is not substantive knowledge that is later prized. For example, Pole (2000: 109) demonstrates that:

> the esoteric nature of the substantive knowledge gained was seen to be of limited use after the completion of the doctorate. In such cases the substantive

knowledge gained from the doctorate was seen as less important or valuable than other forms of knowledge and skills.

Conventional doctoral students' work is likely to be theoretically positioned within a disciplinary framework. The DProf and more recent forms of other doctoral programmes develop theory that arises from practice rather than being discipline-led. Some universities have found ways of drawing on the knowledge within their own institutions and from professional fields external to the university by reconsidering their regulations and systems, accessing people and resources from a whole university perspective rather than through schools or faculties. Universities have not historically taken form in a way that easily affords these kinds of arrangements and so constructing a programme like the DProf is as much a feat of organisation, leadership and organisational positioning as it is of curriculum development and innovation.

The success of the DProf and the benefits it brings to the field of doctoral learning appear to come from greater self-confidence, intellectual development and commitment to further self-development as well as significant 'new' professional learning where direct positive change is made in the candidates' organisation or professional field, confirming Scott et al.'s (2004: 158) claim that 'co-production of knowledge has the potential to enrich the workplace'. These benefits clearly overlap with and support the outcome of other kinds of doctorate. It might be that the DProf has simply found a way to enable this kind of outcome for a wider range of professional areas.

Conclusion

Candidates are the primary agents of control and the exercise of this agency within critical academic and professional environments is the basis of the impacts that the doctorate has upon both the individual and their workplace or professional area. The 'project of self' is therefore seen as a necessary undertaking that takes place in a localised setting which is distinguishable and where candidates have a certain positionality. The focus on this new 'impacting self' adds a particular slant to current debates about professional doctorates. The doctorate work involves processes that develop the practitioner, enhancing their abilities to manage and produce projects that can have potential impact on their organisation, that involves not just seeking to find out what works in what circumstances, but how to develop themselves as practitioners. DProf programmes are able to afford successful substantiation of capacity at doctorate level in both academic ability and professional expertise. The process is itself an important part of the outcome – scholarship based on one's self achievements, work engagement and own continuing development.

DProf programmes are characterised by a number of features such as gaining self-knowledge, and working collaboratively with others in an intricate and dynamic community of practice to create new learning and thus increase the essential resources of that community. We have seen engagement with abstract, human-related, previously undervalued knowledge. The knowledge created by synthesising diverse information has led to outcomes of real-time projects with tangible results that have a useful purpose within a responsible set of values and ethical considerations. Such diverse and critical thinking, group knowledge building, and open-ended processes where everything that will happen cannot be planned, can result in high-value learning.

The facility to offer enhanced opportunity and development to professional people and their organisations and/or professional fields involves utilising the valuable resources that higher education has to offer to engage fruitfully with practitioners in every field. Universities have to think across the disciplines in terms of structure and in terms of knowledge creation, recognition and use. The programmes offer a means to innovate and become creators and critical users of knowledge and thus to bring about change and make positive impact on professional practice. This is done by locating the focus of the programme within the context of work, external to the university whilst recognising and linking the critical thinking, research expertise and other hallmarks of academia with real-world issues confronting communities and professional areas.

References

Antonacopoulou, E. (2004) On the virtues of practising scholarship: a tribute to Chris Argyris, a 'timeless learner', *Management Learning*, 35(4): 381–395.

Antonacopoulou, E., Jarvis, P., Andersen, V., Elkjaer, B. and Høyrup, S. (2005) *Learning, Working and Living: Mapping the Terrain of Working Life Learning*, London: Palgrave.

Armsby, P., Costley, C. and Garnett, J. (2006) The legitimisation of knowledge: a work-based learning perspective of APEL, *International Journal of Lifelong Education*, 25(4): 369–383.

Barnett, R. (2000) *Realizing the University in an Age of Supercomplexity*, Buckingham: SRHE and Open University Press.

Bernstein, B. (1999) Vertical and horizontal discourse: an essay, *British Journal of Sociology of Education*, 20(2): 157–173.

Billett, S. (2006) Relational interdependence between social and individual agency in work and working life, *Mind, Culture and Activity*, 13(1): 53–69.

Boud, D. and Lee, A. (2005) 'Peer learning' as pedagogic discourse for research education, *Studies in Higher Education*, 30(5): 501–516.

Boud, D. and Solomon, N. (2001) *Work-based Learning: A New Higher Education?*, Buckingham: Society for Research into Higher Education and the Open University Press.

Boud, D. and Tennant, M. (2006) Putting doctoral education to work: challenges to academic practice, *Higher Education Research and Development*, 25(3): 293–306.

Costley, C. and Armsby, P. (2007) Research influences on a professional doctorate, *Research in Post-Compulsory Education*, 12(3): 343–355.

Costley, C. and Armsby, P. (forthcoming) Developing work-based learning at doctoral level, in J. Garnett, C. Costley and B. Workman (eds), *Taking Work Based Learning to the Core of Higher Education*, London: Middlesex University Press.

Costley, C. and Gibbs, P. (2006) Researching others: care as an ethic for practitioner researchers, *Studies in Higher Education*, 31(1): 89–98.

DeFillippi, R.J. (2001) Introduction: project-based learning, reflective practices and learning outcomes, *Management Learning*, 32(1): 5–10.

Doncaster, K. (2000) The Middlesex University Professional doctorate: a case study, *Continuing Professional Development*, 3(1): 1–6.

Doncaster, K. and Lester, S. (2002) Capability and its development: experiences from a work-based doctorate, *Studies in Higher Education*, 27(1): 91–101.

Doncaster, K. and Thorne L. (2000) Reflection and planning: essential elements of professional doctorates, *Reflective Practice*, 1(3): 391–399.

Eraut, M. (2004) Informal learning in the workplace, *Studies in Continuing Education*, 26(2): 247–273.

Eraut, M., Steadman, S., Furner, J., Maillardet, F., Miller, C. and Blackman, C. (2004) *Learning in the Professional Workplace: Relationships between Learning Factors and Contextual Factors*, Division I Paper Session, 12 April, AERA Conference, San Diego.

Gibbons, M., Limoges, C., Nowotny, H., Schwartzman, S., Scott, P. and Trow, M. (1994) *The New Production of Knowledge: The Dynamics of Science and Research in Contemporary Societies*, London: Sage.

Gibbs, P., Costley, C., Armsby, P. and Trakakis, A. (2007) Developing the ethics of worker-researchers through phronesis *Teaching in Higher Education*, 12(3): 365–375.

Glasgow Caledonian University (2007) Scottish Centre for Work Based Learning, Doctorate in Professional Practice, at: http://www.caledonian.ac.uk/scwbl/progs/pglf.html.

Gustavs, J. and Clegg, S. (2005) Working the knowledge game?, Universities and corporate organizations in partnership, *Management Learning*, 36(1): 9–30.

Learning Through Work (2007) http://www.learndirect-ltw.co.uk/ep/web/home/ltwhome/homepage/.

Lester, S. (2004) Conceptualising the practitioner doctorate, *Studies in Higher Education*, 29(6): 757–770.

Malfroy, J. and Yates, L. (2003) Knowledge in action: doctoral programmes forging new identities, *Journal of Higher Education Policy and Management* , 25(2): 119–129.

Middlesex University (2007) Institute for Work Based Learning, Doctorate in Professional Studies, at: http://www.mdx.ac.uk/wbl/courses/dprof/dprof.asp.

Murray, L. and Lawrence, B. (2000) The basis of critique of practitioner-based enquiry, in L. Murray and B. Lawrence (eds), *Practitioner-based Enquiry: Principles for postgraduate research,* London: Falmer Press, pp. 18–41.

Pole, C. (2000) Technicians and scholars in pursuit of the PhD: some reflections on doctoral study, *Research Papers in Education*, 15(1): 95–111.

QAA (2000) The framework for higher education qualifications in England, Wales and Northern Ireland, at: http://www.qaa.ac.uk/academicinfrastructure/FHEQ/background/ewni/2000/default.asp#annex1.

QAA (2005) Code of practice for the assurance of academic quality and standards in higher education, Section 1: Postgraduate research programmes, at: http://www.qaa.ac.uk/academicinfrastructure/codeofpractice/section1/postgrad2004.pdf.

Raelin, J.A. (1997) A model of work-based learning, *Organisation Science*, 8(6): 563–578.

Scott, D., Brown, A., Lunt, I. and Thorne, L. (2004) *Professional Doctorates: Integrating Professional and Academic Knowledge*, Buckingham: Society for Research into Higher Education and the Open University Press.

Stephenson, J. and Costley, C. (2007) The impact of a professional doctorate centred on the candidates' work, *Work Based Learning*, 1(1), at: http://test.cy-designs.com/middlesex.

Stephenson, J. and Foster, E. (1998) Work-based learning and universities in the UK: a review of current practice and trends, *Higher Education Research and Development*, 17(2): 155–170.

Stephenson J., Malloch, M. and Cairns, L. (2006) Managing their own programme: a case study of the first graduates of a new kind of doctorate in professional practice, *Studies in Continuing Education*, 28(1): 17–32.

Tennant, M. (2004) Doctoring the knowledge worker, *Studies in Continuing Education*, 26(3): 431–441.

Thorne, L.E. (2001) Doctoral level learning: customization for communities of practice, in B. Green, T. W. Maxwell and P. Shanahan (eds), *Doctoral Education and Professional Practice: The Next Generation*, Armidale: Kardoorair Press, pp. 247–274.

UKCGE (2002) Professional doctorates, at: http://www.ukcge.ac.uk/NR/rdonlyres/53BE34C8-EBDD-47E1-B1C7-F80B45D25E20/0/ProfessionalDoctorates2002.pdf.

Young, D. and Stephenson, J. (2007) The use of an interactive learning environment to support learning through work, in D. Young and J. Garnett (eds), *Work-based Learning Futures*, Bolton: University Vocational Awards Council.

Part IV

Policy and governance

Chapter 14

Doctoral education in risky times

Erica McWilliam

As any academic research manager will tell you, doctoral students *count*. They count in *intellectual terms* as contributors to a culture of research and scholarship, and they count literally as *performance indicators*, as quantifiable units of enrolments and timely completions. This naming of doctoral student as performance indicators (along with grants and publications) does a particular kind of work in the contemporary university, and it is the nature and purpose of this work that is elaborated in this chapter. In broad terms, I am interested in how the university becomes *visible and calculable* to itself as an efficient and effective higher education organisation – *how it performs itself to itself and others* as a 'quality institution'. In particular I am interested in the way *risk-consciousness* provides scripts for performing this task through the management of doctoral education.

What does performative mean?

I do not intend here to embark on a lengthy treatise on performativity a la Austin or Lyotard or Butler. Nor do I intend to elaborate on how these scholars differ in the ways that they understand and use the term 'performativity', because that would be a treatise in itself. However, I do intend, before moving to interrogate how doctoral education works as a performance indicator of higher education, to establish a few key premises about the notion of *performativity* drawn from all three authors.

In broad terms, *performatives* (i.e., what counts as needing to be performed and brought into being through being enacted or performed) are intelligible as effects produced out of a complex web of social relations that render them thinkable, sayable and doable. Counting *timeliness* as a measure of a high quality doctorate, for example, might well have been thought bizarre rather than desirable just a few decades ago when Margaret Mead's doctoral work was inspiring so many other doctoral students – rightly or wrongly – to engage in long-term ethnographic research in far-flung fields. Now timeliness has morphed from an ideal into a performed calculation, i.e., it is eminently thinkable and doable in the higher education sector. And as such it can have the effect of changing what doctoral students and their supervisors actually decide to do or not to do as higher degree research. The imperative to timeliness is inextricably caught up with the doctoral experience as a set of discrete units of time (Stage 1, pre-confirmation and so on), each of which is very important in signalling what is to be done when, how and by whom.

In saying this, I am not arguing that the requirement that doctorates be produced in a timely way is simply an effect of performativity. Good supervisors have always understood that it is in a candidate's interest to work efficiently towards an intended completion date. Financial and other pressures also militate against tardiness in relation to completion. So pragmatism on the part of supervisor and student may be just as productive in this sense as 'performativity'. Nevertheless, my interest is to focus on performativity as one powerful logic for changing how good supervision and good student-ing is being understood.

Performative acts are not wilful or arbitrary, but are acts performed *in* saying something, arising at a particular moment of historical time to constitute what is normal and acceptable practice. As normalising practices, performative acts do the work of excluding the 'unintelligible' as well as shoring up new practices that in other times might be impossible to think of. (For example, it is now being suggested in the UK that schools should be funded, at least in part, on the basis of their capacity to lower the mean Body Mass Index of their students, an idea/social practice that is still unthinkable in many quarters, but is working its way towards intelligibility.)

In computerised societies, performatives make it possible to commodify knowledge, 'exteriorising' it by moving it beyond particular knowers and particular knowledge domains. An example of this would be the way expert medical knowledge is standardised and routinised so that it can be used to diagnose, classify and treat generic categories of 'client', changing the focus of professional service from the client to *information about* the client. This makes it possible to supplant a wide range of arbitrary practices for managing individual clients (e.g., patients or students), by managing instead those aggregated *factors* which are deemed most liable to be effective in delivering organisational targets. Categories like mature-aged, part-time, international, low SES are examples of aggregates that are applied to doctoral candidacy and that do a particular kind of work in framing students as more or less 'problematic'. An effect of this performative work, according to Robert Castel (1991), is the mutation of the practitioner–client relationship (or in terms of doctoral education, the supervisor–student relationship) into a relationship with a flow of exteriorised client information. Put another way, the direct relation with the assisted subject that has characterised classical forms of treatment is transmuted into a relationship of *practitioner-to-information*. Castel elaborates:

> The essential component of intervention no longer takes the form of the direct face-to-face relationship between the . . . professional and the client. It comes instead to reside in the establishing of *flows of population* based on the collation of a range of abstract factors deemed liable to produce risk in general. . . . These items of information are then stockpiled, processed and distributed along channels completely disconnected from those of professional practice, using in particular the medium of computerized data handling.
>
> (Castel, 1991: 281, 293, emphasis original)

Castel's theorising, focused as it is on changing practices in the field of mental medicine, imagines the real possibility of the 'client-as-case' continuing to have a life of its own well beyond and outside the death of the patient's body. The 'real' and most important relationship in terms of managing services to the client is with the growing body of information *about* the client. This helps me to understand how my own doctor has come to spend so little time looking at me when I have an appointment and so much time looking at her computer screen. She 'knows' me better as screen-accessible information and can add to and learn from that knowledge store by focusing on the screen. This does not mean that she cares less about me (although I find this somewhat irritating in terms of interpersonal exchange!) – on the contrary – it is because she understands the importance of 'knowing all about me' that she so seldom makes eye contact.

This mutation of social relations between doctoral experts and their 'clients' is increasingly evident, I would argue, in the university. It is now both normal and acceptable for good supervisors to pay close attention to the range of abstract factors that, when taken together, define a student/client as a case of (more or less) potential risk – risk of failing the course, of wasting university resources, of producing poor quality research). Through statistical correlations of heterogeneous elements, supervisors are, as indicated earlier, invited to differentiate our student population categories (off-campus, on-line), and so determine the modality or intervention that is commensurate with the risks deemed to be associated with that population category. We are still expected to 'know' our students. It is what counts as 'knowing' them that is changed by these performative acts of research management within the university. I am not arguing that we are prevented from having pleasant social relationships with our students. It is simply that the relationship that counts in the management of doctoral education is with student information. This relationship is one we perform through acts of stock-piling and reading data – it is not about what passes privately or in confidence between student and supervisor. What passes privately does not need to be made visible unless it comes forward as alleged misconduct. In general terms warmth, empathy and so on do not count, except when mentioned in student evaluations. I am not arguing that we ought to forget about these aspects of supervision, merely that we should not expect to be acknowledged for them in the management records of the university. Of course, if we are awarded 'Supervisor of the Year', then that makes possible another performative event.

Performing (risk) management

Where has all this come from – or, in performativity terms, how has this new relationship with *flows of information* become thinkable as effective doctoral education practice? To explore this question, we need to understand the political and moral climate of our historical times, and how this climate produces particular logics for managing the organisation. According to Anthony Giddens (2002) and Ulrich Beck (1992), organisational life at the turn of this century is characterised by *risk-consciousness*, a negative logic that shifts attention away from the management and distribution of material/industrial 'goods' to the management and distribution of 'bads', i.e. to the control of knowledge about what can go wrong and what systems are needed to guard against such a possibility.

All social organisations, including universities, are now risk organisations. This is because all organisations need rational systems for calculating and managing threats to viability and reputation in whatever form they may come. In her anthropological studies of social and cultural life, Mary Douglas argues that risk is no longer about the probability of losses and gains – risk simply means *danger*. She states:

> The modern risk concept, parsed now as danger, is invoked to protect individuals against encroachments of others. It is part of the system of thought that upholds the type of individualist culture which sustains an expanding industrial system.
>
> (Douglas, 1992: 7)

As a logic of organisational management, risk-consciousness serves the 'forensic needs' (ibid.) of a new and expanding global culture which demands alertness to the danger of not performing in ways that are morally and politically acceptable, as well as economically viable.

This negative connotation of 'risk' runs counter to the logic that characterised its historic emergence in pre-capitalist times. According to Bernstein (1998), 'risk' evoked a condition of excited anticipation in relation to sixteenth-century seafaring, a more positive connotation than the modern notion of risk as hazard minimisation. As Giddens (2002: 22) reminds us, the modernist notion of risk – of 'hazards that are actively assessed in relation to future possibilities' – is one that could only be thought after magic, cosmology and the fates had given way to the sort of scientific calculation that gave rise to forecasting, book-keeping and insurance. What we have witnessed in more recent times is a shift from risk as 'tak[ing] a chance' to risk as 'cold calculation' (Keynes, in Bernstein, 1998: 12). According to Giddens (2002: 29), this modernist climate of cold, calculated risk is 'marked by a push and pull between accusations of scaremongering on the one hand, and of cover-ups on the other.' The push and pull of risk is evidenced both within and outside organisational life, with claims and counter-claims constituting certain matters as more or less 'risky' or certain people as more or less 'at risk'. This does not mean that risk-as-danger is not 'real'. Rather, it means that risk-consciousness as a moral climate of cold calculation is now an undisputed logic for thinking social and organisational good.

Risk-management-as-risk-minimisation has become a high priority, institution-wide system of communication in all Western organisations, including universities. While in theory one might expect risk management seminars to invite risk-taking, as well as risk minimisation, in practice risk management and risk minimisation have become synonymous.

Although the logic of risk management has been characterised as negative, it does not present as a negative, re-framed as it is through its articulation as effective institutional policy and practice. As 'a system of regulatory measures intended to shape who can take what risks and how' (Pidgeon et al., 1992: 136), risk management comes couched in the language of efficiency and good governance. It comes to us as 'developmental knowledge' (Hobart, 1993) that we apply for our own good and the good of our students. As developmental knowledge, it is couched 'predominantly in the idiom of economics, technology and management' (p. 2), rather than the idiom of academic, theoretical or disciplinary knowledge, drawing on conceptual models that are 'generalisable or appear to offer the greatest predictability or the semblance of control over events' (p. 9). Because publicly-funded organisations like universities need to manage reputation as vigorously as they manage their internal processes, they 'have to work within pre-established guidelines and assume that particular conditions fit a general mould' (p. 9). In Vitebsky's (1993) terms, this involves utilising models of management that 'apply . . . to everywhere and nowhere, everybody and nobody' (p. 100).

The mobilisation of risk minimisation through economic, technological and management knowledge is occurring, not coincidentally, at a time when Western governments are re-positioning themselves as buyers of education services rather than patrons of education. In the new educational market, 'post-welfare' universities are scrambling to demonstrate their utility to any and all potential sponsors. This means, among other things, a new vision of the university and its management, which demands, in turn, the denunciation of traditionally accepted forms of organisation (du Gay, 1994). As social organisations, universities have been called upon to 're-vision' themselves as workplaces with much to learn from 'studies of other businesses' about the relation between employees' attitudes and company performance (Ramsden, 1998: 39). A key proposition here is that universities 'are not intrinsically different from other organisations' (op. cit.) and so the generic language of good business practice is, it goes without saying, always applicable.

Once this proposition comes to count as true, then much can flow from it in terms of the changing culture of the university into a business model, in which all inputs and throughputs must be calculable. In some senses, doctoral education may be understood as the last bastion of a monastic order protected or hidden from this managerial logic. Much of the pedagogical work of doctoral supervision has been conducted in private spaces (like the professor's office) far from the harsh glare of public scrutiny. However, once a funding model like Australia's Research Training Scheme puts dollar values against inputs and throughputs, then it becomes increasingly impossible to think arbitrary, idiosyncratic and drawn out candidature as good doctoral education practice. With doctoral education laid out on the forensic table of accountability, it becomes possible – indeed, necessary – to identify those doctoral practices that are ripe for risk management. The good academic in a good (i.e. risk-conscious) university comes to share with other 'learning managers' an 'attentional economy' (Taylor, 2005) that is focused on minimizing risk to the institution, and is therefore plugged into the burgeoning systems of accountability that are now being used to 'diagnose, classify and treat' (Ericson and Haggerty, 1997: 104) doctoral students (see also McWilliams et al., 2005).

Risk and audit

The 'audit explosion' (Strathern, 1997) that has been occurring for some time now in higher education management is evidence of this imperative at work, not just in doctoral education but in all levels of the university as a risk-conscious organisation. As Marilyn Strathern (1997, 2000) explains, the audit culture works to defend against systemic arbitrariness, applying mechanisms designed to ensure organisational precision for coping with social imprecision. The logic, Strathern argues, is that systems of management need to be uniform because individuals are not, nor are they likely to be. While the audit explosion may have depersonalising effects, the logic of the intensive bureaucratic monitoring that characterises audit culture is not, according to Strathern, 'one-size-fits-all' in terms of the individuals who are its 'products'. What is standard is the particular model for measuring organisational performance. This allows us to speak of 'individual differences' being catered for at the same time that we aggregate large sets of student risk management data in league tables and similar comparative data systems. In this way each university can perform its own effectiveness in performing its accountability to itself as well as to external others.

While few would deny the importance of an ethic of public accountability, it is important to understand what else has been made thinkable through the logic of audit-as-risk-minimisation. The rise of a public demand for waste identification and eradication does more than require accountability. As Alan Lawson (1999: 11) points out, it frames higher education in general as a 'scarce' resource rather than as available to the many:

> Because higher education is valued, it is potentially a commodity. But it is only a commodity worth paying for if it can be made to seem scarce. Once it is scarce it can be competed for, accounted for, and subjected to audits that will inevitably disclose how those scarce resources are being wasted . . . higher degree education . . . has been redefined as a 'scarce' commodity which we can ill-afford to 'waste'.

Lawson argues that conflations of higher degree student data relating to attrition and completion rates make the entire field vulnerable to accusations of waste. Crucially, he indicates that such accusations, once made, continue to be abetted by claims about the irrelevance of much higher degree study and employer dissatisfaction with higher degree graduates (op. cit.). His argument draws attention to the way the performing of effective risk minimisation in higher education works as a tactic for de-limiting what individual universities, and the sector itself, will be allocated. Universities are under greater pressure to consider cutting back on certain services and functions and this logic is utilised for making decisions about whether and how those cutbacks get operationalised. Governments certainly can and do 'interfere' directly in the internal workings of performative universities, but much of the activity attributed to government interference is in fact an effect of risk-minimisation policy in action. In general terms, and with some exceptions, funding flows to those universities that are seen to be the most effective performers, with effective performance being framed by standard measures of 'productivity'. The logic here is thoroughly rational: the stronger the quality case, the more funding can be anticipated. So the negative logic of risk gets translated and made palatable through the positive logic of quality, excellence and productivity.

It is important to understand that there is no space 'outside' this logic – it is a condition of un-freedom within which all publicly-funded universities do their daily work.

And increasingly that work is to require at every level the sort of tough self-regulation that can identify 'waste' and guard against declining standards. In terms of doctoral education, 'waste' can be identified indirectly through the identification of apparently frivolous thesis topics. Journalists on the hunt for evidence of this sort are unlikely to read beyond an abstract, or indeed a title, in asserting their suspicions that frivolity is alive and well and living in doctoral programs.

This does not mean that there are no competing logics. Journalists may also be on the look-out for stories about triumphing over adversity; students may be voting with their feet towards some courses and away for others regardless of the relevance of certain programs (e.g. forensic science) to employability; and academics may continue to ignore compliance requests and retain their jobs. However, we do know that the university is under pressure to be seen to be performing itself intelligently and efficiently, and this means that anything that smacks of indulgence or frivolity is fair game.

It comes as no surprise that the bulk of media accusations of doctoral frivolity or inappropriateness target the humanities in general and cultural studies in particular. Some such allegations have gone as far as to pit an apparently serious, weighty and industry-relevant doctoral research against apparently vapid and ephemeral scholarship. For example, 'Super PhD loses out to blondes and vampires' (*Sun Herald*, 13 July 2003, p. 15) frames a 'boring though worthy' PhD about superannuation being written by a 'talented commerce graduate' as losing out to 'a PhD about the supposed homosexuality of Jesus', 'the desirability . . . of blondes', 'Tattoos', 'the divorce of Nicole Kidman and Tom Cruise', the 'neo-spiritualism of Wonder Woman and Xena, Warrior Princess', the 'surf culture of Bali' and 'vampires' (ibid.). Once this is set against claims about the costs of public education (e.g. in the *Sun Herald* article, the list of unworthy topics above precedes the assertion that there are currently '1550 Australian Postgraduate Awards at a cost of $87 million'), the whole sector stands accused of mismanagement and/or cover-up, and the push and pull around whether or not doctoral education as an area in need of risk management becomes a public matter.

Risk 'events'

Every allegation of this type, once made in the public domain, does the work of a 'risk event' (Kasperson et al., 1998), with serious implications for the individuals or departments involved and for university management in general, especially if it is alleged to be 'typical' of universities in general or even of a sub-set of universities. The problem is exacerbated if the accusations follow close on the heels of similar allegations or negative reports about the activities of the sector.

The fact that a risk event has occurred does not mean that the allegation is true, but it does mean trouble for the university as an organisation. Risk events work both as 'a scientific activity and an expression of culture' (Kasperson et al., 1998: 149). According to Kasperson et al., a risk event is usually 'specific to a particular time and location', but comes to 'interact with psychological, social and cultural processes' so as to 'heighten or attenuate public perceptions of risk and related risk behaviour' (p. 150). Any allegation of inappropriateness, then, gains the status of a risk event if and when it interacts with other socio-cultural processes to produce behaviours that serve to increase the perceived danger to the organisation, triggering demands for 'additional organizational response and protective actions or impeding needed protective actions' (op. cit.). Thus, for example, if there is already widespread public anxiety about the labour market in general, and for 'degreed' professional workers in particular, an allegation of impropriety (like a false claim to have a PhD) is likely to have a more powerful impact both outside and within the sector under scrutiny. Moreover, any further pushes and pulls are likely to generate new risks for the sector, as risk loops back upon itself in a double play, proliferating the actions and reactions that constitute its management.

An interesting case in point is the 'CCTV voyeur scandal' at the University of Warwick (see Williams, 2005). The university attempted to attend to the risk of the less-than-satisfactory security that existed for students who were campus residents. After installing security cameras, it received allegations from student residents that the cameras had allowed individual members of the security staff to engage in voyeuristic activity. The risk event escalated further when staff members who were 'caught zooming security cameras into students' rooms' accused the university of 'bullying' them into resignation during the inquiry into this allegation. Allegations of a 'cover-up' created yet another problem for university managers, who chose not to 'complicate the issue' by informing the 'victims', who were 'now in their latter years of study'. For managers seeking to do the least reputational and personal harm, the on-going challenges were not inconsiderable. Whether they chose a course of action or inaction, the university continued to be 'at risk', with each new action generating a further set of 'risk-minimisation' responses that produced new organisational risks.

Risky doctorates

Doctoral education has a special place in university risk management, because of the fact that the doctorate is the flagship degree of any university, and it should, according to insiders and outsiders, be above reproach in terms of processes and outcomes. When a 'doctoral' risk event occurs, it may well reinforce the myth that standards have fallen from a once glorious and inviolate place. Yet it takes only a limited foray into the doctorate's shady past to see that the doctorate, far from being inviolate, has always been from its inception a risky and flawed enterprise for universities.

At the turn of the twentieth century, for example, it was deemed within the academy that original investigation, the art and science of true research, would never be forthcoming from 'mere training' of the sort that was represented by the PhD (Rae, 2002). For Hoyle and others of his time, training could only mean 'damage to originality that slavish pursuit of [a] degree has caused' (Hoyle, cited in Rae, 2002: 131). The PhD remained suspect for decades in terms of its legitimacy as an induction into the mysterious and tightly bounded world called 'research'. 'Training-in-originality' was deemed to be oxymoronic by many distinguished persons within the academy. As a teaching qualification in earlier times, the doctorate also suffered from the fact that 'bribery was by no means unknown' (Haskins, 1963: 230) in its conferral.

This history is conveniently absent when high protestant appeals are made in the name of shoring up the standards that used to be so squeaky clean. Such appeals, evident in media reports, such as 'Thesis preaches gay gospel on Jesus' (*Hobart Mercury*, 29 May 2003, p. 2), 'Cappuccino courses not Nelson's cup of tea' (*South China Morning Post*, 25 October 2003, p. 2), and '"Silly" degrees face the chop' (*Sunday Herald Sun*, 19 October 2003, p. 1), reiterate the same claims about falling standards using the same doctoral theses to support such claims. 'Gay Jesus' is a notable example, working as both a signifier of silliness and a symptom of post-Christian moral decay. As a 'whacky subject' (*South China Morning Post*, 25 October 2003, p. 2) it evokes a broader problem of 'bizarre degrees' (*Sunday Herald Sun*, 19 October 2003, p. 1), now being undertaken in universities that are 'silly enough to offer a particular course ...' (ibid.).

While academic insiders might well bemoan this as another threat to academic freedom, it cannot be ignored in a performative organisational context. It must be risk managed to mitigate the negative effects on the doctoral program, the faculty, the university and the sector. In the case of the 'Gay Jesus' risk event, academics reacted by 'warn[ing] against students being banned from freedom of thought' (*Sunday Herald Sun*, 19 October 2003, p. 1), while a political opponent of the then federal minister declared the accusation to be 'an astounding attack on academic freedom' (ibid.). However, the push and pull is not a once-off moment. Once it has developed momentum, it can have a life of its own, much like that of the patient whose body has died but whose case can have a life of its own.

Risk as 'softness'

A similar push and pull has been evident around allegations of 'soft' or 'dumbed down' doctoral programs in general. It goes without saying that 'silly' doctorates would, ipso facto, be vulnerable to charges of 'softness'. But 'softness' is an allegation that extends its reach beyond dubious research topics. Accusations of 'soft marking' in the Australian media, e.g. 'Failed students make the grade' (*The Courier Mail*, 3 February 2001, p. 1), 'Universities' testing times' (*The Advertiser*, 10 February 2001, p. 67), 'Marking inquiry exposes glitches' (*The Australian*, 6 June 2001, p. 23), 'Unis get poor marks for evaluation practices' (*The Australian*, 27 June 2001, p. 31) tend to target one alleged instance, but implicate all public universities in 'perpetuating a fraud' (*The Courier Mail*, 3 February 2001, p. 1), and thereby abusing the public trust that is made tangible in government funding.

Such allegations, when they appear, do a particular kind of work in identifying certain client groups as 'riskier' than others in terms of the extent to which they threaten 'standards'. An often reiterated connection continues to be drawn, for example between 'soft marking' in Australian universities and 'exclusive, fee-paying overseas students' (*The Courier Mail*, 3 February 2001, p. 1). Allegations that 'Students' free ride unis "favour fee-payers"' (*Herald Sun*, 16 May 2001, p. 29), in a way that constitutes a 'dark side to export boom' (*The Australian* 20 June 2001, p. 34) in Australian higher education, have prompted media questions such as, 'Are international students getting a better deal?' (*Australian Financial Review*, 13 September 2003, p. 19).

Once universities are called on to 'Lift uni standards . . .' (*Australian Financial Review,* 27 October 2003, p. 1) in response to the issue of 'softness' in relation to overseas students, they are quick to shore up against reputational damage. When challenged in relation to this issue, the University of New South Wales, for example, quickly provided an assurance that the 'enforcement of English language requirements for international students [would] . . . be tightened', in line with 'toughened written English requirements' (*The Australian,* 6 June 2001, p. 23). What the sector cannot afford is to have accusations of special 'soft marking' deals for 'exclusive, fee-paying overseas students' stick, but nor can it risk any loss of income for the university sector if this highly profitable client market is threatened. When doctoral programs are implicated in 'softness' allegations of this sort, the problem is compounded because of the status that such a program has as the most prestigious in the university.

Performing doctoral education

What the above discussion has attempted to flesh out is the way that risk works as a script for thinking, speaking and doing doctoral education. It interrogates the conditions under which doctoral education 'offers itself to be, necessarily, thought' (Foucault, 1985: 11). In so doing, it draws attention to what counts as effective management and supervision of doctoral students, and what counts as a 'good' doctorate. In framing doctoral education as a risk-conscious performance, I have foregrounded some 'prescriptive texts . . . that elaborate rules, opinions and advice as to how to behave as one should' (ibid.: 12), when one is engaged in doctoral education in the academy. My argument is that the scripts that are produced out of risk as a contemporary managerial logic allow all those engaged in this complex work to 'question their own conduct, to watch over and give shape to it, and to shape themselves as ethical subjects' (p. 13). In other words, the proper comportment of the academic supervisor is to take on the moral ethical responsibility of risk-conscious management.

In naming risk as a key imperative in doctoral education I am not arguing for or against this development. It is the condition in which we perform doctoral education, rather than a problem to be solved. This does not mean that we should swallow it in bird-throat fashion. We do need to pay attention to the ironies that attend any set of practices that purport to 'deliver us from evil', and that includes risk-consciousness.

G. K. Chesterton (1909) cautions that 'the real trouble with this world of ours is not that it is an unreasonable world, nor even that it is a reasonable one. The commonest kind of trouble is that it is *nearly reasonable* but not quite' (p. 149). When totally reasonable systems are put in place to manage nearly reasonable people, charming absurdities are pretty much inevitable. Risk both enables and constrains what academics pay attention to, and how we understand what it means to be an effective teacher or researcher. Both friend *and* foe, enabler *and* constrainer, risk is everyone's business.

References

Beck, U. (1992) *Risk Society: Towards a New Modernity*, London: Sage.

Bernstein, P.L. (1998) *Against the Gods: The Remarkable Story of Risk*, New York: John Wiley.

Castel, R. (1991) From dangerousness to risk, in G. Burchell, C. Gordon and P. Miller (eds), *The Foucault Effect: Studies in Governmentality*, London: Harvester Wheatsheaf, pp. 281–298.

Chesterton, G.K. (1909) *Orthodoxy*, New York: Lore Press (reprinted by Greenwood Press, Westgport, 1774, pp. 147–150).

Douglas, M. (1992) *Risk and Blame*, London: Routledge.

du Gay, P. (1994) Making up managers: bureaucracy, enterprise and the liberal art of separation. *British Journal of Sociology*, 45(4): 655–674.

Ericson, R.V. and Haggerty, K.D. (1997) *Policing the Risk Society*, Toronto: University of Toronto Press.

Foucault, M. (1985) *The Use of Pleasure: The History of Sexuality, Volume 2*, translated by Robert Hurley. London: Penguin.

Giddens, A. (2002) *Runaway World: How Globalisation is reshaping our lives*, London: Profile Books.

Haskins, C.H. (1963) *The Rise of Universities*, Ithaca, NY: Great Seal Books, Cornell Press.

Hobart, M. (ed.) (1993) *An Anthropological Critique of Development: The Growth of Ignorance*, London: Routledge.

Lawson, A. (1999) From West to waste through dirty data, *Campus Review*, April 7–13, p. 11.

Kasperson, R.E., Renn, O., Slovic, P., Brown, H.S., Emel, J., Goble, R., Kasperson, J.X. and Ratick, S. (1998) The importance of the media and the social amplification of risk, in R.E. Lofstedt and L. Frewer (eds), *The Earthscan Reader in Risk and Modern Society*, London: Earthscan Publications, pp.149–180.

McWilliam, E., Lawson, A., Evans, T. and Taylor, P.G. (2005) Silly, soft and otherwise suspect: doctoral education as risky business, *Australian Journal of Education*, 49(2): 214–227.

Pidgeon, N., Hood, C.C., Jones, D., Turner, B. and Gibson, R. (1992) Risk perception, in *Risk Analysis, Perception and Management*, London: The Royal Society, pp. 89–134.

Rae, I.D. (2002) False start for the PhD in Australia, *Historical Records of Australian Science*, 14: 129–141.

Ramsden, P. (1998) Out of the wilderness, *The Australian*, 29 April, pp. 39–41.

Strathern, M. (1997) 'Improving ratings': audit in the British University system, *European Review*, 5(3): 305–321.

Strathern, M. (2000) The tyranny of transparency, *British Educational Research Journal*, 26(3): 310–323.

Taylor P.G. (2005) Managing our attentional economy in a changing landscape: complexity, learning and leadership, keynote presentation at QTU's Leadership – The Changing Landscape Conference for Educational Administrators, Brisbane Convention and Exhibition Centre, 19 August.

Vitebsky, P. (1993) Is death the same everywhere: contexts of knowing and doubting, in M. Hobart (ed.), *An Anthropological Critique of Development: The Growth of Ignorance*, London: Routledge, pp. 100–115.

Williams, C. (2005) Cover up revealed after two security guards were forced out for using cameras to spy on bedrooms, Warwick Boar, 27 September, at: http://www.warwickboar.co.uk/boar/news/cctv_voyeur_scandal/.

Chapter 15

New challenges in doctoral education in Europe[1]

Alexandra Bitusikova

The development of higher education and science in Europe has been influenced by two major initiatives in recent years: the Bologna process, leading to the creation of the European Higher Education Area (EHEA) and the Lisbon Strategy, aiming at building the European Research Area (ERA). Both initiatives have had a significant impact on doctoral education that is seen as the bridge between the two processes.

The Bologna process started in 1999 as an inter-governmental process that aimed to develop, guide and promote reforms in higher education, involving small and large countries within Europe. It has quite rapidly broadened and evolved its geographical scope, as well as areas of activities. It is remarkable that, despite the fact that higher education is an area of national sovereignty and differs from country to country, the commitment of European education ministers towards harmonisation of higher education in the framework of the Bologna process has remained strong. The European Commission was initially just a distant observer, but its role as a leading supporting partner has increased in recent years. Forty-six countries are now members of the Bologna process. They include countries from west and east, north and south, countries that have had a long history of the continuous development of higher education as well as countries that less than two decades ago became free from Communist rule and joined the European mainstream. The Bologna process became an influential instrument for promoting reforms of higher education all over Europe. Increasingly, the process has had an impact beyond Europe, especially in patterns and flows of international student and staff mobility, degree structures, and increasing global competition and co-operation both in education and research.

In the early stages, the Bologna process had concentrated on structuring university studies in two cycles of higher education – the Bachelors and the Masters phases. It was only at the meeting of education ministers in Berlin in 2003 (the Berlin Communiqué) that it was agreed to extend the process to the third cycle – the Doctoral phase. This step strengthened the link between the higher education and research missions of universities in Europe, initiating further discussions about the necessity of reforms in the training of young researchers and the importance of enhancing their career opportunities.

The inclusion of doctoral education in the Bologna process has followed, and been closely related to, the policy objectives of the European Union Lisbon Strategy (2000) to make Europe the most competitive knowledge-based economy and society by increasing the number of researchers and enhancing research capacity, innovation and economic growth. Doctoral education can be viewed as a cornerstone in meeting these ambitious objectives. Europe needs a sustainable supply of highly qualified and committed researchers with doctoral degrees, capable of working in different sectors of the economy. At the same time, it has to face the challenge of demographic stagnation, the decreasing interest of young people in research careers and growing global competition for the best academic talent. These pressures are the main drivers of change in doctoral education. The changing demands on the number of researchers and their broader, more flexible profile have triggered a significant re-thinking of doctoral education in Europe.

European universities, as key knowledge-intensive institutions awarding doctoral degrees, play a crucial role in the process of doctoral education reform. In recent years they have been deeply involved in a series of debates and projects initiated by the European University Association (EUA), the main independent representative body of higher education institutions in Europe. In this process, EUA has co-operated also with other stakeholders – national education ministries, the Bologna Follow-Up Group, organisations of students and young researchers (ESU and EURODOC), other university and research associations and the European Union institutions, mainly the European Commission and the European Parliament.

Promoting closer links between the European Higher Education and Research Areas, as a means of strengthening Europe's research capacity, and improving the quality and attractiveness of European higher education, has become a major priority for the European University Association (EUA Graz Declaration 2003). Since 2003, the EUA has developed a framework for intense discussions on the development and future direction of doctoral programmes. The main objective of all EUA initiatives has been to promote the exchange of examples of good practice and to encourage institutional, national and European co-operation in the development of doctoral education.

Results of EUA doctoral debates and projects have fed into the Bologna policy dialogue and the formulation of recommendations for the conference of education ministers held in Bergen in 2005. At this meeting, the ministers stated:

> ... doctoral level qualifications need to be fully aligned with the EHEA overarching framework for qualifications using the outcomes-based approach. The core component of doctoral training is the advancement of knowledge through original research. Considering the need for structured doctoral programmes and the need for transparent supervision and assessment, we note that the normal workload of the third cycle in most countries would correspond to 3–4 years full time. We urge universities to ensure that their doctoral programmes promote interdisciplinary training and the development of transferable skills, thus meeting the needs of the wider employment market. We need to achieve an overall increase in the numbers of doctoral candidates taking up research careers within the EHEA. We consider participants in third cycle programmes both as students and as early stage researchers.
>
> (Communiqué of the Conference of European Ministers
> Responsible for Higher Education, 2005: 4)

The EUA was given a mandate to continue in debates on the further development of doctoral education in Europe and to prepare a report to be presented to ministers at the meeting in London in 2007. The following sections present the results of recent university discourse on the trends in doctoral education in Europe organised by EUA.

Achievements

The first and most obvious conclusion to make from all European debates on doctoral education, is that there is a considerable diversity of organising doctoral education not only across different countries within Europe, but also across different universities within the same country, across different faculties and institutes within the same university, and across different disciplines. Diversity of education and research traditions in Europe can be considered a strength, but it can also lead to fragmentation if it is not managed properly. The Bologna process may be a useful tool for managing diversity of doctoral education traditions. Its objective is harmonisation (not uniformity) achieved through different routes within a common framework (Chambaz et al., 2006).

The third cycle – the doctoral phase – is seen as a crucial part of the Bologna process. However, it differs markedly from the first and second cycles. What makes it specific is that the predominant and most crucial component of the doctorate is research. Originality of research remains the characteristic feature of the doctorate. Universities have to recognise their responsibility to offer doctoral candidates a high quality training to develop their research skills based on doing research, but also to organise courses teaching transferable skills preparing young researchers for their careers in different sectors. The doctorate of today is not based purely on curiosity-driven research as it used to be in the past, but it is often driven also by the needs of stakeholders including governments, industry and commerce – 'real world needs' as described by Taylor and Beasley (2005: 11).

Structure and organisation of doctoral education in Europe

The choice of the most appropriate organisational structures of doctoral education has been one of the key questions in all of the debates in universities across Europe. Organisational structures must demonstrate added value for the institution and for doctoral candidates: to improve transparency, quality, and admission and assessment procedures; and to create synergies regarding transferable skills development. Individual study programmes based on a traditional model of a working alliance between the doctoral candidate and the supervisor without a structured coursework phase, often called an apprenticeship model, are being increasingly questioned and criticised as being inappropriate to meet challenges of training for multiple careers in a global labour market. However, in some disciplines (mainly in social sciences and humanities) individual study programmes are still a prevalent model.

Recent developments, and an analysis of practice across Europe, point to an increasing tendency in many European countries towards structured programmes, with doctoral candidates grouped in doctoral/graduate/research schools. The EUA TRENDS V Report (Crosier et al., 2007) shows that 30 per cent of European higher education institutions surveyed say they have established some kind of doctoral, graduate or research school. This question was also asked in the survey of Bologna process member countries carried out in 2006.[2] Out of the 37 countries that responded, 16 reported that their institutions have introduced doctoral, graduate or research schools alongside existing models, such as traditional individual training or 'stand-alone' structured doctoral programmes. This tendency reflects the need to achieve a critical mass of doctoral candidates and to create an active and internationally recognised research environment which stimulates research co-operation at regional, national and international levels. At the same time it is believed that organisation of doctoral education in a structured way can reduce completion time to degree and increase completion rates.

Two main organisational structures emerge in Europe as vehicles for promoting high quality and internationally oriented doctoral studies:

- *Graduate school* – an organisational structure that includes doctoral candidates and often also Masters students. It provides administrative, development and transferable skills development support, organises admission, courses and seminars, and takes responsibility for quality assurance.
- *Doctoral/research school* – an organisational structure that includes only doctoral students. It may be organised around a particular discipline, research theme or a cross-disciplinary research area and/or it is focused on creating a research group/ network and is project-driven. It may involve one institution or several institutions and organise co-operation among them.

Duration of doctoral programs

Duration has become a subject of closer investigation only in recent decades, mainly as a consequence of governments' scrutiny of public spending. It is an important issue in relation to the funding of doctoral candidates and doctoral programmes. Full-time doctoral programmes in Europe are usually of three to four years' duration; part-time studies take longer. In most countries, however, time to degree (TTD) tends to be longer (sometimes much longer) than the average duration of funding for doctoral candidates and programmes. In addition, only about half of doctoral candidates complete their education with a doctorate (Taylor and Beasley, 2005: 10). As Golde (2000) points out, 'the most academically capable, most academically successful, most stringently evaluated and most carefully selected students in the entire higher education system – doctoral students – (were the) least likely to complete their chosen academic goals' (Golde, 2000: 199, cited in Taylor and Beasley, 2005: 10). These alarming data suggest that it is increasingly important for universities to monitor carefully the development of time to degree and also completion rates. According to the EUA survey from 2006 (Doctoral Programs in Europe's Universities: Achievements and Challenges, 2007), only 18 Bologna countries monitor the completion rate of doctoral candidates. Experience in North America, but also in some European countries, shows that monitoring and improving completion rates can be done more successfully within the graduate, doctoral or research school structures.

Supervision, monitoring and assessment

The question of supervision, monitoring and assessment of doctoral candidates' progress as an important measure of quality of doctoral programmes has been a major topic of discussion for universities. Recent debates at universities and with representatives of the doctoral candidates' organisation, EURODOC, but also several national evaluation reports, show that there is a great need to improve standards of supervision and to develop new supervision practices in doctoral training.

As examples from a number of universities suggest, arrangements based upon a transparent contract of shared responsibilities and rights signed by the doctoral candidate, the supervisor and the institution is good practice. More and more attention is paid to the introduction of multiple supervision arrangements in order to improve transparency and fairness of supervision. It should be encouraged at international and inter-sectoral level through tutoring and co-tutoring by supervisors from academic and research institutions, but also non-academic organisations (such as industry and commerce) in different European countries.

In the light of the reform of doctoral education responding to changes in the global labour market, the role of the supervisor is changing, too. There is a growing awareness among some European universities of the importance of the continuous professional skills development for, as well as performance reviews of, supervisors. This discussion is, however, in its early stages and has not yet begun in many European countries. The UK successfully introduced professional skills development for supervisors in 2004 on the basis of a Code of Practice developed specifically for doctoral programmes by the UK Quality Assurance Agency.[3] Such training is usually organised in an informal way, as one-day-out meetings, based on case studies, discussions, sharing of good practice and experience. Innovative ways of motivating supervisors to introduce effective and high quality practices of supervision also include practices such as annual awards/incentives for the best supervisors.

Transferable skills development

The need to introduce training in transferable skills has emerged after increased complaints of industry and other stakeholders that the traditional doctorate does not meet the challenges of careers outside academia. If Europe wants to become a leading knowledge-based economy and society, it is crucial to train young researchers who can bring expertise to various sectors. As Taylor and Beasley (2005: 12) put it, while the traditional PhD was about producing academics, the new knowledge economy needs research entrepreneurs.

Transferable (generic, life) skills development should be an integral part of all three cycles. The main goal at the level of doctoral education should be to raise awareness among doctoral candidates of the importance of both recognising and enhancing the skills that they develop and acquire through research. Transferable skills development can be organised in different ways, ranging from traditional courses and lectures to more student-centred interactive methods, especially through learning by doing at institutional, inter-institutional and international summer schools or through specialised institutional or inter-institutional support and personal development centres, as offered in the UK by the UK GRAD programmes and the UK Council for Graduate Education (UKCGE). An important element of transferable skills development is bringing together doctoral candidates from different disciplines and different levels (1–3 year) to encourage interdisciplinary dialogue and to foster creative thinking and innovation.

Transferable skills training requires adequate funding. It is important to ensure that reference to transferable skills development is embedded in institutional quality assessment procedures. Academic staff involved in skills development should include both academics who are active in research and understand the need to teach other skills, and external consultants (e.g. industry, companies, etc.). Teaching transferable skills should be recognised in evaluation and promotion of academic staff involved.

Internationalisation of doctoral education

One of the main objectives of the Bologna process is to enhance the attraction and international competitiveness of European higher education. Internationalisation of doctoral education and support of international mobility has become a central component of institutional strategies. European universities entered the competition for the best doctoral candidates as part of the global 'war for academic talent' (Scott, 2006: 4) by encouraging mobility within doctoral programmes and supporting European and international joint doctoral programmes and co-tutelle arrangements. International mobility (including trans-sectoral and transdisciplinary mobility) should be recognised as an added value for the career development of young researchers.

For smaller institutions and countries, mobility may also be a means of training their own young researchers in disciplines and transdisciplinary research areas where a critical mass of doctoral candidates, or capacities or infrastructure do not exist or are very limited.

Universities and public authorities at national and European level introduce and offer funding instruments facilitating the mobility of doctoral candidates from all 46 Bologna countries. However, legal, administrative and social obstacles (for example, obstacles concerning visas, work permits and social security issues) remain problems that have to be addressed by all partners in the process.

In addition to support for international mobility, increasing internationalisation inside universities, especially at doctoral level is also important. Doctoral training and research is *per se* international in nature. Sufficient and diverse opportunities should be provided for doctoral candidates to engage internationally. This can be done through the recruitment of more international staff; the organisation of international workshops, conferences and summer schools; and the development of more European and international joint doctoral programmes. The use of new technologies, such as using teleconferences, e-learning, etc., can also be used to foster the internationalisation of doctoral programmes.

Challenges

Despite the fact that many European universities have achieved common understanding of the need for the reform of doctoral education and have agreed on important aspects of this reform, there are still challenges that need to be discussed and addressed.

Masters–PhD transition

According to the Bologna process, the Masters degree gives access to the third cycle. In most European countries it really is the main entry point for doctoral education. In some countries a fast track to doctoral education from the Bachelors degree is possible for excellent students. Universities in Europe agree that, even if the Masters degree is a common entry requirement for the third cycle, access should not be restricted just to this route.

Following the Bologna development of the three cycles, the first two cycles in many European countries are seen as an interlinked entity and doctoral education as a separate and different entity. With growing international mobility and collaboration at the level of doctoral education, it will be important to clarify the role of the Masters degree and its relation to the doctorate, mainly for the reason that doctoral/graduate education outside Europe covers both the Masters and the doctoral phase. It seems that in some European countries there has been a paradigm shift occurring from 'Bachelor–Master/PhD' to 'Bachelor/Master–PhD'. Many universities are starting to link the second and third cycle activities. This change needs to be investigated and discussed at an international level.

Development of new doctorates

With the changing demands of a fast-evolving global labour market, a range of innovative doctoral programmes has emerged in some European countries. Employability of doctoral candidates within and outside academic institutions, as well as individual and societal needs for lifelong learning, have acted as a catalyst for the development of new programmes, including professional doctorates, more university–industry collaboration-based doctorates and increased European and international co-operation, often leading to joint or European doctorates. Diversity of doctoral programmes and doctorates reflects the increasing diversity of the European higher education landscape in which universities have the autonomy to develop their own missions and profiles and thus their own priorities in terms of programs and research.

The trend towards more diverse doctorates is not welcome by all universities. The emergence of professional doctorates in the UK and Ireland is observed in parts of continental Europe with suspicion. Professional doctorates are practice-based doctorates that focus on embedding research in a reflective manner into another professional practice. They meet the demands of today's labour market as they address issues such as interdisciplinarity, employability and entrepreneurship, while keeping a strong research emphasis. Critics of professional doctorates, however, question the quality and scope of research that is carried out in professional doctorates. European discussion on different new developments including professional doctorates has led to the consensus that original research has to remain the main component of all doctorates and that all awards described as doctorates (no matter what their type or form) should be based on a core of processes and outcomes (EUA, Bologna Seminar on Doctoral Programs: Final Conclusions, 2006). These include the completion of an individual thesis (based upon an original contribution to knowledge or original application of knowledge) that passes evaluation by an expert university committee with external representation.

Status of doctoral candidates

Doctoral candidates in Europe are considered young or early stage researchers who contribute significantly to knowledge production and innovation and are vital to Europe's development. Ensuring appropriate working conditions, rights and career prospects for young researchers, both in academia and in a range of other sectors, is of the highest importance and one of the crucial preconditions for success. As young researchers at the first stage of their career, or at different stages in their career, doctoral candidates should all have commensurate rights. Universities and public authorities in Europe share a collective responsibility to address the status and conditions of doctoral candidates.

The question of the status of doctoral candidates has been discussed at many fora and often with doctoral candidates themselves. In different European countries, doctoral candidates are seen and recognised in different ways. The results of the EUA survey among the Bologna Process member countries in 2006 indicates that, out of 37 participating countries, in 22 countries the status of a doctoral candidate is mixed, which means that doctoral candidates are officially recognised both as students and employees. In nine countries doctoral candidates are seen only as students and in three countries only as employees. Whatever the status of a doctoral candidate is, it is crucial that he or she is given all commensurate rights including healthcare, social security and pension rights. The social dimension of doctoral education in Europe has to remain an important component of institutional, national and European policies.

Career development

Promotion of attractive research careers and other career perspectives for doctoral candidates is the collective responsibility of universities and other stakeholders, including national and European authorities. The European Charter for Researchers and the Code of Conduct for the Recruitment of Researchers (European Commission, 2005), which is a set of recommendations published by the European Commission, stresses the importance of sustainability and continuity of career development for researchers at all stages of their career, including early stage researchers (doctoral candidates and post-doctoral researchers). Development of career opportunities for doctoral candidates should be done in collaboration with partners outside academia in order to implement clear career paths inside and outside academia, and between academia and other sectors of employment. Some European countries established organisations dedicated to career development of researchers (such as UK GRAD or CRAC) and many universities introduced career development services for their students, but there are still many universities and countries in Europe that are only at the beginning of this process.

Funding of doctoral education

Given the crucial role of doctoral education as the key formative stage of a research career in both academia and non-academic sectors, and the importance of doctoral education for Europe's future development, appropriate and sustainable funding of doctoral education and doctoral candidates is absolutely fundamental. However, the differences in funding among different European countries are large and can be considered a serious obstacle in achieving the common objectives of the Bologna process and the Lisbon Strategy. On the basis of the analysis of the questionnaires received from the Bologna Follow-Up Group member countries,[4] it is clear that scholarships/fellowships/grants are the main mode of funding doctoral candidates, although, in about half of the countries, salaries or teaching assistantships are also offered. The grant amounts for doctoral candidates vary considerably in different countries – from less than 5,000 euro to almost 30,000 euro annually. With such a low level of grants in some countries it is difficult to attract the most talented people, to ensure sustainable education and research development, and to stop 'brain drain' from economically poorer countries. Funding for doctoral candidates should be stable, covering the full period of the doctoral programme, and provide sufficient means to live and work in decent conditions.

A large diversity exists in how doctoral education is funded in European countries. Some governments give funds in a lump sum to institutions; in others, institutions are funded by competitive grants or by a combination of both mechanisms. When grants are given to doctoral programmes, more often these are dedicated to particular research projects (and doctoral programmes related to them) rather than to universities. In addition to direct government funding, a number of national or private foundations, research councils, grant agencies and other entities, as well as the European Science Foundation (ESF), provide additional funding sources.

Diversity in funding sources, channels, mechanisms and modes is not a bad thing. As this is probably an irreversible trend, greater consultation and co-ordination between government ministries, research councils and other funding bodies to bring about optimum modes of funding of doctoral candidates and doctoral education will become an increasingly important, but complex issue.

Conclusion

The latest developments in doctoral education in Europe clearly demonstrate the significant transformation of the third cycle. The Bologna process and the Lisbon Strategy have been the main drivers of changes in European doctoral education, although global external forces such as globalisation, demographic prognoses, and social, economic and cultural changes across the globe also have an impact on third cycle reform. Doctoral education is no longer just the responsibility of a university department or faculty but has become a crucial component of an institutional strategy at each university that wants to attract the best talent from all over the world and to belong to the category of internationally recognised research universities with high reputations. National and European policy makers also realise the importance of doctoral education for the knowledge-based society and economy and include it in national and transnational strategies for research, innovation and competitiveness. The European transformation of the third cycle is, however, part of a broader global transition of doctoral education. Institutional and international competitiveness has to go hand in hand with increasing collaboration between universities and other stakeholders at the global level. Sharing good practice, discussing trends in doctoral education development in different world regions, and acting locally and globally is the only way of improving and strengthening doctoral education and to contributing to global knowledge production.

References

Chambaz, J., Biaudet, P. and Collonge, S. (2006) Developing the doctorate, in *Bologna Handbook*, Berlin: Raabe Academic Publishers, C 4.4–2, pp. 1–18.

Communiqué of the Conference of European Ministers Responsible for Higher Education (2005) *The European Higher Education Area: Achieving the goals*, at: http://www.bologna-bergen2005.no/

Crosier, D., Purser, L. and Smidt, H. (2007) *TRENDS V: Universities shaping the European Higher Education Area*, Brussels: European University Association.

European Commission (2005) *The Charter for Researchers and the Code of Conduct for the Recruitment of Researchers*, Brussels: European Commission.

European University Association (EVA) (2003) *Graz Declaration*, at: www.eua.be.

European University Association (2005) *Doctoral Programmes for the European Knowledge Society*, EUA Report, at: www.eua.be.

European University Association (2006) *Bologna Seminar on Doctoral Programmes: Final Conclusions. Matching Ambition with Responsibilities and Resources*, at: http://www.eua.be/fileadmin/user_upload/files/Nice_doctorates_seminar/final_recommendations_in_EUAtemplate.pdf.

European University Association (2007) *Doctoral Programmes in Europe's Universities: Achievements and Challenges*, EUA report prepared for European Universities and Ministers of Higher Education, at: www.eua.be.

Golde, C. (2000) 'Should I stay or should I go?': student descriptions of the doctoral attrition process, *Review of Higher Education*, 23(2): 199–227.

Quality Assurance Agency for Higher Education (QAAHE) (2004) *Code of Practice for the*

Assurance of Academic Quality and Standards in Higher Education, Section 1: Postgraduate Research Programmes, at: http://www.qaa.ac.uk/academicinfrastructure/codeOfPractice/section1/postgrad2004.pdf.

Scott, P. (2006) The global context of doctoral education, in *Bologna Handbook*, Berlin: Raabe Academic Publishers, C 4.4-1, pp. 1–12.

Taylor, S. and Beasley, N. (2005) A *Handbook for Doctoral Supervisors*, London and New York: Routledge.

Chapter 16

Policy driving change in doctoral education

An Australian case study

Ruth Neumann

This chapter provides an insight into Australian doctoral education in the early twenty-first century, as a case study of the global changes in doctoral education policy. It presents findings from a national study on the doctoral education experience (Neumann, 2003) in the context of emerging government policy on doctoral education. It demonstrates the state of rapid transition in doctoral education and highlights the diversity and flexibility of the Australian doctoral education scene. Change has been triggered by altered federal government funding policy on higher education. Universities must adapt from a time of funding enrolled doctoral places to an era of competitive performance-based allocations calculated on actual doctoral completions. The challenge for universities and the country is that diversity not be sacrificed in the process as university management is tempted to adopt risk minimisation strategies under the pressures of more competitive funding and narrow outcomes-based performance measures.

While the focus in this chapter is specifically on developments in doctoral education in Australia, the period in which the study was conducted reflects change in doctoral education internationally. In the US, the Carnegie Foundation embarked on a study of the future of doctoral education investigating six disciplines in university departments with forward-looking doctoral programs (Golde and Walker, 2006). In Europe, the Bologna process, initiated in 1999, is driving many countries to re-examine their doctoral programs with a view to developing a European framework for program length and quality assurance (EUA, 2007). In England, the Higher Education Funding Council has studied doctoral completions and supervision quality (HEFCE, 2005). Doctoral education has moved further centre stage internationally. However, responses to change take on national and local features, providing comparative relevance.

This chapter looks firstly at the national policy context for doctoral education since 1990. It then presents an overview of some key developments in Australian doctoral education in practice from the national study. Two main areas are highlighted. The first is the diversity of the structure of doctoral research influenced by both discipline and institutional context. The second area is the changing nature of doctoral research and supervision practices across the disciplines. The study findings provide an insight into the variety of student experiences and changing practices influenced by the broader policy environment, disciplines and specific institutional contexts. The chapter concludes with a discussion of the implications for the diversity of doctoral education.

The policy context

The Australian government White Paper (Kemp, 1999) on research and research training introduced radical policies on the funding of doctoral students. Arguably the most fundamental change since the Federal Government commenced funding research training through scholarships and stipends in the 1950s (Murray, 1957), it strongly focused the attention of universities and university management on doctoral education.

In the period 1991–2000 the number of research students virtually doubled to reach more than 37,000 (DETYA, 2001), of whom three-quarters (28,000) were doctoral students. Increased student diversity accompanied this growth. In addition to the traditional full-time students moving from undergraduate and honours research to the PhD, part-time and distance students enrolled in PhDs or professional doctorates became part of the national profile. Increasing numbers of international students, as well as a greater age range, added to the diversity of profile.

An important feature of this decade of growth and diversification of doctoral students is also the expansion in the range of disciplines providing doctoral research. New professional fields, many in the social sciences, joined the traditional science and humanities disciplines in providing opportunities for doctoral study. The expansion of disciplines for doctoral research includes a diversification of structure and type of doctorate, either PhD or professional doctorate. This diversification resulted from two important reviews at the commencement of the 1990s. The discussion paper, *Review of Australian Graduate Studies and Higher Degrees* (NBEET, 1989) and the subsequent report *Higher Education Courses and Graduate Studies* (NBEET, 1990), assessed the scope and structure of doctoral research and recommended the diversification of doctoral structures, particularly through the introduction of professional doctorates. Professional doctorates were seen to have multiple purposes. Key among them were the provision of opportunities for doctoral research in non-traditional disciplines and professional fields, and the creation of a fast-track doctoral qualification for the projected shortfall of academic staff at that time (NBEET, 1989, 1990). By early 2001, 131 professional doctorate programs in education, health, law, psychology, management, the creative arts and science were on offer (McWilliam et al., 2002). More recently, professional doctorates are being offered in areas such as public health and tropical medicine. In general, professional doctorates have been seen by policy makers and advisers as a means of attracting fee income and adding 'relevance' to doctoral research training (Neumann, 2002a).

The period of 1991–2000 can be characterised as a vibrant and dynamic time for doctoral education. Increasing growth and diversity took place within a tight agenda of government fiscal constraint (ibid., 2002a). In the late 1990s, however, overall higher education policy in Australia became even more strongly focused on questions of funding, accountability and value for money, as judged by measured outcomes and contribution to the Australian economy (Neumann, 2007). The late 1990s witnessed significant funding reductions in operating grants to universities. Disciplines in the humanities in particular, but also in costly science and engineering fields, experienced financial constraints and were forced to down-size their departments (Illing, 1997; Wells, 1996).

While the increases in doctoral students during the decade were strong, representing an increasing percentage of all student enrolments in universities, the percentage of doctoral completions as a proportion of all student completions increased more slowly (DETYA, 2001). In keeping with the stronger performance focus of the government, the government introduced the far-reaching and contentious decision to include research student completions as a key measure in calculating annual government research funding to individual universities (Kemp, 1999). Up to that point, the practice had been to provide annual funding based on numbers of students enrolled in research degrees. This practice was seen to have encouraged complacency among universities in the quality of research supervision and was argued to encourage long completion times and high attrition rates (DETYA, 2001; Gordon, 2000; Kemp, 1999). The introduction, from 2001, of the Research Training Scheme (RTS) provided universities with funding allocated on a competitive performance basis, calculated on institutional completions in the previous two years. The maximum time of funding for a candidate under the RTS was reduced from five to four years. The expectation was that three years would be the norm.

Understandably there were concerns among universities with this change of funding practice. The effect of competitively allocated doctoral places among all universities based on institutional performance was to focus the attention of universities on the management of their doctoral practices. There were broader concerns about the impact on diversity in terms of type of student and breadth of research fields, topics and research approach (Neumann, 2002a; Smith, 2000). The temptation for universities to minimise risk in order to maximise completion numbers and hence research funding was argued to be strong (Chubb, 2000). This was an ideal opportunity to examine doctoral education, as institutions adapted their practices from the end of one funding era (i.e. funding enrolments) to the beginning of another (i.e. competitive funding of completions). Thus, the study of the diversity of the doctoral education experience examined institutional practices and procedures in relation to doctoral education at a time which still reflected the practices of one era and revealed institutional positioning to take best advantage of the next.

Doctoral education in practice

The doctoral education experience project

The radical funding policy introduced by the 1999 White Paper, and its potential impact on the development of doctoral education, provided the impetus for a national study on the doctoral education experience. The aim was to gain a deeper understanding of students' perspectives on their doctoral education experiences. It considered the influences of type of doctorate (PhD or professional doctorate), the mode of enrolment (full time or part time), and the stage of the research process (early, middle or late) on student experiences. These were contextualised for both discipline and institution. Interview and documentary data from six different universities covering the broad mix of disciplines were analysed. Over 130 interviews were conducted, two-thirds with students. The study focused on four disciplinary groups: the sciences (represented by physics and biological sciences); the science-based professions (engineering – chemical, civil, electrical, mechanical); the humanities and social sciences (history, political science, cultural studies, creative arts); and the social science-based professions (education, law, management). Participating institutions were selected to ensure diversity of institutional research approach and different eras of establishment, student numbers and government research funding allocation. Institutional location reflected urban and regional universities, as well as single- and multi-campus institutions. At the two largest universities, annual doctoral enrolments were in the range of 2000–4000 with annual enrolments at the other universities in the range of 500–900. The two different research doctorates formed central elements in the study's design. Accordingly, it sought to include faculties and departments that offered both a PhD and a professional doctorate in their field.

The sections below highlight the key findings on program structure and on changes in research topics and supervision practices.

Doctoral structures and models

The reviews of graduate studies in the early 1990s aimed to generate discussion on the appropriateness of the existing doctoral course structure for future employment and career paths. The reviews did not propose a particular structure, but anticipated that professional doctorates would provide 'professional training which will probably require substantial pieces of investigative work, projects and exercises, in addition to straight coursework' (NBEET, 1989: 28). Thus, the structure and organisation of PhD and professional doctorate programs were reviewed across the discipline groups and institutions in the study. Professional doctorate programs from five of the six universities were included in the study. Not all universities offered professional doctorates and, where these programs existed, they were not offered across each of the discipline groups. The professional doctorates were in the humanities/social sciences and the social science-based professions and included the creative arts (Doctor of Creative Arts, DCA), education (Doctor of Education, EdD), management (Doctor of Business Administration, DBA) and law (Doctor of Juridical Science/Studies, SJD).

A common perception has been that PhDs are entirely research-focused, with the possibility of coursework dependent either on practice within a particular discipline or department or undertaken on an individual needs basis. Professional doctorates, on the other hand, are seen to have a more varied structure. This study did not identify any major distinction between the structure of PhD and professional doctorate programs. Nearly 50 per cent of the PhD programs across the four discipline groups had a formal coursework component. The remainder were research-only, with the possibility for candidates to undertake coursework if necessary. Whether a coursework component was included in a PhD program was dependent on the particular faculty. Thus there were PhDs in, for example, physics that were research-only and also with a coursework component across the universities studied. Within the same university, faculties varied as to whether their PhD programs included coursework.

Three types of coursework were found in PhD programs. The first, found almost exclusively in social science-based professions, incorporated formal research methods courses. The second type of coursework, found in both the social science-based professional doctorates as well as in the humanities/social sciences, focused on how to undertake, develop and structure a PhD thesis. The third, essentially a broadening of content and factual disciplinary knowledge, was prevalent in the science and engineering fields. The timing of coursework also varied, being related to its purpose. Thus programs with research methods courses generally provided them at the beginning of the PhD program, while courses designed to inculcate students into the PhD process generally occurred over the first half of the candidature. Programs that required a broadening of content knowledge could be undertaken by students at any stage of their candidature.

In professional doctorates, while a coursework component was expected, not all had programs of compulsory coursework: one was by research only. In the social science-based professional fields and in the humanities/social sciences, the coursework structures in professional doctorates were the same as those found in the corresponding PhD programs, namely courses on research methods and on how to undertake a thesis. Some programs also had a small number of content broadening courses. Only in one university was a portfolio model adopted for professional doctorates. It was explained that:

> [The] model is meant to be for a person in a profession with a contribution to the profession; . . . they are required to do one or two research projects and . . . they work through a series of experiences which lead to the development of a portfolio. So the portfolio includes . . . and it may be a bit tough, it includes four refereed journal articles at least.
>
> (Deputy Vice-Chancellor)

The requirements of this portfolio model were recognised as onerous, and the publication requirement was also seen as problematic. In this university, and in two others, professional doctorates were described as 'under review' or 'on hold'. Experienced supervisors pointed to arduous workload requirements. This may in part be the explanation for why the numbers of active students (compared with the numbers 'on the books') in several of the professional doctorate programs were low. Yet other comments from experienced supervisors argued that structures such as the portfolio model gave rise to confusion and ambiguity for both students and potentially examiners:

> You think of the joke, you walk on one side of the road, you walk on the other side of the road, you walk down the middle and you're going to get killed, right. I think that's what's going on with some of the DBA programs. They haven't got it clear

in their own mind. They're certainly not clear when they're communicating to students as to what these things are all about and consequently people are wandering all over the highway here and somebody's going to get hurt. . . . I think the thing is that there is no clean, clear distinction between a DBA and a PhD between universities.

(Academic 129, Management)

However, the educational discussions on doctoral thesis and portfolio structure will continue as faculties and institutions review and adapt their doctoral programs (see e.g. Maxwell and Kupczyk-Romanczuk, 2007).

Doctoral research topics

In addition to program structure as a differentiating feature between PhDs and professional doctorates, there is also argued to be a difference in the nature of the research topic. In the initial NBEET reports (1989, 1990), it was envisaged that in professional doctorates the research activity would be applied, profession- or practice-oriented and not necessarily based within the university. A theme of much recent discussion on professional doctorates in Australia and the UK (see e.g. Bourner et al., 2001; Lee et al., 2000; Scott et al., 2004) emphasises the importance of the connection with practice through the research topic. More diversified research investigations – for example through portfolios and the adoption of a more reflective, practitioner-oriented mode of research education (Maxwell and Kupczyk-Romanczuk, 2007; Morley and Priest, 2001) – are developments reflecting these views.

Within the professional doctorate programs in this study, however, the research thesis dominated. As with the PhD, the success of a student's doctorate rested on it. In terms of substantive issues such as types of research topic or research method, there was claimed to be no difference between the PhD and the professional doctorate. All students within the professional doctorate programs studied maintained that their research could be accommodated in a PhD and that even in such areas as the creative arts there was scope within PhDs for 'non-traditional exploration' (Student 112, Creative Arts). There were cases of transfer between the two doctorates across all universities and all disciplines. In transferring into a PhD from, for example, a DBA or a DCA, 'the thrust of the key nature of my research' could be maintained (Student 128, Cultural Studies). Similarly in moving from a PhD to a professional doctorate, the nature and scope of the research topic remained unaltered:

> I liked the idea of being in the DCA rather than a straight PhD, which seemed to be much more based on studying other people's work. I wanted to do that but I also wanted to look at my own writing as well.

(Student 112, Creative Arts)

Within the management discipline in particular, students had selected a DBA because they liked the idea of undertaking research of direct relevance to their workplace.

However, especially in the case of later transfers into a PhD, such research was equally possible within a traditional program. Aside from personal student preference for enrolling in a professional doctorate as compared with a PhD program, the nature, scope and manner of research were not differentiating aspects.

A further notable feature was the lack of close involvement with industry or profession. In none of the professional doctorate programs was there evidence of a contribution from a student's workplace, employer, or other professional connection. Although most students' research topics derived from their professional interest and experience, none of them were undertaking work- or industry-based research, as might have been expected from the rationale for professional doctorates. Similar findings were made in another study at that time (McWilliam et al., 2002), as well as earlier studies (Maxwell and Shanahan, 2001; Trigwell et al., 1997). The small number of students who were testing their research in their workplace held senior positions that enabled them to explore its applicability in practice and provided them with a budget to do so. They described their employers as being aware of their research but only mildly interested. However, holding such senior positions did not prevent students from being retrenched by their employers in the course of their candidature, as was the case with several management students in the study. Similar situations were found with students undertaking PhDs in the social science-based professions that were funded by industry, but did not occur among industry-funded PhDs in the sciences and engineering.

The study had expected to find diversity in doctoral structures and research topics, based on the differing rationales for PhDs and professional doctorates. While the study did find diversity of doctoral structures, this diversity was not based on the differentiation between the two types of doctorates. The diversity in structure is clearly related to type of discipline combined with institutional context. Most doctorates have a coursework component and the type and timing of the coursework in relation to the research is discipline-dependent. As with program structures, doctoral research topics are accommodated across the two types of doctorates. There were no underlying differences based on doctoral type. In fact students moved seamlessly between doctoral programs with no change in research topic required.

Research topics and supervision practices

The introduction of a competitive completions-based model to fund doctoral education is seen by the government to reduce the time taken for a doctoral degree and to provide an incentive to universities to manage the doctoral process more efficiently. As discussed earlier, stakeholders were also concerned that there was the potential to reduce the diversity of research fields and approaches, while there has been discussion of risk management in doctoral education in the recent academic literature (Evans et al., 2005; McWilliam et al., 2005). The research findings confirm that strong pressures are exercised by senior management within all institutions for doctoral topics to be scaled down to a reasonable size. There was ready acknowledgment that universities, supervisors and students have expectations about research topics beyond what is manageable in the timeframe of a PhD, and in particular the timeframe to be funded by the new policy:

> I think people have got to learn to pick a topic that is manageable in the time that they've got, to pick objectives which are realistic – again within the time and the resources they've got – and the sooner they do that and hone down the dimensions of their investigation the better for them.
>
> (Senior manager 132)

The focus of management was to ensure a shorter and tighter timeframe for topic refinement. The aim was to complete in 3–6 months the early topic refinement stage from the accepted 12–18 months. If this process was to take longer than 6 months, then it was thought that students would need to take periods of leave of absence to enable them to refine their topic in their own time. In all but one of the universities there was evidence that the scope of the research topic had changed. In disciplinary terms, the effect in the humanities and social science-based professions is to encourage less ambitious projects in terms of scale. The days of the 'blockbuster thesis' are over and the focus is on 'do-able' projects within the government's specified timeframe of three years. In science fields the trend is also to 'downsize' projects and make them 'significantly less significant'. The pressures in costly research areas of the experimental sciences and science-based professions call for a more pragmatic approach to doctoral research topics. One experienced supervisor in the sciences explained:

> ... [there are] a number of pressures on the university and so now supervisors tend to try and slot students into things that minimise the risk of a delay and so we tend to put them on projects where we've already got the funding for the equipment or we've already got the equipment and so basically we're trying to fit round pegs into round holes – peg is the student, hole is the project ...
>
> (Academic 57 Science)

In fact, in the science and science-based professions, government funding pressures in the past few years have already forced two very large engineering and physics faculties to only undertake doctoral research topics that were sponsored by industry, and where the focus was on research of immediate relevance to industry:

> ... they always have a strong element [relating to practice] and ... students do only projects that we can get funding for. If you want to have funding for your students you have to have a project that someone is willing to pay for. If you find someone who is willing to pay for it, they are not willing to wait indefinitely for it. ... I think 80 per cent of [the topics] are somehow connected to industry ... we are not encouraging topics without an industry connection too much because they are the areas that effectively the supervisor cannot top up if they have no money ...
>
> (Academic 34 Dean, Engineering)

Associated with the trend to obtain industry funding for doctoral student research, supervisors have become increasingly concerned to select and allocate doctoral projects that are more circumscribed and less risky than in the past. There were some supervisors who referred disparagingly to this practice as 'tick the boxes' research or research on a 'production line':

> [The] recipe for success [is] to have a very well designed project, where, in that area [of physics] essentially you are exploring the properties of different samples. . . . [So it's] a well-defined path, and you just tick the boxes as you go along, and after three or so years you write it up and you'd have your results. And, you know, the methods were well proven because many people before had used the same equipment to measure other samples, and it gives them a training – . . . it's more of a factory type approach to PhD research – like a production line in a car factory. . . . The threat is this: it's very difficult to put your finger on, but it's the ability to think for yourself and develop ideas by yourself, innovation. You know I think if you have a factory approach then innovation just goes out the window, because you're not encouraging people to think for themselves and develop new ideas.
>
> (Academic 58 Science)

Clearly, doctoral research topics in these fields and these departments are seen as less substantial than topics in other science fields and departments and also from what they have been in the past. Some of the students interviewed in departments where this type of research had become standard questioned whether their topic was in fact worthy of a PhD:

> I'm not sure, sometimes I think, 'well, is this really good enough to be a PhD?' Because to me it's no massive jump in understanding or intuition or anything like that. It's no massive leap. It's just applying a different area to solving your problem, so to speak. I'm a little bit, 'maybe, maybe this isn't PhD. Maybe this isn't good enough'.
>
> (Student 80 Engineering).

With these pressures on research topics and funding, there were also clear repercussions on doctoral student selection. The focus on industry-supported research and tight timeframes meant that it was important to select the 'right type of student', able to complete in a maximum three-year timeframe. The specific rules of student selection were in all cases unofficial and tacit university, faculty and departmental policy. In general, candidates applying for part-time status were not accepted, since part-timers, it was argued, take longer to complete. A rare part-time student in one engineering faculty explained how she had survived as a part-timer:

> I enrolled as a full-time student and almost immediately got pregnant with my second daughter. So, I did the first year full time . . . I think I officially kept going until whenever the next semester started in the next year, and took six months off then

. . . . And at this university, certainly in engineering, one of the few criteria, for doing a PhD part time is full-time care of, like, an elderly or disabled person, or a child under five. . . . Certainly within Engineering they want you full time unless there's some sort of circumstance, and that's one of the few circumstances, is care of a child under five . . . that's in writing. So, you're not allowed to work. Having to work to support yourself isn't an excuse to go to part time, they won't accept that. So, I switched to part time, and that's sort of how I ended up how I am today.

(Student 44 Engineering)

As well as a strong preference for full-time students, there was also an avoidance of international students and a preference for local Australian, or at least native English-speaking, candidates. A very experienced supervisor in one of Australia's largest engineering faculties explained:

We have consciously gone for local students because they are more self starting, they have got the right background skills, they have the ability to tell a staff member they are wrong, whereas the foreign students wouldn't dare do that. And so the students have to be more self reliant because we have to jack up the numbers with fewer staff and so, yeah, it is a matter of getting more confident students who basically can run the projects to a substantial degree themselves.

(Academic 65 Engineering)

The response indicates a pragmatic approach in a faculty under great staffing and research funding pressure. Similar reactions to staffing and funding pressures were also evident in at least two other large engineering faculties.

Pressures to be more selective in enrolling doctoral students were also evident in the humanities and social sciences in four universities where there were long and well-established traditions of research. The pressure to scale down the size and scope of the research was clearly evident, as was the move to more closely align student research interests with the departmental research profile. This partly involved a change in supervisory style, with a move towards a 'science model' for supervision. Supervisors aimed to have a mix of individual and group sessions with their research students. The group meetings – a novel arrangement in the humanities – were intended to build a supportive peer group and one where ideas on similar topics could be exchanged and explored.

There are implications for departmental size in such a supervisory approach in humanities and social science fields. Where it was being tried, departments tended to be larger, with a wider range of research areas to be covered. The aim in these cases was to build functional 'cohorts' in broadly defined areas through the introduction of coursework requirements. In those universities where the humanities departments were smaller, or had an emerging research profile, the smaller numbers of staff able to supervise made this approach unfeasible. There were strong resource pressures on staff in these situations with students commenting unfavourably on the frequency of supervision meetings and the overall research support available through the department or faculty.

Conclusion

The discussion has focused on core aspects of doctoral education: program structures, research topics and supervision practices. This snapshot of early twenty-first century doctoral education prompts considerations of the ongoing development of doctoral education, in particular the maintenance of diversity. The emergence of countervailing forces of risk-minimisation through increased student and research topic selectivity can operate to impinge on diversity. The Australian case may illustrate pertinent developments of interest to European universities, as the pressures for change in doctoral program structures and duration, to facilitate translation across national systems, compel institutions to examine their practices. In particular, where tighter, outcomes-based government funding accompanies this pressure, the Australian example may provide useful insights.

Diversity was evident in doctoral program structures and can be argued to be one of the most important outcomes of the development of doctoral education during the 1990s. This diversity was shown to be discipline-related rather than dependent on type of doctorate. Initially proposed as an alternative to the PhD, professional doctorates were seen as a means of fast-tracking doctoral research through the introduction of coursework, as well as a means of introducing greater relevance into doctoral research topics for industry and the professions. A growing academic literature promoted the distinctiveness of research undertaken within the professional doctorate. The findings of this study reveal that there is no longer a 'traditional' PhD and that structural variation is essentially discipline-dependent, with variations based on institutional contexts. Coursework components are a feature of most doctoral education, although the type and timing of the coursework vary depending on discipline type.

Similarly, it can be argued that disciplines underpin the nature of research questions more strongly than doctoral type. It has been argued that research topics in professional doctorates have a closer connection and more relevance to the workplace than do research questions within the same disciplines in the PhD. However, all the professional doctorate students in this study maintained that their research topic could appropriately be undertaken either in a PhD or in the professional doctorate. Experienced doctoral supervisors endorsed this. The ready movement of students between the two degrees during candidature stood out. Further, the concern to link research relevance with industry, the professions and the workplace was shown to be tenuous and difficult to achieve in practice. Where there was any direct connection between profession or workplace and research, it had been created by individual student interest. In general, the lack of involvement of professional doctorate programs in industry, workplace or profession was striking. It is important in discussions on research across the disciplines to distinguish between discipline-driven (pure) and social- or practice-driven (applied) research. In professional disciplines the link between theory and practice is by definition inextricably close (Becher, 1989; Neumann, 2002b). But while the distinctions between pure and applied, theory and practice appear neat and clear-cut for discussion purposes, in actuality they overlap and blur (Neumann, 1992, 1993; Rip, 2000).

Given the intertwining of theory and practice in professional fields, it could be argued that the award in these disciplines should be a professional doctorate rather than a PhD. However, the important question is really whether the distinction between PhDs and professional doctorates continues to serve an educational purpose. A more productive approach would be to argue for the maintenance of diversity in doctoral structures within organisational structures that are open to change and flexible in operation. The support of an artificial distinction between PhDs and professional doctorates may mean that the remaining point of distinction between PhDs and professional doctorates lies in the charging of fees for professional doctorates. Promoted by government policy advisers partly as a means of raising revenue, professional doctorates notably in the management field have been established as fee-paying research programs. In this study, university managers in some engineering and humanities faculties were considering introducing professional doctorates marketed as fee-paying programs to the professions. Recently fee-paying professional doctorates in public health have been introduced. However, in this wider study, only in the management field were professional doctorates fee-paying programs. Even here, the capacity and willingness of students to pay was restricted to a very small number of programs, while the evidence from previous work on the DBA (Neumann and Goldstein, 2002) found barely a handful of viable programs able to charge significant fees.

Within this context, it is important to consider the forces operating to restrict diversity. Changed government funding of doctoral education, together with funding reductions to universities in earlier years, were clearly influencing supervision practices, the scale and management of doctoral research topics and student selection as universities prepared themselves for the coming funding era. The increased emphasis on initial topic selection, scale of research topic, and reduction in the time taken for topic refinement were evident across all discipline groups, either as already enforced practices or as strategies ready for implementation. The effects flowing from the broader government institutional funding reductions of the late 1990s were particularly powerful in science and engineering. Research topics providing quick results to industrial sponsors were described as 'pre-structured' and 'production line'. The main concerns were to minimise risk in research topic selection, and to identify students who were likely to require minimum supervision with maximum chance of rapid completion. For the humanities, the move was to adopt a science or cohort model of supervision. The resulting risk-minimisation strategies called for an approach to student selection based on those most likely to complete within a finite three- to four-year timeframe. Institutional risk management approaches also required students who could function with minimal supervision and direction. The unspoken policy was to give preference to full-time students likely to need only limited supervision. Selecting students from a non-English speaking background who would require more supervisory support was also avoided.

This chapter has adopted the view that doctoral education is at a time of transition, driven strongly by government and global policy. In particular, the direct government funding intervention on doctoral education has swiftly prompted universities to re-assess their approaches to, and practices of, doctoral education. The competitive funding of doctoral outcomes through timely completions has the potential to bring about far-reaching change in core areas of the doctoral research process. The challenge for universities is to ensure that the positive aspects of diversity in all its forms, which have developed so strongly over the past decade, are retained.

Acknowledgements

The study, *The Doctoral Education Experience: Diversity and Complexity*, was funded by the federal Department of Education Science and Training (DEST). The contribution of project staff Clare Holland, Anna Isaacs, Hellen Morgan-Harris and Sarah Wilks is acknowledged.

References

Becher, T. (1989) *Academic Tribes and Territories: Intellectual inquiry and the cultures of disciplines*, Milton Keynes: Society for Research into Higher Education and Open University Press.

Bourner, T., Bowden, R. and Laing, S. (2001) Professional doctorates in England, *Studies in Higher Education*, 26(1): 65–83.

Chubb, I. (2000) The challenge of making ends meet in postgraduate research training, in M. Kiley and G. Mullins (eds), *Quality in Postgraduate Research: Making Ends Meet*, proceedings of the 2000 Quality in Postgraduate Research Conference, Adelaide, 13–14 April, University of Adelaide, pp. 15–23.

Department of Education, Training and Youth Affairs (DETYA) (2001) *Higher Education: Report for the 2001–2003 Triennium*, Canberra: DETYA.

European University Association (EUA) (2007) *Doctoral Programmes in Europe's Universities: Achievements and Challenges*, report prepared for European Universities and Ministers of Higher Education. Brussels: EUA.

Evans, T., Lawson, A., McWilliam, E. and Taylor, P. (2005) Understanding the management of doctoral studies in Australia as risk management, *Studies in Research*, 1: 1–11.

Golde, C. and Walker, G. (2006) *Envisioning the Future of Doctoral Education: Preparing Stewards of the Discipline. Carnegie Essays on the Doctorate*, San Francisco, CA: Jossey-Bass.

Gordon, J. (2000) The challenges facing higher education research training, in M. Kiley and G. Mullins (eds), *Quality in Postgraduate Research: Making Ends Meet*, Adelaide: University of Adelaide, pp. 9–13.

Higher Education Funding Council for England (HEFCE) (2005) *PhD Research Degrees: Entry and Completion*, at: http://www.hefce.ac.uk/pubs/hefce/2005/.

Illing, D. (1997) Further 1pc cut with few sweetners, *Australian Higher Education Supplement*, 14 May, p. 27.

Kemp, D. (1999) *Knowledge and Innovation: A Policy Statement on Research and Research Training*, Canberra: Commonwealth of Australia.

Lee, A., Green, B. and Brennan, M. (2000) Organisational knowledge, professional practice and the professional doctorate at work, in J. Carrick and C. Rhodes (eds), *Research and Knowledge at Work: Perspectives, Case Studies and Innovative Strategies*, London and New York: Routledge, pp. 117–136.

Maxwell, T. and Kupczyk-Romanczuk, G. (2007) *The professional doctorate: defining the portfolio as a legitimate alternative to the dissertation*, at: http://www.une.edu.au/ehps/staff/tmaxwellpubs.php#item2.

Maxwell, T. and Shanahan, P. (2001) Professional doctoral education in Australia and New Zealand: reviewing the scene, in B. Green, T. Maxwell and P. Shanahan (eds), *Doctoral Education and Professional Practice: The Next Generation?*, Armidale, NSW: Kardoorair Press, pp. 17–38.

McWilliam, E., Lawson, A., Evans, T. and Taylor, P. (2005) 'Silly, soft and otherwise suspect': doctoral education as risky business, *Australian Journal of Education*, 49(2): 214–228.

McWilliam, E., Taylor, P., Thomson, P., Green, B., Maxwell, T., Wildy, H. and Simons, D. (2002) *Research Training and Doctoral Programs: What can be Learned from Professional Doctorates?*, Canberra: Department of Education, Science and Training.

Morley, C. and Priest, J. (2001) Developing a professional doctorate in Business Administration: reflection and the 'executive scholar', in B. Green, R. Maxwell and P. Shanahan (eds), *Doctoral Education and Professional Practice: The Next Generation?*, Armidale, NSW: Kardoorair Press, pp. 163–185.

Murray, K. (Chairman) (1957) *Report of the Committee on Australian Universities*, Canberra: Commonwealth Government Printer.

NBEET (National Board of Employment, Education and Training) (1989) *Review of Australian Graduate Studies and Higher Degrees*, Canberra: NBEET.

NBEET (1990) *Higher Education Courses and Graduate Studies*, Canberra: NBEET.

Neumann, R. (1992) Research and scholarship: perceptions of senior academic administrators, *Higher Education*, 25: 97–110.

Neumann, R. (1993) Academic work: perceptions of senior academic administrators. *Australian Educational Researcher*, 20(1): 33–47.

Neumann, R. (2002a) Diversity, doctoral education and policy, *Higher Education Research and Development*, 21(2): 167–178.

Neumann, R. (2002b) A disciplinary perspective on university teaching and learning, in M. Tight (ed.), *Access and Exclusion*, Sydney: Elsevier, pp. 217–245.

Neumann, R. (2003) *The Doctoral Education Experience: Diversity and Complexity*, Evaluations and Investigations Programme, Research, Analysis and Evaluation Group, Canberra: Department of Education, Science and Training.

Neumann, R. (2007) Policy and practice in doctoral education, *Studies in Higher Education*, 32(4): 459–473.

Neumann, R. and Goldstein, M. (2002) Issues in the ongoing development of professional doctorates: the DBA example, *Journal of Institutional Research*, 11(1): 23–37.

Rip, A. (2000) Fashions, lock-ins and the heterogeneity of knowledge production, in M. Jacob and T. Hellstrom (eds), *The Future of Knowledge Production in the Academy*, Buckingham: Society for Research into Higher Education and Open University Press, pp. 28–39.

Scott, D,., Brown, A., Lunt, I. and Thorne, L. (2004) *Professional Doctorates: Integrating Professional and Academic Knowledge*, Maidenhead: Society for Research into Higher Education and Open University Press.

Smith, B. (2000) The challenge of making ends meet in postgraduate research training, in M. Kiley and G. Mullins (eds), *Quality in Postgraduate Research: Making Ends Meet*, Adelaide: University of Adelaide, pp. 25–29.

Trigwell, K., Shannon, T. and Maurizi, R. (1997) *Research-coursework Doctoral Programmes in Australian Universities*, Canberra: EIP, DEETYA.

Wells, J. (1996) Cuts reduce uni flexibility, *Australian Higher Education Supplement*, August 14, p. 36.

Chapter 17

Regulatory regimes in doctoral education

Mark Tennant

Doctoral education has been increasingly the object of public scrutiny, policy debate and academic analysis. Critical appraisals are being made of the traditional PhD; new programs and new professional doctorates are being established; the role of supervisors is being examined and challenged; and the need for doctorates to support innovation and economic development is being actively promoted. All this is occurring in a period of significant growth in student numbers, increasing diversity in the student population, and a burgeoning international student demand.

This activity has occurred in the context of a more concerted effort by governments, accreditation agencies, and peak bodies to regulate and control universities, largely through more rigorous accreditation provisions, audit mechanisms, and requirements relating to standards and quality assurance processes. Indeed, universities themselves have moved to intensify central regulation and control over the activities of departments and schools.

This is certainly the case with doctoral education, one feature of which has been the centralisation and standardisation of institutional practices, enshrined in the establishment in universities of central units operating across all academic areas which have responsibility for establishing institution-wide strategic directions, policies and procedures for managing candidatures, and for reporting on, managing and improving whole-of-university quality and performance. Such central units (sometimes constituted as Graduate Schools) are certainly becoming more widespread as universities seek to control, regulate and measure the core elements of doctoral education, often at the behest of national governments, inter-governmental agencies and/or peak bodies. The focus of this chapter is on the functions of these units and how they sit within broader policy and regulatory frameworks. Following McWilliam et al. (2002), I understand regulation and control as a 'risk management' response to the perceived dangers wrought by contemporary trends in higher education more broadly and in doctoral education in particular. They argue that a concern with risk management is a feature of contemporary higher education worldwide and draw attention to the way in which a more 'risk conscious' higher education policy environment has an impact on the management of higher degrees by research (McWilliam, 2006). In this chapter I argue that such risk management is at best contradictory and at worst self-defeating, in that it negates the risks necessary for creative and innovative doctoral work.

Some drivers of risk management

The global knowledge economy

Recent changes in the management of research education need to be seen in the context of the impact of broader global trends and globalising forces in higher education. For example, the so-called 'knowledge economy' places new demands on universities, who no longer enjoy a monopoly on the production of knowledge through research and the distribution of knowledge through publishing and teaching. There is a growing expectation that universities should provide research and education that is more relevant and pertinent to the needs of the contemporary knowledge economy. Workers in this economy are represented as being innovative and entrepreneurial, collaborative yet self-motivated and self-managed, flexible and reflexive, and with an international perspective on their work. The knowledge economy also challenges the traditional role of the university as a gatekeeper of 'legitimate' knowledge, with the growing recognition of the value of the workplace as a site of knowledge production and innovation – hence the term 'working knowledge' (McIntyre and Symes, 2000). Related to this is the increasing recognition that the kinds of problems faced by communities, industry and the professions do not fall neatly into disciplinary categories. Rather, they call for cross-disciplinary or trans-disciplinary solutions. In this new economic landscape, both the domestic and international demand for higher education has grown – and much of this demand is from 'non-traditional' students.

Traditional forms of communicating knowledge have of course been completely transformed by new information and communication technologies that have also allowed more flexible forms of delivering education to a global market. These trends have resulted in universities needing to compete for students in a global marketplace, to provide educational opportunities for a more diverse student population, to ensure employment outcomes through developing relevant graduate attributes, to provide both online and face-to-face learning opportunities in both on-shore and off-shore locations, and to foster trans-disciplinary learning and research.

Growth and diversity

In recent years much has been written about the increasing diversity of doctoral education (Bourner et al., 2001; Pearson, 1999; Tennant, 2004; Usher, 2002; Winter et al., 2000). There is diversity in the form of provision (such as the traditional PhD by thesis, professional doctorates, and generic work-based doctorates), diversity within forms of provision (e.g. practice-based PhDs; PhDs by project; 'new route' PhDs; different mixes of coursework, artefact and thesis in professional doctorates), and diversity in the student population (increasing participation of women, more part-time students and greater age mix). In the US, the annual survey of graduate enrolment conducted by the Council of Graduate Schools in conjunction with the Graduate Record Examinations Board summarises the trend towards 'non-traditional' domestic graduate students since 1986: notably a growth in minority students at an average annual rate between 4 and 6 per cent (African American, American Indian, Asian, and Hispanic/Latino), with women accounting for most of this growth. At the same time, white enrolment was unchanged (see Brown, 2006: 31).

In addition, overseas students make up 16 per cent of the total graduate enrolment and 26 per cent of graduate enrolment in designated research universities. Nerad (2006) points to the increase in PhD production worldwide and to the growth in international students undertaking doctoral education. She reports that the following percentages of earned doctoral degrees were completed by international students in 2003: Germany 13%, Japan 13%, the UK 39% and the US 30%.

As McWilliam et al. (2002: 123) comment, diversity is not seen as something undesirable. Rather, it is a welcomed danger – it serves both an economic purpose (new markets are opened up for universities) and a social purpose (the promotion of a just and equitable society through access to educational opportunities for all):

> The aim is not to 'overcome' the diversity that is increasingly a feature of university student populations . . . the potential threat for universities as organizations lies not in diversity of student or staff populations but in systemic arbitrariness – in (inappropriate) organisational imprecision in the context of (appropriate) social imprecision. Put simply, the logic is that systems of management need to be uniform because individuals are not, nor are likely to be.

And so a uniformity of processes, procedures, standards and general outcomes will permit diversity in doctoral provision and in the population of doctoral candidates, while at the same time provide assurance about the nature and worthiness of a doctoral qualification.

McWilliam et al. (ibid.) cite the work of Douglas (1992), in which risk is conceptualised as 'danger' as opposed to the balance of probabilities for losses and gains. She points to the dangers associated with the increasing number and diversity of students undertaking doctoral studies. McWilliam et al. (2002: 120) see risk management as a system of rules, formats and technologies that are brought to bear on the development, maintenance and evaluation of doctoral programs. Such systems can be found in codes of practices adopted at national or institutional level; in new management, administrative and funding arrangements; in reporting requirements; in quality audits, in evaluation and monitoring mechanisms; and in the production of a range of best practice guidelines. Generally speaking, external arrangements and processes of risk management tend to drive internal institutional arrangements. The remainder of this chapter illustrates and examines the different ways in which risk has been managed through the establishment of regimes of uniformity at national, regional and institutional levels. Of course, the relationship between risk management, creativity and innovation is complex and open to debate. As such I will leave it to the reader to judge whether the kinds of regulatory instruments and practices described below appear to contain the features of what Roffe (1999) identifies as barriers to creativity and innovation in organisations: placing creative processes into systematic and rational sequences, reward and control systems that reinforce regularity, overly bureaucratic rules and processes, and a strongly risk-averse environment.

The code of practice – UK

Perhaps the best example of a national approach to risk management can be found in the precepts for research education developed by the UK Quality Assurance Agency for Higher Education (QAAHE). These precepts have force because they are used by the QAAHE to evaluate university performance. The Foreword provides the setting:

> The Code assumes that, taking into account principles and practices agreed UK-wide, each institution has its own systems for independent verification both of its quality and standards and of the effectiveness of its quality assurance systems. . . . The precepts express key matters of principle that the higher education community has identified as important for the assurance of quality and academic standards. Individual institutions should be able to demonstrate they are addressing the matters tackled by the precepts effectively, through their own management and organisational processes . . .
>
> (QAAHE, 2004: 1–2)

Immediately, the Code places responsibility on individual universities to establish internal mechanisms of quality control but there is an expectation that such internal mechanisms follow the 27 precepts outlined in the Code – and this is largely guaranteed, given that subsequent audits by the QAAHE will use the precepts as a guide (see, for example, the Report on the Review of Research Degree Programmes: England and Northern Ireland, 2007). The 27 precepts cover the areas of institutional arrangements (four precepts), the research environment (one precept), selection, admission and induction of students (six precepts), supervision (four precepts), student progress and review arrangements (three precepts), development of research and other skills (three precepts), feedback mechanisms, assessment (three precepts), student representation, complaints and appeals (three precepts). The precepts themselves are so detailed that there are very few degrees of freedom left for universities. For example, one precept under the category of 'institutional arrangements' states in part that, 'Institutions will develop, implement and keep under review a code or codes of practice *applicable across the institution* which *includes the area(s) covered by this document*' (italics added). Firstly, the national Code stipulates that individual institutions must have an institution-wide code (leaving little space for local practices in departments or schools) and, secondly, the content of individual institutional codes must include the precepts of the national Code. Yet these precepts are elaborated in such detail that they fill 29 pages of text (excluding the introductory pages and the appendices), which is more than one page of elaboration per precept.

This is not the end of the story. The Code makes cross-reference to other documents developed for the national approach to postgraduate research education. Most notably, Appendix 3 reproduces a document on generic skills titled 'Skills Training

Requirements for Research Students, Joint Statement by Research Councils/Arts and Humanities Research Board (AHRB)'. This document specifies the 'skills that doctoral research students funded by the research councils/AHR would be expected to develop during their research training' – what are often referred to as 'generic skills'. These comprise 35 separately listed skills, styled 'to be able to . . .', and categorised under the following headings:

1   Research skills and techniques, e.g. to be able to demonstrate original, independent and critical thinking.
2   Research environment, e.g. to be able to understand the processes for funding and evaluation of research.
3   Research management, e.g. to be able to apply effective project management through the setting of research goals, intermediate milestones and prioritisation of activities.
4   Personal effectiveness, e.g. to be able to demonstrate flexibility and open-mindedness.
5   Communication skills, e.g. to be able to write clearly and in a style appropriate to purpose.
6   Networking and teamworking, e.g. to be able to develop and maintain co-operative networks, working relationships with supervisors, colleagues and peers, within the institution and wider research community.
7   Career management, e.g. to be able to appreciate the need and show commitment to continued professional development.

(QAAHE, 2004: 34–35)

These skills reflect another public policy agenda in Europe and in Australia: the concern with the limitations of narrow doctoral programs that focus only on the production of a dissertation but neglect the development of employment-related and personal skills.

Overall, it is easy to see how strong, co-ordinated national government interventions in the quality and standards of research degrees, coupled with funding provisions, lead to institutional alignment with national policy. This is certainly the case in England and Northern Ireland, as described in the Report on the Review of Research Degree Programmes: England and Northern Ireland (2007), which reviewed 86 doctoral granting institutions and subsequently reported, 'Most institutions now have formal training programmes that are informed by the Research Councils UK Joint Skills Statement' (p. 11) and that 'Institutions show good levels of engagement with the Code of practice in a thoughtful manner' (p. 22). Significantly, in commenting on different institutional arrangements for managing doctoral education, the report reveals the underlying concerns that such institutional arrangements address:

> This section considers the arrangements that institutions have in place to *safeguard* the academic standards of their RDPs and enable these to be delivered successfully according to national and, where relevant, international *expectations*.
>
> (QAAHE, 2007: 3 italics added)

The concern here seems to be to 'safeguard' against possible threats (read here the diversity of students and programs) and to meet national and international 'expectations' (read here the competition for research students in a global marketplace).

Differing approaches to quality assurance – Europe and the US

Co-ordinated national government intervention in doctoral education is an increasing feature (in varying degrees) of other European countries and in Australia. In France, where there is strong state control over higher education, doctoral education is organised in 'doctoral schools' and legal regulations cover key aspects of doctoral education such as admission and examination requirements and procedures, how studies are organised, and the confirmation of the degree. Thus quality assurance is largely through legal regulation rather than through national codes, national reporting mechanisms and audits. Doctoral schools have existed since 1998, and as Lemerle (2004: 42) describes:

> They are very useful for structuring research activities in universities and are very important in the negotiation of a university's institutional strategic plans. There are more than three-hundred doctoral schools in France.

By way of contrast, in Germany, although detailed regulations for awarding doctoral degrees exist in each of the 16 German states, the requirements differ in different states, universities, and even faculties within universities. Hufner (2004) reports that doctoral education is, in the main, highly decentralised and individualised without much national or institutional planning. However, a number of peak bodies have signalled a need for reform, which is underway. For example the peak body of rectors and presidents has recommended the establishment of doctoral schools and the Science Council has made recommendations for reform of doctoral education. Graduate colleges (*Graduiertenkollegs*) are thematically oriented research groups, of which there are now over 283 – although it should be noted that different approaches exist, as reflected in the different names given for doctoral schools (*Promotionskollegs*, *Graduiertenzentren* and *Graduiertenkollegs*). Although not yet realised, there is certainly an awareness in Germany of a need for a more structured and transparent approach to doctoral education if it is to participate fully on the European and international stage.

Contributing to a major UNESCO comparative study of doctoral education in Europe and the US, Kehm (2004: 283) summarises what she sees as the trend in the 13 countries represented in a major UNESCO study of doctoral education:

> The trend . . . is to establish a relatively formal structure for Doctoral education, ie abolishing the traditional 'apprenticeship model', consisting of a professorial supervisor and independent research, in favour of more structured research education and training within disciplinary or interdisciplinary programmes or graduate schools.

In the US there is a long history of structured postgraduate education within graduate schools. However, this occurs in a higher education system where there is no established national system of accreditation or national approach to quality assurance. Accreditation of higher education institutions, for example, is carried out by regional accrediting agencies (six in all), which are private organisations controlled by the academic community. Some fields of study have additional accreditation requirements from professional bodies or state licensing agencies, for example Engineering, Business, Law and Teacher Education. The various states have an accrediting role and/or play an active role in quality assessment and performance-based funding so that the state higher education institutions are accountable for the use of public funds (see Rhoades and Sporn, 2002).

Altbach (2004: 266) summarises the situation with respect to doctoral programs:

> No national or state quality assessment of Doctoral programmes in any discipline takes place . . . The basic fact, however, is that the US has a complex and highly effective set of accrediting arrangements, sponsored and managed by the academic community, that provides a basic 'floor' concerning academic quality and resources at all levels of the post-secondary system, but very little in terms of quality assurance or assessment.

Having said this, there are some national approaches to evaluation and quality assessment, as exemplified by the US News and World Report's comprehensive ranking process for postgraduate education, the National Research Council's evaluation of doctoral programmes (Goldberger et al., 1995) and the annual Council of Graduate Schools reports (Brown, 2006). The US also faces significant issues in common with its counterparts in other countries: the transition from doctoral education to work, the increasing international student cohort (almost 50 per cent in Engineering and at 40 per cent for physical sciences), generally a more diverse student body, and concerns about the length of time it takes to complete a doctorate (six to nine years).

Generally speaking, such issues are being addressed at institutional level through established strategic planning and quality assurance mechanisms. In the US such mechanisms are partly driven by the market and partly driven by public accountability – but not driven by national audits, national codes of practice or national policies and guidelines, as elsewhere.

Recent Australian experience

In Australia there exist a peculiar and somewhat uncoordinated mix of instruments that give effect to the national policy agenda. There is a performance-based funding mechanism in place, the Research Training Scheme (soon to be partly replaced by the Excellence in Research for Australia–ERA initiative); there is a national audit body, the Australian Universities Quality Assurance Agency; there were for many years annual reporting requirements through the Research and Research Training Management Plans submitted to the Department of Education, Science and Training (DEST); and there is a national survey of graduate satisfaction, the Postgraduate Research Experience Questionnaire, administered by Graduate Careers Australia. In addition there are peak bodies that produce guidelines for good practice such as the Australian Vice-Chancellor's Committee and the Council of Deans and Directors of Graduate Schools (see Council of Australian Deans and Directors of Graduate Studies, 2005). These instruments have been developed to monitor and assess the extent to which universities are aligning themselves with national priorities in research education: reducing the time taken to complete, linking research education more effectively with research agendas and quality research environments, providing generic employment skills training for research students, increasing the quality and quantity of research degree graduates, ensuring quality supervision and support is provided, maximising opportunities for the commercialisation of research, and improving retention.

Arthur (2002), a senior official in the education bureaucracy in Australia, points to the major concerns driving reforms in doctoral education: unacceptably low retention and completion rates, poor supervision, insufficient departmental support, impoverished infrastructure, inadequate links between research strengths and research education, a lack of employability and commercialisation skills (p. 33). Chubb (2006: 17), Vice-Chancellor of the Australian National University, adds to this list the looming dangers of global competition:

> Given the scale and pace of investment in leading universities and technical institutes in the northern hemisphere – especially in China, India, Europe and North America – and the intensifying international competition for intellectual talent, Australia is at serious risk of becoming a backwater.

The problem with the mix of instruments in Australia is that they drive different behaviours, some of which are contradictory and some of which are unintended and arguably work against the improvement of quality and standards. The instruments in play have driven universities to centralise the management and organisation of research degree programs in Australia, largely because the university as a whole is used as the unit of measurement (with the exception of the planned ERA exercise). Graduate schools or their equivalent have now been established in most universities, and there is a peak body, the Council of Deans and Directors of Graduate Schools, which has developed national guidelines and policies for its members. Set out in Table 17. 1 below is a brief description of each of these instruments.

The Research Training Scheme (RTS), which was introduced in 2001, has arguably had the most impact on universities, mainly because it is a performance-based funding scheme. The only doctoral program metric used is completions – basically, more completions mean more funding, irrespective of whether the completions are from domestic or international students. Given that increased completions can only come from three sources: higher retention, reduced time-to-complete and increased enrolment, the RTS has driven strategies to improve these metrics. The easiest metric to influence is enrolment, so it is no surprise that universities have been enrolling students in excess of the funding available to support students and that there has been rapid growth in

Table 17.1 Quality assurance, funding and reporting instruments for doctoral education in Australia

Instrument/agency	Measures/reporting related to research degrees
RTS – a government funding scheme. Funding for research programs is based on performance metrics.	Research degree completions 50% (other components being research grant income – 40%, and staff publications – 10%)
RRTMR – an annual report prepared for DEST.	Report on areas such as management and administrative arrangements for research degrees, planning and resource allocation, programs to develop generic skills of students, supervisor development, graduate attributes, supervisor qualifications and research activity, load and completions.
PREQ – a national survey administered by Graduate Careers Australia. The results are publicly available.	Recent graduates complete a 28-item questionnaire in the areas of supervision, the thesis, infrastructure, generic skills, and research climate.
AUQA – a national quality agency that conducts audits of universities once every five years and produces a publicly available report.	Universities prepare self-reports on their quality assurance processes and outcomes. The focus is on whether the processes are appropriate to the aims and objectives of the institution.
ERA (planned) – a government-sponsored funding scheme for research and research training. The funding is for general research support and is based on an assessment of research quality.	It is likely that metrics based on research outputs will be used.

international student numbers. This has placed additional strain on the system, with questionable implications for the quality of programs. The emphasis on time-to-complete has led some commentators to argue that this militates against innovation and risk taking in research in favour of 'doable' but mundane projects that can easily be managed within the time-frame allowed (see Council of Australian Postgraduate Associations, 2000). There is more emphasis placed on structured milestones in research degree programs and the reporting and monitoring of progress – managing out the risk of failing to progress in an orderly and predictable way.

The burden of monitoring quality and ensuring outcomes other than increased completions is placed on the other instruments – the RRTMR, AUQA and PREQ. Even though these instruments are not connected to funding, universities neverthe-less have been keen to align themselves with the general thrust of the instruments: to measure quality in terms of the process and strategies used to support a high quality research education. An AUQA audit begins with the audited university preparing a performance portfolio, which is basically a self-assessment of its performance, with an emphasis on the relationship between its performance and its quality assurance processes. At the completion of an AUQA audit, a public institutional report is produced, which contains a set of commendations, affirmations and recommendations. As a result, universities across the higher education sector are introducing the kinds of things that the auditors like to see with respect to research education. For example, most universities now have centralised university units being responsible for establishing whole-of-university quality assurance processes and standardised administrative procedures. There is a strong emphasis on supervisor training and registration and/or accreditation. Universities have introduced processes for entry and removal from the Supervisor Register, largely because the register is not seen to be robust without a performance-based threat of removal. This seems to be peculiar to research education (it is certainly not the case with coursework teaching) and, as such, signals the special status given to supervision. Other recent actions that universities have taken include performance-based processes for resourcing research students, a variety of funding and policy attempts to link research education more strongly with research strengths, a more rigorous monitoring of progress, the establishment of structured programs for skills training (including employability and commercialisation skills), and the use of student evaluations for planning improvements.

In the Australian system, there appears to be a fundamental contradiction between the drive for more completions and other policy agendas, such as the development of broader skills during doctoral candidature. One could argue that such broader skills should be embedded into the design of the thesis, but there is a limit to the extent to which this can be done and in reality many generic skills are taught separately, as an additional curriculum component of undertaking a doctoral program. The AUQA reports document and encourage many of these schemes and the government has encouraged and funded efforts by the sector to provide training in generic skills. For example, funding has been provided for the establishment of an e-Grad School, which provides online modules for research students in areas such as project management, entrepreneurship, leadership, public policy and commercialisation (cf. UK GRAD). The government has also developed its own scheme to encourage research students to learn about commercialisation – even to the extent of providing scholarships for students to take 'time out' from their thesis to undertake a formal qualification in research commercialisation. Such schemes, because they make significant demands on students' time, seem to militate against the drive for completions. The apparent contradictions between the various regulatory instruments are the outcome of shifts in policy focus over time – in the case of Australia, the shift has been from retention and completions towards alignment with research strengths, quality outcomes (including the impact of research) and employability.

Concluding comments

I commenced this chapter with the observation that doctoral education in contemporary times is being scrutinised as never before. I argued that this is a response to the risks arising from growing student numbers, more diversity in the student population, international competition in a global marketplace, and the need for doctoral education to be relevant to the needs of the global economy. While different countries have very different quality assurance arrangements, a common thrust is to standardise, regulate, measure and control the key aspects of doctoral education – admission, induction, progression, supervision, resourcing, graduate attributes, thesis requirements, and the examination process. Typically, this standardisation is exercised through centralised rules, regulations and quality assurance processes that apply to all departments and schools – often organised through central administrative units such as Graduate Schools. Overall, the various stakeholders may send out contradictory messages about what constitutes quality research education (e.g. there is likely to be a trade off between completing early and developing a range of skills relevant to employment). Moreover, and somewhat ironically, creative and innovative doctoral research arguably requires the kind of risk taking that is now being managed so arduously.

References

Altbach, P. (2004) The United States: present realities and future trends, in J. Sadlak (ed.), *Doctoral Studies and Qualifications in Europe and the United States: Status and Prospects*, Bucharest: UNESCO, pp. 259–278.

Arthur, E. (2002) The Commonwealth's role in assuring quality in postgraduate research education, in M. Kiley and G. Mullins (eds), *Quality in Postgraduate Research: Integrating Perspectives*, Canberra: CELTS, pp. 32–40.

Bourner, T., Bowden, R. and Laing, S. (2001) Professional doctorates in England, *Studies in Higher Education*, 26(1): 65–83.

Brown, H. (2006) Graduate Enrolment and Degrees: 1986 to 2005, Washington, DC: Council of Graduate Schools, Office of Research and Information Services.

Chubb, I. (2006) The future of research education, in M. Kiley and G. Mullins (eds), *Quality in Postgraduate Research: Knowledge Creation in Testing Times*, Canberra: pp. 17–26.

Council of Australian Deans and Directors of Graduate Studies (2005) Framework for Best Practice in Doctoral Education in Australia, at: www.ddogs.edv.au/download/207271667.

Council of Australian Postgraduate Associations (2000) Submission to DETYA on the proposed implementation of the Research Training Scheme, at: www.capa.edu.au.

Douglas, M. (1992) *Risk and Blame*, London: Routledge.

Goldberger, M., Maher, B. and Flattau, P. (eds) (1995) *Research-doctoral Programs in the United States: Continuity and Change*, Washington, DC: National Academy Press.

Hufner, K. (2004) Germany, in J. Sadlak (ed.), *Doctoral Studies and Qualifications in Europe and the United States: Status and Prospects*, Bucharest: UNESCO, pp. 51–62.

Kehm, B. (2004) Developing doctoral degrees and qualifications in Europe: good practice and issues of concern – a comparative analysis, in J. Sadlak (ed.), *Doctoral Studies and Qualifications in Europe and the United States: Status and Prospects*, Bucharest: UNESCO, pp. 279–298.

Lemerle, J. (2004) France, in J. Sadlak (ed.), *Doctoral Studies and Qualifications in Europe and the United States: Status and Prospects*, Bucharest: UNESCO, pp. 37–50.

McIntyre, J. and Symes, C. (eds) (2000) *Working Knowledge: The New Vocationalism and Higher Education*, Buckingham: Open University Press.

McWilliam, E., Singh, P. and Taylor, P. (2002) Doctoral education, danger and risk management, *Higher Education Research and Development*, 21(2): 119–129.

McWilliam, E., Taylor, P., Lawson, A. and Evans, T. (2006) University risk management and higher degree research, abstract of symposium, in M. Kiley and G. Mullins (eds), *Quality in Postgraduate Research: Knowledge Creation in Testing Times*, Canberra ANU, p. 231.

Nerad, M. (2006) Globalization and its impact on research education: trends and emerging best practices for the doctorate of the future, in M. Kiley and G. Mullins (eds), *Quality in Postgraduate Research: Knowledge Creation in Testing Times*, Canberra: ANU, pp. 5–12.

Pearson, M. (1999) The changing environment for doctoral education in Australia: implications for quality management, improvement and innovation, *Higher Education Research and Development*, 18(3): 269–288.

QAAHE (2007) *Report on the Review of Research Degree Programmes: England and Northern Ireland*, Mansfield: QAAHE.

Quality Assurance Agency for Higher Education (QAAHE) (2004) Code of practice for the assurance of academic quality and standards in higher education, Section 1 – Postgraduate research programmes, UK, September, pp. 1–39.

Rhoades, G. and Sporn, B. (2002) Quality assurance in Europe and the US: professional and political economic framing of higher education policy, *Higher Education*, 43: 355–390.

Roffe, I. (1999) Innovation and creativity in organisations: a review of the implications for training and development, *Journal of European Industrial Training*, 23(4/5): 224–241.

Tennant, M. (2004) Doctoring the knowledge worker, *Studies in Continuing Education*, 26(2): 432–441.

Usher, R. (2002) A diversity of doctorates: fitness for the knowledge economy?, *Higher Education Research and Development*, 21(2): 143–153.

Winter, R., Griffiths, M. and Green, K. (2000) The 'academic' qualities of practice: what are the criteria for a practice-based PhD?, *Studies in Higher Education*, 25(1): 25–37.

Part V

Reflections

Chapter 18

Challenging perspectives, changing practices

Doctoral education in transition

Bill Green

What is happening with the PhD? With research supervision and its oversight? With doctoral education? These are some of the key questions animating and energising this engaging, timely and important collection. Clearly, the field of doctoral studies is undergoing a significant transitional phase. We are currently in the midst of what seems quite momentous change, even as we struggle to make sense not only of what is happening in this recently emergent scholarly field of inquiry but also of where we have been and where we are going. Partly we are driven by forces beyond us; and partly we ourselves are driving change, as scholars and as practitioners in a range of associated activities that include research supervision, program development, policy formation, higher education studies, academic leadership and university management.

Knowledge, research and the doctorate: a world in motion

It is becoming very clear, and is emphatically outlined in this book, that the scene is changing in all sorts of ways, across a range of scales, from the macro-contextual through to the micro-practices of everyday life and learning in the postmodern university. On the largest scale, there have in recent decades been momentous shifts in the prevailing modes of knowledge, its production and also its circulation and use-value. Congruent with the emergence of what Castells (1996) calls the Network Society has been the accelerated opening up of a new dynamic sociotechnical space of flows of knowledge, and new global networks of research and education. Perhaps one of the strongest accounts in this regard, albeit one of the more controversial, has been an argument by Gibbons and Nowotny, and their various associates (Gibbons et al., 1994; Nowotny et al., 2001), concerning a shift in operational and evaluative focus between quite distinctive knowledge modes, or orientations. This has involved moving, meta-paradigmatically, from the still current traditional focus on disciplinarity and the perceived hegemony of the modern research university ('Mode 1') to a new programmatic focus on the emergence of what might be called more secular, worldly forms of research and knowledge ('Mode 2'). Of course, the case is better realised in critical-dialectical terms and needs to be properly historicised. For many, nonetheless, this argument remains persuasive and even compelling, and certainly challenging (Nowotny et al., 2003).

Linked to this, in ways still to be fully articulated, is a growing body of work addressed to the notion of the knowledge economy, itself a phenomenon that cannot be understood outside of an engagement with the globalisation thesis. All this was foreshadowed almost three decades ago now in Lyotard's (1984) eloquent and still pertinent analysis of what he called postmodernity and the changing forms and conditions of knowledge production and consumption in 'the most highly developed societies', originally prepared for the Quebec government's Council of Universities. In particular, Lyotard's account of the emergence of a new social logic of performativity continues to have striking relevance in and for the twenty-first century world of the postmodern university. A new sense of the role and significance of knowledge has emerged as the leitmotif of the age. Yet, at the very time and indeed in the very same action as knowledge is thus thematised, it has become both commodified and fetishised, and accordingly both re-valued and de-valued. Knowledge is now important, and desired, not so much for what it *is* but for what it *does*. The overriding context for this is the economy, yet this too must now be seen for what it must be in the new *doxa* – a transcendental object, a black hole that draws everything into its alchemical ambit. It is supremely ironic that, just when knowledge as such comes emphatically onto the front-end agenda of governments and corporations alike, of business and the polity, globally, the university is effectively displaced as an authoritative institution in this regard, or at least re-positioned – including in its historic role in doctoral and research education. Yet, as Lee and Boud note here and as others imply (e.g., see Chapter 11), doctoral research *is* nonetheless knowledge work – indeed, an exemplary form of knowledge work. Finding a way to better understand what this means, now and in the future, is precisely the challenge that confronts us.

As well as such important shifts in knowledge production and its validation, there are also profound changes to be observed in the more specific space of doctoral work itself. Perhaps most critically, the traditional PhD is no longer the sole object of concern, nor the singular sign of value. Just as there has been proliferation and differentiation at the macro level, the doctoral award now extends beyond the PhD as such to include such innovations as the new professional doctorate in fields such as Education and Engineering (e.g. EdD, EngD), project- and design-based doctorates, doctorates by publication and the like – a new 'family of doctorates', in fact, which also takes in what has been called 'new variant' PhDs (Park, 2005), and mutations within the PhD itself.

This latter point is worth a brief comment. Whether there was ever the degree of unanimity and homogeneity with regard to the identity of the PhD that is sometimes imagined, or 'remembered', is debatable. Nonetheless, this does not mean that such a fantasy did not have very real effects, in policy and practice alike. The push for internal innovation in the PhD is to be welcomed, although it should not be used simply as an excuse to retain the status quo. The situation as it is unfolding along these lines does make for managerial complexity, especially in the context of a new risk economy, as McWilliam outlines it (Chapter 14); but perhaps this should be seen as more of an opportunity than anything else, given all the possibilities of self-organisation and emergence. A new sensibility is required of researchers and research managers alike: a new reflexive research subjectivity, fully attuned to the challenges of complexity. Revisioning the PhD has a key role to play here – perhaps going beyond the recent Carnegie emphases on 'stewardship' and (traditional) 'disciplinarity'.

Of particular note in terms of a continuing opening up of new opportunities and challenges, is the work reported here on practice and project. I want to address the former category in more depth and detail in a moment. With regard to the latter, the emergence of what is described here as 'project-based research within creative disciplines' (Allpress and Barnacle, Chapter 12) is especially interesting. This is not just for its own sake – that is, with regard to work in fields such as Architecture and Design, or the Visual and Performing Arts – but also for what it might imply for other practice-oriented fields, which also operate with different or alternative rationalities. This is referred to in Chapter 12 as 'the role of different ways of knowing in knowledge generation', or 'alternative knowledge generation', and it remains a complex and vexed issue in universities and other institutional contexts. What is the place and value in the overall (doctoral) research economy of what has been described as 'material thinking' (Carter, 2004), embodied knowing, emergent arts-based inquiry (Somerville, 2007), performative knowledges, and 'non-representational thinking' (Thrift, 1996)? This question is particularly important at a time when doctoral scholars, across a range of fields, are increasingly seeking to broaden the scope of intellectual expression and presenting for examination what are, for many 'old-timers', challenging and innovative portrayals of knowledge, learning and insight. A further point to note, and applaud, in the account of RMIT's program in this chapter is not just that it is addressed to 'a broader definition of research by project that encompasses, but is not restricted to, professional practice undertaken in an industry context', but also that it deliberately allows for non-instrumental, 'speculative research' as a legitimate form of inquiry. This is something all too often overlooked, or suppressed, in practice-referenced doctoral studies. Again this raises all sorts of questions and problems for research supervision and management.

(Re)turning to education

I want to turn now to what I see as a decisive breakthrough in the overall project of the book: the strong and programmatic focus on *education* as an organising frame of reference. This is described in the Introduction as 'a shift from the organising idea of postgraduate research' to an emphasis on 'the educative work involved in preparing doctoral graduates' and in doctoral programs more generally. Doctoral research studies as a field of interest is named explicitly, that is, as *doctoral education*. This is something I welcome, and indeed have long argued for (Green, 2005; Green and Lee, 1995).

It is worth noting here that to date there has been a curious reluctance within published scholarship in the field to embrace the educational, or the educative, as a principle of unity and identity, or to see this work as in dialogue with the established field of educational research. This made, at times, for a curious tendency for researchers of doctoral education to seemingly re-invent the wheel. At the same time there has been no doubt a measure of strategic distancing from the more normative school-centric forms of educational research that characterise the work done in many Schools of Education, although to this must be added the fact that relatively low status is afforded to such schools in universities more generally. Also relevant, and arguably even more important, is the auratic quality of research itself, as a defining feature in the modern university's characteristic charisma. I have elsewhere suggested that, within this symbolic economy, research is set (up) against the seemingly more mundane activity of education, or the educational practices that underpin and sustain the advanced knowledge work of the university – something that Hoskin (1993) and others have clearly discerned in the historical record (e.g. Clark, 2006). Hence, disciplinarity as an organising idea has been deliberately counter-pointed with pedagogy, although the relationship between the two is better realised as a complex dialectic than as a simple binary. Given the value placed on research, however, it may be understandable that the field has sometimes sought to distance itself from education *per se*.

But here, the focus is squarely on doctoral (research) education. This means that the field has the full resources of educational research to draw on, as both an archive and a practice, and also, more specifically, those of the field of curriculum inquiry. This includes a long history of engagement with two key concepts that are perhaps among the very few that are genuinely indigenous to education as a field of inquiry and praxis, namely *curriculum* and *pedagogy*. It needs to be said that, for me, these are to be understood in a quite specific sense as two sides of the one coin, or perhaps as different but related lenses.[1] I have already indicated that, in my work with Alison Lee, I have been exploring the significance of pedagogy as a productive resource for (re)thinking research supervision (Green, 2005; Green and Lee, 1995, 1999), and I take up this matter again in a moment, from a slightly different angle.

Two of the chapters in this volume directly address issues of curriculum, although a number of others, in their concern with program development, might also be said to be working with(in) the concept. Gilbert provides a useful review of what might be called mainstream curriculum inquiry and design (Chapter 5). His account of the doctorate *as* curriculum focuses on 'what it is that graduates learn in their courses of study', suggesting that, while this is now becoming a much more articulated, formalised matter, it has always been operating in doctoral work, however implicitly or tacitly. Recognising that disciplinary knowledges and cultures have traditionally served as frames and resources of this kind, he describes the doctoral curriculum as 'the systematic selection and articulation of experience in order to produce the intended outcomes of doctoral research training'. The question of what knowledge is at issue in doctoral studies – that is, the relationship between curriculum and knowledge in doctoral education – is also taken up in the chapter by Scott and his colleagues, in their account of the new professional doctorate (Chapter 11). While focusing their discussion on 'professional study at doctoral level in two occupational fields' (Education and Engineering), they look specifically at the question of knowledge, drawing on the later ideas of Bernstein's sociology of knowledge. Their concern is with the specialist and specialised knowledge that characterises professional practice fields, and hence – like the professional doctorate itself – the relationship between knowledge and practice. Although this is not in fact engaged with in their work, there is a further relationship to consider here, perhaps more specifically of a curriculum-theoretical nature: between knowledge and identity. Indeed, this set of relationships is something that clearly warrants further exploration.

To do so, however, is likely to require other theoretical resources and perspectives than those mobilised here. Pinar's (2004: 2) view of curriculum theory as 'the interdisciplinary study of educational experience' offers much in this regard, I suggest. Drawing significantly though not exclusively on the arts and humanities, theory and philosophy, he argues that the focus of concern for curriculum scholars should be on *understanding* educational phenomena – in this case, what goes on in doctoral education, or what is happening and what might be its significance and meaning. Pinar sees curriculum inquiry as intellectual work. It involves asking questions that go beyond the utilitarian, the pragmatic, the narrowly relevant; that is, it seeks 'investigations of more fundamental questions of human experience that might not lead directly to economic development and increased productivity'. 'Such a view of curriculum inquiry and research,' he writes, 'is akin to what in the natural sciences would be termed basic research, wherein destinations are not necessarily known in advance' (p. 29). Where is the 'basic research', then, the speculative inquiry, in doctoral education?[2]

This question opens up, further, the issue of what is the *vision* that shapes and informs education, and therefore doctoral education, in these complex and risky times. It is arguably one that has at its heart a will to audit and accountability, and a passionate enthusiasm for performativity. Drawing on Derrida and Deleuze, humanities scholar Hainge (2004: 38) writes of philosophy and the university and presents what might be seen as a truly radical vision of education:

> Do we not believe that education has the capacity to interrupt the ordinary course of historical temporality, that many of the radical breaks in history that have appeared through massive social change or technological innovation have often been (at least in part) the result of education?

For Hainge, education has what he calls 'an unconditional purity', at least potentially, and also as it were philosophically. He sets this against its local realisation, in Australia (but clearly elsewhere as well), and asks, '[h]ow can education be reinvested with a sense of absolute purity to counterbalance the excessive pragmatism under which it is currently suffering and suffocating?' (p. 39). He goes on to propose that education is best seen as situated in 'the tension born of the seemingly oppositional conflict of an absolute purity and an empirical pragmatics' (p. 40). Notwithstanding the insistence of knowledge economy rhetorics in the discourse of the contemporary university, 'research and education should not have to obey this particular pragmatic, [and] income generation is not the only way for research education to play a pragmatic role in society' (p. 41). This seems to me to have special and specific relevance for doctoral education and the postmodern university. As documented clearly here in this volume, there is an intensifying governmental interest in doctoral studies and research education, and programmatic moves towards their professionalisation and rationalisation, their re-framing within a supra-logic of productivity. It is surely timely to ask about what gets left out of, or lost from, such an agenda. Might not doctoral research education be better conceived less instrumentally and more aspirationally – more philosophically?

Practice theory and doctoral studies

To be sure, this is partly what this book as a whole is on about. It is made clear, early on, that it is motivated towards a strong re-valuation of the concept of *practice*, and hence it very usefully draws on recent work from what has been called practice theory and philosophy (e.g. Schatzki, 1996, 2001). This is inquiry that ranges from poetics to politics, across the arts and sciences, and with particular value, it seems to me, for the re-assessment of the advanced knowledge work of the professions. As noted in the Introduction, '[p]ractice is an over-arching conceptual frame for the sets of key themes that organise the book'. This is elaborated in Chapter 2, which seeks to present a view of doctoral education as, firstly, a form of social practice and, secondly, as itself comprising a range (or 'bundle') of distinct research, pedagogic and administrative practices, within an overall context of 'an expansion, distribution and diversification of the practices of doctoral education'. An important distinction is made between doctoral education *as* practice and *for* practice, although it seems to me that work still needs to be done to bring the two together, or at least to indicate the relationship that might be observed *and* forged between them. What is important to understand is that what such a practice-theoretical perspective offers, and what sets it apart from other accounts that have been offered with regard to doctoral education, is its focus on the *vernacular*, on the mundane practices of everyday life, in all their routine and materiality, and also on the material practices that *contextualise* it. What is said and what is done in doctoral education, where and when, repeatedly, as an ongoing activity-system?

Elsewhere Alison Lee and I have drawn attention to the seminar as a distinctive feature of doctoral work, where would-be researchers and scholars look and learn who they must become, in the company of their mentors and their peers:

> The seminar is a powerful means whereby what counts as academic-intellectual work is represented and authorised. . . . It is for students a matter of often watching and learning how to be, how to interact and intervene. How to introduce and develop a commentary however attenuated it might need to be in the circumstances, how to work with difference and disputation, how to speak and when, even how to hold one's body or deploy certain mannerisms or gestures ('impatience' for instance).
>
> (Green and Lee, 1995: 134)

What is clearer to me, now, is that this is always a performance, a *practice*, something that not only happens, in time and space, a choreography of bodies and voices, but is repeated, rehearsed and *cited*. Academic subjects are thereby formed, and deformed, differentiated, distinguished; careers unfold and follow, or don't. The politics of reputation and disputation begins, and is thereafter carried out, in the practice of academic presencing. What is also clear to me, now, is that this practice is offered mainly in those on-campus circumstances, arguably ideal, and that it is a minority, privileged opportunity when it occurs. For many doctoral scholars, however, those studying at a distance or on a part-time basis, or in relative isolation – the majority? – it is much more difficult to imagine oneself as the Subject of Knowledge, and to indwell in the virtual company of other Subjects. Yet it is always, I suggest, just such an act of *imagination* that is required in doctoral work, intermingled with fantasy and desire.

Rather than discuss further here what a practice-theoretical account of doctoral education entails and offers, I will now go on to explore just one aspect. Building on the observation made in Chapter 2 that there is 'at the heart of the doctorate a set of practices that produce both objects . . . and subjects . . .', I want to focus on the distinctive 'object' of the dissertation. It needs to be acknowledged, though, that the actual dissertation itself does not figure equally significantly in all fields, or indeed across the broad divide of the arts and sciences. Moreover, as Rip (2004: 165) observes, there are questions to be asked, even now, as to the long-term viability or value of the dissertation in doctoral research education, as 'a type of product that will never be required in the later career'. So it is important to be clear that what I am referring to here as the 'dissertation' is to be understood as at once the monograph that is, conventionally, the tangible outcome of doctoral research, and a more conceptual 'knowledge object', in Knorr-Cetina's (2001) sense. At issue is the notion of 'epistemic practice', or 'knowledge-centred practice', which Knorr-Cetina proposes in bringing together knowledge society arguments, research work and practice theory. What is important in the case that she develops is her emphasis on the creative, innovative and constructive side of practice rather than on its more routine, recurrent and (ir)regular aspects. Her focus is on the 'knowledge object', as a distinctive form of objecthood, one characterised by ontological incompleteness and non-identity. As she writes: 'objects of knowledge are characteristically open, question-generating and complex'. Moreover, '[t]hey are processes and projections rather than definitive things' (Knorr-Cetina, 2001: 181). Importantly, knowledge objects 'are meaning-producing and practice-generating; they provide for the concatenation and constructive extension of practice' (p. 183). They are thus incitements for further learning and thinking, beyond the specific enactment of (research) practice they relate to, at the same time as being bounded instances of that particular (objectual) practice. With regard to doctoral research education, they also must be seen as marking out a pedagogic space of being and becoming, a new academic 'identity'.

Here, it needs to be said that, while Knorr-Cetina is not herself concerned with research education, the implications are clear, and her argument is likely to have particular value in better understanding doctoral studies. The researcher interacting with an emerging knowledge object operates similarly, it seems to me, to the becoming-researcher, the novitiate, although it should not be forgotten that such interaction is precisely what the latter is engaged in learning how to do. Knorr-Cetina stresses that what is at issue in research practice is a key *relationality*, which she describes as an 'expert-object' relationship and as a fundamental feature of 'epistemic environments' (Knorr-Cetina, 2001: 187). It should be borne in mind that, for the established (i.e. 'licensed') researcher, the focus is on the research itself and its worldly consequences, and not so much on its record. That is certainly the case in the sciences, generally speaking, although in the arts and humanities the situation is complicated by the fact that the research, in and of itself, is more often than not to be identified with the (written) record, ideally the 'book' – although this is further complicated, in turn, by poststructuralist arguments regarding the 'text' and the 'work' (e.g. Barthes). Whereas much scholarship in the field of doctoral education to date has focused on the formation of subjectivity, and appropriately so, it may be that just as important is the peculiar 'object-ivity' involved in doctoral research education. What is the relational dynamic that is realised in doctoral work, conceived as objectual, epistemic practice?

The question might also be stated thus: What can be said about the relation of the doctoral scholar, the 'candidate', to the dissertation? The first thing to say is that it is an object of *examination*, both literally and in a more Foucaultian sense. Examination is arguably specific to the pedagogic register, in this form at least, as part of the formal apparatus of curriculum and assessment that Gilbert evokes in Chapter 5. As such, it is a mechanism of classification and judgement, of authorisation and accreditation. But it is also a matter of *reading*: the examiner 'reads' the text of the dissertation, and s/he either 'passes' it or s/he doesn't. Hence the question can be further rephrased to refer to the doctoral scholar's relationship to reading and writing, to language.

What then is the relational dynamic between candidature of this kind and *language*? At issue here is a particular view of language, as a Symbolic practice, an abyss of signification. This seems a long way from more instrumental views and usages of language, as might be observed for instance in accounts of academic literacy or, indeed, of doctoral writing (Chapter 8). Yet caution should be exercised in this regard, because there is in fact a connection, or rather it can be constructed as such. This would be to see the mundane practices of writing (and reading) of the doctoral candidate and their associated anxieties as a practical engagement with the Symbolic. But candidature is also an instance of the distinctive kind of relationality with a 'knowledge object' that Knorr-Cetina has described, referring to 'the unfolding, dispersed, and signifying (meaning producing) character of epistemic objects', which includes 'their non-identity with themselves' (Knorr-Cetina, 2001: 184). The dissertation-text is to be seen therefore as a thing in itself, a 'knowledge object', *and* also as standing in for the research at issue, the object of inquiry, and hence also a 'knowledge object', though differently. It is characterised by incompleteness, non-identity, *différance*.

What Knorr-Cetina (2001: 185) paraphrases nicely as 'objectual relations', as a feature of epistemic practice, applies to research pedagogy as much as it does to research practice. As she writes, 'objects of knowledge structure desire, and provide for the continuation and unfolding of object-related practice' (Knorr-Cetina, 2001: 185). She draws on Lacan (and also Hegel) in making this argument, referring to 'a structure of wanting' which, as she says, 'implies a continually renewed interest in knowledge that appears never to be fulfilled by final knowledge' (Knorr-Cetina, 2001: 186). Such an account may provide a useful supplement to those already in place, to do with the impossibility of subjectivity in research supervision and the social psychopathology of doctoral work (Lee and Williams, 1999; Green, 2005). What has been identified as a structural lack in the self might well be linked to a lack in the object of knowledge, understood with reference to both practice and representation. The relationship to the knowledge object of doctoral research education is particularly complex, then. Yet engaging such complexity may well prove most productive – and that point itself a fitting conclusion both to this chapter and to the book as a whole.

References

Carter, P. (2004) *Material Thinking*, Melbourne: Melbourne University Press.

Castells, M. (1996) *The Rise of the Network Society*, Cambridge: Blackwell.

Clark, W. (2006) *Academic Charisma and the Origins of the Research University*, Chicago: University of Chicago Press.

Gibbons, M., Limoges, C., Nowotny, H., Schwartzman, S., Scott, P. and Trow, M. (1994) *The New Production of Knowledge: The Dynamics of Science and Research in Contemporary Societies*, London: Sage.

Green, B. (2005) Unfinished business? Subjectivity and supervision, *Higher Education Research and Development*, 24(2): 151–163.

Green, B. and Lee, A. (1995) Theorising Postgraduate Pedagogy, *Australian Universities Review*, 38(2): 40–45.

Green, B. and Lee, A. (1999) Educational research, disciplinarity and postgraduate pedagogy: on the subject of supervision, in A. Holbrook and S. Johnston (eds), *Supervision of Postgraduate Research in Education*, Coldstream, Victoria: Australian Association for Research in Education, pp. 207–222.

Hainge, G. (2004) The death of education, a sad tale (DEST): of anti-pragmatic pragmatics and the loss of the absolute in Australian tertiary education, in J. Kenway, E. Bullen and S. Rob (eds), *Innovation and Tradition: The Arts, Humanities and the Knowledge Economy*, New York: Peter Lang, pp. 35–45.

Hoskin, K. (1993) Education and the genesis of disciplinarity: an unexpected reversal, in E. Messer-Davidow, D. R. Shumway and D. J. Sylvan (eds), *Knowledge: Historical and Critical Studies in Disciplinarity*, Charlottesville: University of Virginia Press, pp. 271–304.

Knorr-Cetina, K. (2001) Objectual relations, in T. R. Schatzki, K. Knorr-Cetina and E. van Savigny (eds), *The Practice Turn in Contemporary Theory*, New York: Routledge, pp. 175–188.

Lee, A. and Williams, C. (1999) 'Forged in fire': narratives of trauma in PhD pedagogy, *Southern Review*, 32(1): 6–26.

Lyotard, J.-F. (1984) *The Postmodern Condition: A Report on Knowledge*, Minneapolis: University of Minnesota Press.

Nowotny, H., Scott, P. and Gibbons, M. (2001) *Re-thinking Science: Knowledge and the Public in an Age of Uncertainty*, Cambridge: Polity Press.

Nowotny, H., Scott, P. and Gibbons, M. (2003) 'Mode 2' revisited: the new production of knowledge, *Minerva*, 41: 179–194.

Park, C. (2005) New variant PhD: the changing nature of the doctorate in the UK, *Journal of Higher Education Policy and Management*, 27(2): 189–207.

Pinar, W. F. (2004) *What Is Curriculum Theory?*, Mahwah, NJ: Lawrence Erlbaum.

Pinar, W. F. (2006) The problem with curriculum and pedagogy, in *The Synoptic Text and Other Essays: Curriculum Development and the Reconceptualization*, New York: Peter Lang, pp. 109–120.

Rip, A. (2004) Strategic research, post-modern universities and research training, *Higher Education Policy*, 17: 153–166.

Schatzki, T. R. (1996) *Social Practices: A Wittgensteinian Approach to Human Activity and the Social*, Cambridge: Cambridge University Press.

Schatzki, T. R. (2001) Practice theory, in T. R. Schatzki, K. Knorr-Cetina and E. van Savigny (eds), *The Practice Turn in Contemporary Theory*, New York: Routledge, pp. 1–14.

Somerville, M. (2007) Postmodern emergence, *Qualitative Studies in Education*, 20(2): 225–243.

Thrift, N. (1996) 'Strange country': meaning, use and style in non-representational theories, in *Spatial Formations*, London: Sage, pp. 1–50.

Notes

5 The doctorate as curriculum: a perspective on goals and outcomes of doctoral education

1 The term 'research training' is consistent with the standard policy terminology in the United Kingdom and Australia. Valid questions can be raised about whether training is an adequate concept to encapsulate the process of doctoral education, but this issue is not taken up here. It is relevant to note the use of the term 'research education' by other contributors to this volume.

8 PhD education in science: producing the scientific mindset in biomedical sciences

1 There were no obvious gender-specific differences, or issues related to the experience of the supervisor (ranging from 1 to 25 students), or length of time the student had been in a PhD program (0.3 to 6.6 years) in the responses to any of the questions.

9 Representing doctoral practice in the laboratory sciences

1 Funded by the Australian Research Council, the aim of this Linkage Project was to develop detailed information from two related studies, in distinctive but complementary sites, about the contemporary doctoral experience. In addition to three chief investigators (Evans, Pearson and Macauley), three postgraduate student associations participated as industry partners. As one of two doctoral candidates engaged in the project my focus was on full-time students while the focus of my counterpart was on part-time students.
2 Stenhouse (1978) has distinguished between case data, case record and case study. In the development of this chapter, three edited and verified transcripts constitute case data; given its polyvocal nature the case narrative is a variation of the case record; and the combination of narrative and interpretation denotes the case study.
3 In order to maintain the confidentiality of informants, certain aspects of this narrative have been modified. For example, pseudonyms have been used for the characters – Jane, Trish and Scott; the tertiary institution – Tinternvale University; the external research agency – Trentham Institute; and the industry groups – the Chicken Consortium and the Fowl Foundation.
4 Scott was also a recipient of an industry-funded scholarship, albeit from a different organisation to those referred to in this narrative. One of the reasons for his accepting the position of research assistant was to secure financial remuneration, given that funding from the original scholarship had expired.

15 New challenges in doctoral education in Europe

1 This chapter is based on the results of the European University Association projects, published in two EUA reports: *Doctoral Programmes for the European Knowledge Society* (2005) and *Doctoral Programmes in Europe's Universities: Achievements and Challenges* (2007). The author was involved in both projects as their coordinator as well as co-author of the reports.

2 The questionnaire on funding of doctoral education was sent to the 46 Bologna Follow-Up Group ministerial members in September 2006. The analysis of the results from 37 countries that responded to the questionnaire was done by Yukiko Fukasaku, Innovmond, France, in 2007 and published in the EUA report, *Doctoral Programmes in Europe's Universities: Achievements and Challenges* (2007).

3 Quality Assurance Agency for Higher Education (2004) *Code of Practice for the Assurance of Academic Quality and Standards in Higher Education, Section 1: Postgraduate Research Programmes*.

4 See Note 2.

18 Challenging perspectives, changing practices: doctoral education in transition

1 Interestingly, Pinar disputes the articulation in this way of curriculum and pedagogy, seeing the latter term more or less simply as 'instruction', or teaching, and therefore linked in his account to learning. He proposes instead a new focus on a reformulated notion of 'study' (Pinar, 2006), which I think can be usefully explored in relation to Clark's (1995) classic notion of the 'research–teaching–study' nexus in the research university – something I leave now for another occasion . . .

2 There may be a useful connection to be made here with Rip's (2004: 155–156) view of 'strategic research' as a renewed concept in the context of new modes of production of knowledge, which he suggests has become 'a new type of basic research'.

Index